EXPECTING TO FLY

In search of the Spirit

Patrick Sheridan

authorHOUSE®

AuthorHouse™ UK Ltd.
500 Avebury Boulevard
Central Milton Keynes, MK9 2BE
www.authorhouse.co.uk
Phone: 08001974150

First published by AuthorHouse 7/22/2011

ISBN: 978-1-4567-7031-0 (sc)

Acknowledgements

Many people have contributed to the completion of this book. In particular I would like to thank my wife Grazyna for her unfailing patience, help and enthusiasm at every stage of the process.

I would also like to thank Caroline Durant for much of the editing and proofreading as well as for all her encouragement, Chris Patmore for graphic design and technical advice, and my son Daniel for the book cover design and artwork.

I am equally grateful for the considerable amount of writing time gained – and the many long commuting drives avoided – thanks to Tim and Christina's hospitality.

In addition I would like to thank Chris and Ruth for early support and editorial advice and Grace, Marilyn, Hania, Ann, Finbar, Linda, Larissa, Sue and Cythare for their useful feedback and suggestions.

Contents

Foreword

I'm not sure why I am attempting to put spiritual experience into words. Words are limited, but I suppose it's the nature of the experience to want to share and communicate. I have also been fortunate. The unsuspecting seeker has to cross something of a minefield in the search for truth, and I have both survived the journey and found what I was looking for.

Spiritual experience itself is not as rare as one might think, much more elusive are the means to evaluate it and, in terms of the evolution of consciousness, how to awaken, sustain and develop it.

A friend who has read the story I am trying to tell suggested half jokingly that I confirm it is a genuine personal account and not a science-fiction novel. I guess it is easy to forget how amazing the truth can actually be. As microscopic and insignificant as we might seem in this enormous universe, even greater dimensions of wonder and purpose can unfold within us. I could not have imagined the divine before I experienced it, but the moment I did it was as if I had always known it. Should anyone wonder, then, everything I have described is the truth as I have experienced it, and the experiences themselves are potentially available to anyone.

The path I have travelled has been a bumpy one, although it started out promisingly enough. I was born in Hong Kong into a comfortable English colonial lifestyle. One of my earliest memories is the intense delight I felt on entering the warm, sparkling water of an outdoor swimming pool. The pool was built into the hillside and the patio overlooked the colourful panorama of Hong Kong harbour spread out far below. Splashing into the sparkling emerald water in my rubber facemask and flippers felt like entering paradise.

Twenty years later, things were very different. I stood despondently in a dark cul-de-sac near Euston Station in central London at three o'clock in the morning. I was shivering in an ankle-length ex-RAF coat (fashionable for some reason) with much split-ended hair flowing haphazardly down towards my waist.

I was on the streets looking for somewhere to sleep, and had ducked into an alley to avoid a policeman as I was high on a cocktail of drugs and had cannabis on me. He had seen me, and the wavering light of his torch signalled his imminent arrival. I got rid of the cannabis as best I could and looked up at the stars watching timelessly in the sky above me. 'This part of the cosmic dream is a bit of a bummer,' I thought.

My life was following its usual pattern of highs and lows. Only two or three years earlier, I had thought I had found the answer to everything. I had exulted in LSD's miraculous gifts and crossed the threshold of humanity's ancient schism with the natural world. I had touched the omniscient and omnipresent one that waited with such infinite patience for us to awaken to our divine nature.

But LSD had a sting in its tail. It created as many questions as it answered and opened the door to hell as well as to heaven. It had promised everything and then reneged on it like a treacherous friend; illuminating unimaginable spiritual heights only to dump me in a ditch, leaving me forever dissatisfied with anything the material world had to offer.

I had crashed and burned in a spectacular manner, yet I could not regret it. To have touched such wonders even for a moment was worth a dozen lifetimes to me. It was not worth an eternity, however, and my perspective began to change further down the line as I became more aware of the effects such rough handling had on subtle aspects of my being. In time I was to realise that with a little more faith and patience (well, OK, a lot from a human perspective) the truth would have unfolded of its own accord. I had tried to open my birthday presents a little too early and done some damage in the process.

Meanwhile, back in Hong Kong at the beginning of my life, a very different image of water was to stick in my mind, some years after the first. This time I was standing on the beach watching shark fins skim through the water where I had been only minutes before. It gave me a horror of sharks that stayed with me for a long time. It could almost have been a portent of things to come, but I remained blissfully ignorant of such things and set forth optimistically on the journey of life.

I had no intention of writing about my youth when I first began to trace the convoluted path of my seeking, but I did not get far before I realised I was talking about an elusive thread that ran from my earliest years. One thing I did know was that I wanted to concentrate on experience rather than speculate about concepts and beliefs, and a kind of retrospective journal wound its way into existence.

Every aspect of my being had played a part in my stumbling quest for completeness, baggage and all. Attempting to follow this thread has proved an interesting exercise in introspection and a rather mortifying reappraisal of the damage I inflicted upon myself on the journey. Some of my behaviour now seems astonishingly reckless and foolish to me.

Of course, I can imagine that another person's history will not be everyone's favourite subject, even though I have tried to avoid too much personal detail. The earlier part can be skipped without missing much of consequence by fast forwarding to chapter six and the part of my life where I began seeking in earnest.

Chapter 1
Bold beginnings

I do not remember much about my earliest years. Most of my memories begin from the age of about five or six, when I was living with my family in a block of flats, one of three standing on a hill which overlooked Happy Valley race course on one side and Hong Kong harbour on the other.

The surrounding hillside dropped away on all sides, its slender trees and bushes, long dry grass and clumps of bamboo exuding a rich, sweet fragrance in the baking-hot sun. It was a place of high adventure. At one place was a steep rock face known as 'dead man's slide', and at another, a long, wide, open slope of wild grass known as the 'roly-poly.'

We clambered daringly about on the 'slide', clinging in fear and excitement to the pleasing roughness of its hot, ancient surfaces, and we rolled down the 'roly-poly' sideways over and over again with our arms and legs stretched out until the grass was flat and smooth, when we could slide down on our backsides at high speed. We also did some sliding down a wide, open drain that ran down the hill, and at another place, where a tree grew on the outside of the wall that encircled the hilltop, we loved to clamber, Indiana Jones style, down its gnarled surface root system to the hillside below. We built huts, hunted snakes and explored Second World War tunnels excavated by the Japanese.

We had Chinese servants who lived in a separate, purpose-built wing of the flats, which was alien territory to me, strange and exciting with squatting toilets and the mysterious smell of incense. I was deeply attached to the Chinese ladies who helped to look after us, and both fascinated and alarmed by everything Chinese. It was a strange situation, to be surrounded everywhere by the exotic sights, sounds and smells of the ancient Chinese culture without really participating in it at all. There was a yawning gap separating the lifestyles of the local Chinese and the colonial English that I could not cross, but its mystique hovered constantly and tantalisingly in the background of my life.

The sights, sounds and smells of Hong Kong filled my childhood; the endless pounding of pile drivers on distant building sites, the garbled sounds of excitement drifting up from the race course in the valley, the universal chirping of the cicadas in the trees. The streets were alive with loud, chaotic activity and colourful sights and aromas, the scent of incense, fish and spices mingling with that of drains to create a heady mix, punctuated from time to time by the raucous sounds of Chinese funerals, magnificently colourful dragon dances and the constant barrage of firecrackers at Chinese New Year. Down at the waterfront, Chinese junks bobbed haphazardly at anchor, their floating families calling out to each other with casual good humour, and distant fires in the hillside squatter camps sometimes lit up the night sky.

I do not remember anything particularly spiritual about my early life. I was somewhat awed by the Catholic religion that my family belonged to, but I did not like it. I suppose I felt it to be one more alarming and incomprehensible institution in a world that seemed filled with such things. I did feel a deeper sense of mystery and attraction on occasion, once or twice at the sight of the huge nativity scene in the church at the Christmas midnight mass, and again during a visit to a monastery, but I somehow did not relate these experiences to the everyday face of the Catholic Church.

Such things belonged to a deeper part of me that I did not understand and rarely acknowledged, to feelings and impressions that felt deeply significant but were not related – or I could not relate – to the world I lived in. They would move me in some profound and nameless way and then fade like a half-remembered dream.

The world of dreams itself was another matter. I often dreamed I could fly, sometimes so vividly I found it hard to believe it wasn't true when I awoke. I would sit staring at my arms, half convinced that if I flapped them hard enough I would rise into the air. Another frequent dream, one that always left me with a strange longing, was of being immersed in a lake of clear still water in which I did not need to breathe. I had bad dreams too, of course, my least favourite featuring an alarming number of poisonous snakes that lay in wait for me everywhere I went.

There was also a strange experience that sometimes took place when I was semi-awake, usually drowsy and about to drift off to sleep. I would feel as if my head and my pillow – and sometimes my whole body – were expanding and contracting, repeatedly growing to a huge size and then shrinking to become tiny. This was slightly scary but also oddly familiar, as though there were something I knew about it that I could not remember.

Something else that seems quite extraordinary looking back on it was the comfort I got from my 'blanket'. This was a special blanket of a particular kind of material, I forget what it was but it had a certain texture absent from 'ordinary' blankets. I would suck my thumb and hold the blanket in both hands, absorbing what I thought of as 'electricity' from it and feeling an intense sense of contentment and fulfilment as it flowed into me. It only worked for a limited period and only if the blanket was 'cool'; after a while it became 'hot' and 'used up', and had to be left to cool down and charge up again. It was an ability that lasted for a surprisingly long time.

Every three or four years, colonial officials had long 'leaves' of many months, with much of this time spent travelling to and from various destinations by ship. On the first leave in which I participated, we travelled to Australia and back, and the second was a return trip to England. The final journey was back to England again, where we settled permanently. I loved these ocean voyages; I have vivid memories of the stately, rolling progress of the ship, the salty tang in the air and the exciting sound of the sea rushing past the porthole at night. The journeys took weeks, and at my young age they seemed to last forever.

The high points of the trip were the exotic foreign ports that the ship called at. It was thrilling to see land appearing as a faint smudge on the distant horizon that slowly took on form until a wonderfully new, unfamiliar landscape crept into view. Ports were endlessly fascinating places, full of the deep bass tones of ships' horns and miscellaneous clanging and banging noises as cranes loaded or unloaded cargo; filled with the exciting sight of boats of all shapes and sizes coming and going. Noisy, optimistic locals would circle the ship calling out and laughing, peddling their wares or diving for coins. Going ashore was a huge adventure; disembarking from the ship to walk in another land seemed incredibly exciting, almost unreal. At different times we stopped at Singapore, Penang, Colombo, Port Said and Genoa, while during the Suez crisis we sailed right round Africa, calling at Cape Town and Durban as well.

I remember life on board ship as a kind of endless holiday. Once I got over my sea-sickness, each day was always novel, fun and charged with a vital sense of joy. Everything was different from life on land, from constantly having to step over the sturdy steel thresholds of the watertight doors to swimming in a collapsible swimming pool on deck filled with seawater. I can still remember the delight I felt as water was pumped up from the sea, abruptly inflating the flat canvas hose to disgorge a flood of salt water into the pool, filling it in minutes. It felt as if the wild essence of the ocean had transferred itself onto the deck and allowed us to revel in its elemental nature.

Even the way the toast was served in the dining room seemed excitingly special (no crusts, neatly cut into triangles and stacked in little metal racks next to curled pats of butter). We played deck quoits, throwing thick, round circlets of rope to slide onto score markings painted on the decks (and losing a few over the side), or sneaked out of the cabin at night with other kids to spy on our parents at fancy dress parties in the ballroom. I also managed to terrify my parents by clambering about outside the ships' railings as we passed through the Suez Canal.

The ship ploughed on day and night, with the deep, steady roar of the engines, felt rather than heard, reverberating through the superstructure like the pulse of an immense living being. The ship was dwarfed in its turn by the enormous mass of water we sailed on. The ocean was a constant companion, a vast primal entity with many moods. I loved the sea, though I was awed by its power. I was not old enough to think much about my feelings, but it both scared and fascinated me. I could sense its indifference to human affairs, yet an unnamed exaltation sometimes filled me at its untamed majesty.

I loved the way flying fish skimmed over the water with sunlight twinkling merrily on the wave crests, and I was awestruck by the raw power of its massive leaden waves in stormy weather. I vividly remember watching through thick, rain-lashed plate glass windows as the ship's bow plunged ponderously down so far below the horizon it seemed impossible it would ever rise again, hang there for a long, long moment and then begin its slow, rolling climb once more.

I remember little about the first trip to Australia, just isolated images of egg-collecting on a farm, dead lizards by the side of the road and waking in a sleeper carriage to find people looking in through the window as our train pulled into a station somewhere between Sydney and Perth. I have more memories of the first trip to England. 'Going home' as it was known in Hong Kong had achieved an almost mythical status in my mind, and I gazed in awe at the miraculous array of red telephone boxes, policemen without guns, bombed-out buildings and conker trees.

Our first stop was a visit to relatives in Sussex, where I was introduced to the amazing phenomenon of 'Jack Frost'. Surprisingly, I do not remember feeling the cold much, just the thrill of the exquisitely beautiful patterns that formed on my bedroom window each morning. We were staying in a hotel and the 'dining room' was a separate, barn-like structure without heating where we went for meals wrapped up in overcoats and scarves, yet my most vivid memory is of the beautiful high wooden ceiling rather than the cold.

Another astonishing new experience was television, which excited me not because of the programmes (which were quite boring) but the extraordinary sense of omnipresence I experienced in front of it. Of course I didn't have a name for it; I just felt very aware that I was entering a domain of shared experience that connected me with people all over the country. It was a kind of womb-like sensation, a feeling of being part of something much greater than myself that gave me a strange sense of comfort and contentment. This awareness receded as I became more familiar with TV, but I have often wondered if it is the real attraction of 'the box'.

Other elderly relatives in Kent fascinated me with their old-world/old-fashioned ways and their 'real English' houses filled with interesting new smells such as wood rot, musty stored fruit and old newspapers. I remember following the progress of a half-crown piece (a coin I had heard about, but never seen before) in the trembling hand of an aged great uncle – it made its way so slowly towards my outstretched palm that I wondered if it would ever actually complete the journey. He not only achieved this much-appreciated transfer of wealth but set out to similarly enrich my sister, with the words, 'and for the girl, ditto repeat-o.'

I recall as a moment of perfect happiness bedding down in the Flying Scotsman at Kings Cross Station, bound for Scotland. We stayed in Scotland for several months, and the astonishing wonder of frost was superseded by the infinitely greater revelation of snow. I was completely amazed by snow; I found it totally magical and have loved it ever since. My first experience of it must have triggered a considerable high in me, I remember feeling totally enthralled at the way it changed the world into a silent, enchanted garden of purity, stillness and beauty. Its pristine loveliness really touched my soul.

An equal and opposite primal element I grew to love in Scotland was the domestic fire. The flickering flames mesmerised me; there was something incredibly beautiful about them that always seemed to hover just beyond the point of recognition. I loved the homely smell of coal burning in the grate and the fitful hissing and crackling it made as it delivered its cosy heat. One of my most magical treats was to have a fire in my bedroom when it was very cold or I was ill. I could imagine nothing better than watching the flickering shadows it threw across the ceiling as I drifted off to sleep.

There were other things about Scotland that were not so nice. I went to a school divided down the middle by a high wall separating Protestants from Catholics. This restriction reduced interaction between the two groups to the mere trading of stones and insults over the wall at break times, but after school the antagonism could spill over into scuffles outside. It did strike me as rather odd, but I was far more concerned with trying to adapt to this new transient life to wonder much about this strange arrangement. I was also introduced to 'the strap', a flat, sturdy length of leather, a substantial part of which was split into nasty strips. The teachers used it on our outstretched hands, and it was extremely painful. It left horrible, swollen white wheals on fingers that could not bend or grip anything for a long time afterwards.

I knew our trip to the UK was temporary and was quite happy to leave it all behind and set off back to Hong Kong. I slipped easily back into shipboard life on the return voyage – and this was the trip that took place during the Suez crisis, which meant we were at sea for eight weeks, sailing around Africa. Arriving back in Hong Kong was a lot more like going home than coming to England had been. I vividly remember looking out of a porthole and watching familiar sights come into view that seemed almost unreal after everything that had happened. My old life came flooding back, filling me with happiness. For a while reality itself became the stuff of dreams and to this day I sometimes dream of finding myself back in Hong Kong where life is wonderfully familiar, alive with colour and exotic fragrance, and full of joy.

The next few years, between the age of about six to ten, is the period I remember most about Hong Kong. I picked up where I had left off, returning to my old school and friends, and things went on as they had before. Life became more interesting as we got older; our explorations of the surrounding territory grew bolder and our games more daring. We succeeded in breaking into a big tunnel under the hillside through a ventilation shaft and explored it in terrified glee; until I boasted about it to my parents and ended up having to lead a posse of adults to it, who unsportingly had it bricked up.

Typhoons were exciting, too. We would stay out for as long as we could as the winds grew in power then rush out afterwards to build camps in blown-down trees. I remember watching a resolute delivery man on a push bike with a big basket in front of it labouring through the winds of an approaching typhoon. He stopped and leaned his bike against the hilltop perimeter wall to deliver something, and had barely left it when a huge gust of wind lifted it straight up in the air and dropped it neatly over the other side, down an eight foot drop to the top of the steep slope of the 'roly-poly'.

Snake hunting figured high in our self-invented mythology, but since our technique was basically to throw fireworks into likely looking holes on the hillside it was unsurprising that we never actually found any. We only came across snakes by accident, one of them a bright green specimen that made its presence known with an indignant hiss as I crouched down over it. (At which point our roles were swiftly reversed and the hunter took off like a rocket.) The largest snake we found was probably already dead, but just to be sure we pushed a heavy grass roller over it. We stuffed it into a large biscuit tin and took it to school to show our nature-study teacher, who was less than pleased when we removed the lid and some kind of reflex action caused it to uncoil out all over the table. There were other fairly exotic creatures in the environment too; wild cats, giant centipedes, glow worms, praying mantis and huge dragon-flies.

I loved fireworks, and for this Hong Kong was a great place to be. Chinese bangers looked like small sticks of dynamite, a nice red colour with long, thin, fizzy grey fuses. The Chinese used to weave the fuses together to create long, densely packed double or triple rows of bangers that looked a bit like belts of machine-gun ammunition. They would hang these fireworks from their balconies at Chinese New Year, where they would go off deafeningly, continuously and endlessly. Having so many bangers all going off in one go seemed a bit of a waste to me, and I liked to take these potent 'ammunition belts' apart to create huge stores of explosives to have more fun with. Guy Fawkes Night was the expats' turn to light up the sky, and it was great to have two firework nights a year. Even the morning after the 5th November was exciting, when I would race around with my friends looking for unexpired fireworks before the school bus arrived.

The ponderous shadow of the Second World War still hung over everything, and it was common for kids to play 'war games', but for some reason we decided only 'real war' was the way to go. The hill where we lived was a natural defensive position, and perhaps we were infected by the restless spirits of the British and Japanese soldiers who had died on its slopes or inspired by the defences with which the Japanese had then honeycombed the hill. We were certainly inspired by the activities of the Hong Kong Defence Force, which involved a certain amount of watching our dads march about in military parades and finding 303 rifle ammunition rolling about in the back of the family car. 'Real war' demanded such things as wedging slivers of glass into the end of our bamboo spears, building HQs that could be set on fire by the enemy and standing in opposing lines firing salvos of rockets at each other. On one occasion, unfortunately, a rocket hit a passing pram just as a set-piece battle was achieving something like the real thing, and an extremely irate mother routed both armies single-handedly.

My love of fire had followed me back to Hong Kong and led to trouble when we were inspired to take turns lighting fires on the hillside and dare each other to wait longer and longer before putting them out. I don't remember who the idiot with the most bottle was, just the panic as the fire spread with increasing ferocity all around us. It was soon frighteningly out of control, and we fled. My parents arrived home to find fire engines hard at work on a sizeable conflagration and my alibi somewhat compromised by me hiding under my bed yelling, 'I didn't do it!'

I also went through a phase where I liked nothing better than shutting myself up in a large built-in cupboard and holding burning matches against the paint to watch it blister. It was fairly typical of my ability to become absorbed in experiences and remain oblivious of the risks involved. Licking the ice-box in the fridge fitted into this category. My tongue froze to the ice and I could not even call out for help, but luckily my frantic 'Ahh! Ahh! Ahh!' noises attracted attention from another room and I was saved by some dexterously applied warm water.

This kind of episode seemed to happen fairly regularly. I remember freewheeling down a hill on a push bike as a teenager and wondering what would happen if I let go of the handlebars and did nothing to steer the bike. The bike kept going for a surprisingly long time but my mood of abstract contemplation lasted longer and the next thing I knew my face was scraping along the surface of the road. I did retain a certain satisfaction from following the experience through to the end, though.

Surprisingly, I do not remember experiencing much regret when the time came to go back to England for good. I mostly remembered the good things about England by then, I imagine, and I was looking forward to being on a ship again. I suppose it seemed to me that travelling from one part of the world to another was not particularly difficult, and I airily assumed I would return to Hong Kong sooner or later. The voyage back was wonderful as always, although marred a little this time by the thought of sharks lurking in the sea below me. I was older and more independent on this trip; I made friends with other kids, and we had a great time playing and exploring all around the ship. Alas, though, once I was back in England a curtain came down on my old, carefree, globetrotting life, and a new more difficult and painful existence began.

Chapter 2
Home is where the heart is

I did not comprehend how much things had changed at first, being fully occupied with surviving the fire-fight I was dropped into at a decidedly provincial village school in Sussex. Here my sisters and I had an insurmountable problem. We talked 'posh', or at least differently, and the teacher did the worst thing imaginable by asking us to stand up and hold forth about all of the interesting things we had seen in our travels.

Most of the kids who had not hated us on sight hated us after that, and it marked the beginning of an endless three months of taunting, nasty jokes and snubs. The kids there (with a few exceptions) went to extraordinary lengths to make us feel unwelcome. Out of school hours they would follow and harass us, and even threw stones at my mother pushing my younger brother in a pram.

Little did they know that they were dealing with the veteran of a Hong Kong battle group, however, and I armed myself with a mace and chain I made to keep them at bay. (Luckily I never actually tried to use it.) One day I received an invitation to meet a large group of the kids at the village playing fields because they 'wanted to make friends'. Naturally I was honour-bound to go unarmed, and, when I got there, true to form they locked me into a barn and loudly debated my fate outside the doors. It was obviously a situation calling for my jungle warfare skills to kick in, and I managed not only to escape from the barn through some loose boards at the back but also to evade a hot pursuit by the whole pack of them and work my way back home without being caught. I felt quite pleased at this success and was beginning to feel I could hold my own in this hostile environment, when suddenly it was time for a change again.

For some reason it was decided we were going to live in Somerset, and off we went house hunting. We stayed in a hotel, and a house was eventually chosen, but I didn't get to move into it with the rest of the family. Instead, at age ten, I was sent off to boarding school. Somehow I did not question the idea, events moved with a kind of dreamlike inevitability and I was dropped off by my father, astonished and bewildered and despondently clutching the amazingly large sum of ten shillings.

The desolation I felt at being left on my own in this strange institution was extraordinary. I hung about in a kind of stunned stupor for a while and then wondered aimlessly off to some nearby shops where I spent part of my newfound wealth on some sugared almonds. I remember vividly how profoundly meaningless the money felt to me and how inadequate a compensation were the sugared almonds for this frightening new reality.

At first it was like living in a bad dream from which I could not awaken. For the first year, our dormitories had orange night lights and the worst feeling in the world was to wake up at night and see that hateful orange glow. It was a feeling of total desolation, as if I had been marooned on another planet. I gradually got used to boarding school but I never liked it, although it helped a lot that I shared the ordeal with a lot of other kids in the same situation. I had plenty of friends, and we all contrived to enjoy ourselves as best we could.

Half term plucked me out of purgatory and propelled me into paradise. Going home seemed too good to be true, and family life was rediscovered as a perfect existence that bubbled with magical joy. This perfect happiness was crowned by our new house, which was actually fairly old, quite large and standing in a sizeable garden with a number of outhouses. The bliss of being home did not always survive the everyday realities of family life of course; my three sisters were younger than me, and my brother the youngest, and we loved and fought with each other much as any other family did. Our home in Somerset was the setting for ten years of ups and downs that were shared and remembered fondly by all of us.

All too soon I was whisked back to school and the dreaded orange night-lights, and life settled down into a pattern of chronic home-sickness and joyous homecomings. These mood swings probably made me more introspective; they set me pondering about the nature of happiness, or perhaps the nature of unhappiness as this was the emotion I felt most acutely.

Boarding school was a rather loveless place, sustained by the camaraderie of lonely boys and policed by men in black determined to make us good Catholics. It was run by black-frocked 'brothers' with an air of menace and steely authority, thinly disguised with a brisk and jolly manner. There were some that showed a human side, of course, but they had to work within the strictures of the system, which preached salvation through prayer, sports, examination results and the cane. Even the 'brother' I liked the most once chased me around and around the classroom with his cane when I was cheeky. I eventually managed to make him laugh, though, by acting like an execution victim, using my handkerchief as a blindfold, and he let me off.

One thing was certain; the endlessly stern observance of 'mass' in the church-sized chapel twice a week before breakfast and 'high (interminably long) mass' on Sunday mornings, followed by 'benediction' (groan) in the afternoon, went a long way towards convincing me that religion was utterly boring. The only relief was to take turns pretending to faint and to be helped out by a grateful assistant.

I felt deeply unhappy at being away from home but tried to keep this to myself. I took to identifying various stages of homesickness with particular places in the school and its grounds, and I would brood there on the emotions of the moment. There was the overwhelming misery of the first day back and the sadness of the fading reality of home at the end of the first week, followed by the abstract detachment of the succeeding weeks, punctuated intermittently with poignant letters from home. Finally the glorious last week would arrive, and I would bask in the certain knowledge of '*this time next week*' until the unbelievable day itself would dawn and I would be transported back to paradise by my father in his car.

There was inevitably a flaw in this scenario; there was trouble in this earthly paradise. I knew I was fortunate in many ways, and I enjoyed life with my family in such a lovely, rambling old house and grounds. Despite this I became conscious of a deeper part of myself that was confused, vulnerable and lonely, and looked out at the world, even at family and friends, with various degrees of trepidation and incomprehension. I remember feeling a mixture of surprise and distress one day after becoming embroiled in an argument with my parents within hours of reaching home. 'Well, that didn't last long,' I thought glumly, as I reviewed the speed with which 'end of term bliss' had dissipated.

I wondered about the deep, aching longing I called homesickness as it seemed a big let-down to be at home and still to be unhappy, and I began to feel I wanted something my family could not give me. The mysterious object of this nameless longing could seem tantalisingly close at times, especially when I was at home and relatively happy. On my return to school, its absence became an aching wound that drowned out everything else for days or even weeks, before settling back into a kind of resigned detachment.

The older I became, the more frightening the world appeared to be. I tended to be ill at ease with strangers, particularly elderly people, and I became more aware of this as I grew older. Generally speaking, I found 'grown ups' quite odd; they seemed clumsy, gross and boring, and often had peculiar habits that could seem alarming or even perverse. They often smelt strange, too, of scent, cigarettes, alcohol and other mysterious things, and their important jobs in the great big outside world seemed somehow tedious, frightening and incomprehensible all at the same time.

I had no ambitions in the adult world; in fact, I was not attracted to it at all. I have always had difficulty in understanding why people talk about 'power' in terms of political or social position. To me, having power was being able to walk on water or raise the dead. It was not a religious feeling but a conviction that life should be full of magic and wonder, and it drove me to spend much of my time daydreaming, drawing, reading or writing stories.

I had some kind of vague, unformulated belief that a perfect, magical reality existed somewhere and that sooner or later I was bound to stumble across it. I remember a school text-book containing simple, idyllic sketches of prehistoric humans sitting around a fire or catching fish in a river that transported me into an intense reverie of pure delight. I would literally shiver with ecstasy at the miraculous simplicity that these images conjured within me, and my ability to lose myself in this kind of magical inspiration, real or imagined, led me to develop quite a capacity to escape the more mundane concerns of everyday life. Watching the (1959) movie 'The Time Machine' at the age of about twelve, for instance, held me spellbound to such a degree that it took me a full week to realise it wasn't real.

There was also a more martial side to my imagination, perhaps an echo of my Hong Kong 'militia' days. One of my pastimes was drawing lots of little men engaged in wars with each other. They all wore tunics belted at the waist and had calf-length boots, cloaks and little helmets, and coloured uniforms to tell them apart. As well as this, I delighted in writing dramatic adventures about a not unfamiliar band of schoolboys engaged in epic struggles against fire, flood, earthquakes and mysteriously appearing dinosaurs. We used fountain pens refilled from bottles of ink at the time, and I can still remember the sweet metallic tang of the ink that always conjured up the thrilling sense of limitless creative possibilities.

My artistic and literary efforts tended mostly to be enjoyed only by me, a somewhat unfortunate exception being a Catholic 'brother' at my boarding school, who picked up one of my stories about a school revolt in which every teacher was captured and tortured to death in graphic detail. He informed me I had a dangerous imagination, the subtext being that several of my victims, including him, were men of God. His dour warning did not impress me, of course, my experience with men of God and their nasty swishy canes having convinced me that they deserved anything I could dream up. They literally beat us black and blue at times, although even this had its compensations as communal showers were a great venue for showing off our war wounds.

My thirst for interesting experiences caused me to gravitate towards kindred spirits at school, and a little gang of us developed, each honour-bound to make life as exciting as possible. We kept a weather eye open for suitably interesting places and set about exploring them at every opportunity. The school was situated in a residential suburban area within striking distance of shops, the seaside, cliffs, bracken-covered downs and a river estuary, which gave us plenty of scope for fun.

We had lots of adventures, a couple of which turned out to be a little more exciting than we had bargained for. One of these took place in the roof space of the main school building in the middle of the night. It was a large, old building, and the loft was an extensive labyrinth of interconnecting spaces. We made our way through different parts of it, at one point squeezing through a narrow gap between the rafters and a large water tank, quite convinced we were on the verge of discovering something amazing. Instead, we finally came up against a dead end, and as we shone our only torch onto the rough brickwork of the disappointing gable end wall the light flickered and died.

I remember a moment of pure terror, followed by an eternity of panic-stricken scrabbling about in total darkness as we tried to find our way out. We were quite desperate, and were talking about breaking through the plaster ceilings below the wooden joists we were crawling on when I had a stroke of luck. Crawling blindly along in no particular direction, I touched the water tank we had squeezed past. From there we managed to find our way out, filthy dirty, moderately traumatised and cured of any further ambitions in loft exploration.

Instead, we turned our attention to outdoor pursuits and set off on a carefully planned trip about midnight one Friday the thirteenth to a churchyard, a mile or so from the school, looking for ghosts. We failed to find any, although we did note some suitably mysterious feelings and weird smells, but on our way back to school we were stopped by a policeman. We blithely told him we were coming back from a party, and, despite the image we must have presented as a group of twelve- or thirteen-year-olds wandering about at two o'clock in the morning (it was the early sixties), he surprisingly let us go.

However, word of our escapade got back to the headmaster, and we were hauled before him to have an impressive amount of fire and brimstone heaped upon us and our pocket money cancelled for the foreseeable future. I felt it had been well worth while, though, as it had been amazing fun and had furthered my research into spiritual matters. I had been reading a lot of Dennis Wheatley books about the occult and was spending a great deal of time trying to remember my dreams as this was supposed to be a first step towards taking control and 'waking up' in the astral realm. This excursion had seemed quite Dennis Wheatley-like, and I was hopeful of more exciting things to come, but it was an ambition that became sidelined as the unexpected encroachment of puberty began to claim centre stage.

One of the great things about this school, in the last year I spent there, was that fishing became recognised as an official sport. This unlikely development allowed us to head off down to the river with our fishing tackle on Wednesday afternoons, Saturday afternoons and a large chunk of the day on Sundays. The river opened out into a sizeable estuary and harbour, and surprisingly we were able to hire small motor boats to go fishing in. This was reasonably affordable because the hire charge depended on the number of occupants, and one of us would hire out each boat while the remainder waited to board them further up river.

Even more surprisingly, this led to me getting my first girlfriend. She happened to be on the river bank with a friend when we cruised past in a couple of boats throwing stones at each other, delightful kids that we were, and one of the stones hit me on the head. I hammed up my injury like a football star, which attracted the attention of one of the girls, and the rest was history, albeit a brief one. I had the distinct feeling I was not ready to have a girlfriend, but she wouldn't take no for an answer. She turned out to be full of useful tips such as how to breathe through the nose while kissing; in fact, I suspect that her knowledge was a lot more comprehensive than that, but I was not destined to find out as fate intervened to part us.

The spirit of adventure inspiring the 'gang' I was in developed a darker side as some of the more headstrong characters had begun to steer us into activities of a more destructive and light-fingered nature. On one occasion a fire we accidentally started in a tool shed beside a rubbish dump grew out of control, and we had to run for it, something that left me feeling disturbed and unhappy. We began to break into uninhabited properties instead of just exploring derelict ones and shoplifting instead of looking for flotsam and jetsam on the beach, and finally hit rock bottom when the most reckless character among us pushed us into taking money from somebody's dormitory locker. I felt terrible about this, but did not have the courage to denounce it. Instead, I crept back afterwards and returned my share, deciding at the same time to distance myself from the group I had drifted into. It was a timely decision, as it turned out, and I escaped the consequences of a fairly dramatic episode involving the theft of money from the headmaster's office, flight on a stolen motorbike and the expulsion of a gang member from the school.

However, the activities I had been involved in had not completely escaped the notice of the 'brothers' and had reached my parents' ears in the general fallout from the scandal. Along with all this, I had been conducting a long-term 'anti-boarding school' campaign, bombarding my parents with complaints about being away from home and showering them with letters counting off the days until the end of term. The net result was that, at the end of my third year, life changed abruptly again, and I was whisked out of one Catholic boarding school and put into another nearer home.

Chapter 3
Weekend warrior

In my new school, I was a weekly boarder, and this was a great improvement, or at least the part between Friday evenings and Monday mornings was. I still had to go to church on Sundays with my parents, but now I could see the local convent schoolgirls who went there too. There was no more 'mass' before breakfast on weekdays; instead, a priest flung open the dormitory door every morning booming, 'In the name of the Father and of the Son ...' at the top of his voice, and we all had to scramble out of bed and be on our knees praying by the time he got to '... and the Holy Ghost. Amen.' If we failed, the bed was tipped upside down on top of us.

The school was out in the countryside and a long way from shops, derelict houses and girls, and the relief supplied by my fictional fantasy world was now less satisfactory. I still read and wrote a lot, in fact the school library was pretty well stocked, better stocked than the establishment was aware of, I'm sure, as I came across some fairly explicit novels. I gave up on astral travel and began having romantic day-dreams instead, and wrote adventurous females into my stories who didn't mind being constantly rescued from dinosaurs and aliens. Hormones were starting to run amok and life was becoming increasingly complicated, but despite this, or perhaps because of it, I began looking around for new ways to make things more interesting.

Success proved fairly elusive to begin with. I had actually started this process some time earlier, my first experiment in this line being drinking as much water as I could possibly hold; this had certainly given me a marvellously full feeling, but was not absorbing enough to make up for the endless peeing afterwards. Self-induced laughing fits had seemed promising for a while too, when I found I could work myself up into a kind of hysterical jollity in which anything said to me seemed hilariously funny and sent me off into fits of laughter. Unsurprisingly, this was not universally popular and had had to be abandoned. I was now far more sophisticated than this and started off with smoking dried banana skins, and when that didn't work I dissolved aspirin in Coca Cola. I even tried eating shoe polish wrapped in tissue paper. My first major success was inhaling the gas in the chemistry lab at school, which made me quite satisfyingly dizzy.

Running parallel with these investigative activities, the discordant notes of emerging sexuality were growing in persistence and intensity. I had felt its touch before in strange, infrequent episodes during my childhood when unexpected thoughts and feelings of fearful, guilty excitement had rudely intruded into my life, only to vanish and be forgotten for months or even years as if they had never been. Now such feelings were beginning to intrude in a more regular manner, entwined around highly improbable fantasies about equally fanciful females.

School itself was an irritating impediment to my escapist agenda, and I began a separate investigation into ways of getting ill so that I could stay at home. This ranged from standing on the roof at night in a bowl of cold water, trying to catch a cold, to eating soap. I don't know where I got the idea that eating soap would give me a temperature; I just remember being fixated on the exciting idea that a temperature would guarantee me time off school. I can report, in the unlikely event that anyone else is daft enough to try this, not only does it not work but everything tastes of soap for a week afterwards.

The older I became the more disconcerting and incomprehensible the adult world seemed to be. I felt at times as if I were surrounded by a kind of chaotic, mundane dream in which everyone seemed reconciled to their role except me. I could see no purpose or meaning to any of it and was too busy trying to navigate from one alarming situation to another to try and make sense of it all. I was relatively happy at home, but the thought of being fed to the remorseless adult world of oppressive conformity and financial servitude filled me with gloom.

At the same time, something new and exciting was clamouring for attention, a groundswell of music, rebellion and fun. The swinging sixties were arriving and generating an intensity of excitement that grew with every new hit record or movie released. It is difficult to convey the sheer novelty and exhilaration of those times in these more pedestrian days of saturation computer games, wall-to-wall satellite TV and limitless music channels. I remember having goose bumps, the hair on my body literally standing on end, at the thrill I felt as the tinny sounds of *The House of the Rising Sun* rose from an illicit transistor radio concealed in my blazer at school.

There was no contest as to which world I wanted, and this coincided with the discovery that I was not the lone explorer I thought I was; the entire adult population was ingesting and inhaling noxious substances to make life more interesting, and had been doing so for quite a long time. Getting hold of cigarettes meant that I no longer had to inhale gas from the chemistry lab to get dizzy, and once armed with alcohol I was off on a roller-coaster ride that was to last for twelve years.

Alcohol seemed like a magic elixir that had come to my rescue, and I was too excited by how it made me feel to question its pedigree. Suddenly I had the means to change life into a fun-filled adventure any time I wanted, to liberate energy and emotional intensity at will and forget the scariness and officious oppressiveness of the adult world. It gave me the confidence to be what I felt was my real self, made me less self-conscious with the mysterious opposite sex and seemed an ideal accessory to the electrifying new world of rock and roll.

I didn't wait until I left school to get started and at sixteen was caught smuggling whisky into school concealed cunningly (as I thought) in a shampoo bottle. I ran away from this school twice, something that was relatively easy to do as I always had a return ticket each week and had only to make my way a few miles into Exeter and catch a train. Both events were triggered by incidents in which I felt unjustly treated, the second incident perhaps with less conviction.

In the first instance, I was discovered in the dormitory under a pile of mattresses with lots of people jumping up and down on top of me. I felt outraged that so obviously innocent a victim as myself should be included in the punishment, which was detention on the following Friday evening, and I immediately smuggled myself out on the day boys' bus. My homecoming caused much shock and consternation, and I was sent back the next morning, but apart from a surprisingly humane telling off by the headmaster nothing happened, and I never did stay for the Friday-evening detention.

On the second occasion, a posse of us escaped to a nearby pub and got pretty drunk after finishing our GCE 'O' level exams, then ran into a kind of turkey shoot while trying to sneak back into school late at night, with eagle-eyed 'fathers' pouncing on legless revellers clambering in through various windows. Next morning we were 'gated' for a week, a much greater blow than it sounds as we had finished our exams and were supposed to be leaving school that day, a week before the rest of the school. It was also Sports Day, and my parents were driving down to take me home after admiring my athletic abilities.

Being gated after school had ended was obviously outrageous, and there was only one thing to do, so I promptly ran away again. I hitchhiked into town and arrived at the train station, where I happened to bump into my eldest sister and the girl who lived next door. It turned out that they were making the journey to my school by train so there would be room for my luggage and me to go home in the family car. Looking back, it seems slightly odd that they went at all, but I suppose the prospect of watching lots of boys run around in gym shorts had something to do with it. We had a spirited discussion, but I was outnumbered and the gym shorts prevailed. I reluctantly agreed to come back to my school with them and pinned my hopes on my parents negotiating a reprieve.

This did not materialise, of course, and I vented my anger by putting the minimum possible effort into my sporting activities, forcing my embarrassed parents to watch me do the one hundred yards at a slow trot and cover a total distance of about a metre on the hop, skip and jump. Surprisingly, I quite enjoyed the following week, even though we had to spend some of the time rectifying the results of the high-spirited mayhem we had indulged in on that supposed last wild night of school.

Chapter 4
All you need is love

It was about this time that real girls were starting to appear on my horizon, now promising something very different from the oddly dreamlike liaison I had experienced with my 'girlfriend' at my first boarding school. At the time she had orchestrated most of the proceedings, and I had not been old enough to take the whole thing seriously.

Up until this point, much of my attention on the opposite sex had been focused on the same girl next door I had met at the station with my sister. She was about my age and had been coming over to play with my sisters since she was ten or eleven. I passed through a whole gamut of emotions where she was concerned, and at different times she was a friend, playmate, sexual siren and romantic icon, and sometimes several of them at once. She was also, as she reminded me recently, a good sport, and told her parents she had been bitten by her hamster when I accidentally shot her through the finger with my air rifle.

I remember the earlier years I knew her with most affection, when we would sit out in the fading light on long summer evenings and talk about anything that came to mind. I experienced something amazing in her company when we were about twelve or thirteen. We had made a kind of camp behind some outhouses in her garden, and inside this idyllic little construction I went into a state similar to the one I had experienced at the sight of the prehistoric men in my school text-book. I found myself suddenly in a magical world in which she had become a wonderful, almost holy being, a kind of sacred handmaiden of the Earth Mother (the nearest I can get to describing it). It was unexpected and astonishing, and affected me profoundly, but I made no effort to tell her or anyone else about it. It was very special and seemed to belong to another world entirely. I did not feel capable of communicating it to anyone, and I felt sure I would be laughed at if I tried.

My first couple of encounters with girls were pretty forced and contrived, pursued because I felt it was expected of me as much as anything else and I felt shy and awkward, and unsure about how I was supposed to behave with them. Puberty was in full swing and life was becoming increasingly bewildering. I was surrounded by images of sexual and romantic fulfilment in films, magazines, songs and advertising, and assailed by Catholic conditioning about impurity and sin. A lack of sin did not seem to have much going for it, however, certainly offering no real alternative to the fun everyone else seemed to be having; and the drive towards union with the opposite sex, both carnal and romantic, was just too strong.

My problem was that I didn't know where fantasy ended and reality began. There were times when I would have been happy to get through thirty minutes without thinking about sex, and trying to reconcile randomly rampant physical urges and far-fetched romantic expectations with the fresh-faced, reticent young ladies I could see around me was as confusing as it was daunting. It did not occur to me that trying to engineer a relationship was ridiculous until I met a girl I really did care about, and then everything was very different.

At first life was great. I left school and went to art college. I rode around on my scooter with my friends, sometimes as part of larger packs, went to lots of parties and drank a lot. I lived in the West of England, where there were plenty of nice country pubs to visit and wooded hills and beaches for fire-lit revelry. A fair amount of activity also took place at my home, where there was room for lots of people. My parents were remarkably accommodating, and there were sometimes a dozen scooters and motorbikes parked in the drive, with two or three friends often staying over for the weekend.

We had a sizeable garden with a number of outhouses, and even a swimming pool for which the family had given up a holiday one year to help with its construction. One of the outhouses was a double garage connected in an L shape to another shed, which provided quite a lot of space, and we hung netting and coloured lights everywhere and had garage parties decades before their time.

My first real girlfriend affected me quite profoundly. I was still hopelessly shy and socially inept, but now I felt something amazing. She made me touch base with something special, something deep and simple that seemed almost sacred. Sexuality was relegated to a natural, somehow less imperative role and replaced by something I valued a lot more, a sense of silent companionship, an instinctive trust and an awareness of things beyond words. I did not realise for a long time just how rare this actually was. I saw something so beautiful in her that I found it hard to believe I was looking at flesh and blood, as if there were some mystery about the female form that hovered on the edge of understanding. I was not really aware of how high I was flying; I just accepted it as the natural order of things and basked in a new sun of happiness.

Such a Utopian development was too good to last, of course, and sure enough a cloud appeared on the horizon. Her father took a dislike to me and forbade her to see me. This was unusually draconian even in those days, but her father was a forceful man and she was not really old enough to do as she pleased. Months of agonising intrigue followed, with secret letters and clandestine meetings. Finally, however, the female form turned off the supply to my overflowing cup and dumped me. I had not known how vehemently her father disapproved of me and only learned much later of the lengths to which he had gone to force her into it. It came as a profound shock; I could not believe that something in which I had so much trust could betray me.

It was of course foolish and unfair to have invested all of my faith in the goodness of the world in one person. (But, having said that, I met her again recently and still think she is an angel! She ended up in Australia, where she teaches Hatha Yoga.) At the time, all I knew was that it hurt like hell. For the first time, I got so drunk I lost all memory of what had happened, and the next morning my awestruck sisters had to fill me in on the struggles of my unfortunate parents to calm me down while I screamed and cried my heart out.

The pain lasted for a long time, and I aggravated it by drinking vast quantities of cider and brooding over pop songs that reminded me of her. Life went on and I acquired another girlfriend, largely through her persistence, and I was surprised to find that the more indifferent I was to her, the more she seemed to like me. She was a sweet girl, and I became quite fond of her, but I had no interest in anything serious.

Eventually I did fall in love again, but in quite a different way. This time, I wisely chose a young lady hitchhiking through town in fringed jeans and bare feet. She was fascinatingly different from anyone I had met before, quite precocious, fond of admiring cloud formations and knowledgeable about all sorts of things beyond the horizons of rural West Country life. She was also an attractive girl who enjoyed flirting, drank as much as I did and had a habit of begging money from strangers. When I first met her, she and her friend were being chased around by a hapless policeman trying to get his helmet back from them.

There was obviously no chance of an overbearing father here. There was a strong attraction between us and we got together, but it was a very different relationship from my first. Instead of a sense of joy and fulfilment, there was emotional turmoil and overwhelming need. She found a place to stay and hung out with the gang of people I knew, and the usual round of parties and pub crawls began to be supplemented with trips further afield, hitchhiking or on scooters along with some of my friends.

She continued to flirt and to do outrageous things, but we sought each other out at night. We got drunk together and cried together, with neither of us really knowing why. We spent a fair amount of time crashed out in hay barns, and the two of us were discovered passed out in the street in Edinburgh by the police. (How different those times were; the law woke us up, helped us across the road and arranged for us to sleep in a taxi parked for the night in a yard. They even got a colleague to come around in the morning to make sure we were all right.)

The relationship hit troubled waters when my partner-in-passion discovered she was pregnant. Life was suddenly complicated and confusing, all the more so because she turned out to have a deep complex about babies. The solution was a simple one on the face of it because at that time the accepted convention was either marriage or adoption. The reality was anything but simple, though, as my ever-original other half decided she didn't mind getting married, but wanted the child adopted. It seems quite extraordinary looking back on it, and it was horrendously confusing at the time. Marriage and babies had not figured in my world-view at all up to this point, and I was suddenly confronted by huge decisions about both of these things. I was plunging into a maelstrom of conflicting emotions and drinking more and more recklessly in order to escape them.

My parents were not at all keen on their potential daughter-in-law, but the idea of their first grandchild disappearing into an orphanage horrified them. I floundered hopelessly as high drama and emotional storms swept around the family, and in a kind of numb bemusement I accepted that we would get married and my parents would look after the child initially, with some fairly flexible options awaiting post-natal developments.

Everyone believed my un-blushing bride would change her mind after the child was born, but I was not convinced they were right. Events proved she knew her own mind only too well, and the strange arrangement went ahead, greatly to the credit of my parents. In fairness, I do not believe it was a selfish or perverse decision on my wife's part. She couldn't help her horror of babies. There was a reason for it and it troubled her deeply, and there were tragic episodes in which she tried to take him back but found that she couldn't cope. My long-suffering parents shared in these difficult moments too, and behaved with quite astonishing forbearance and selflessness.

Dramatic events had heralded the birth as my family home was flooded the night our son was born. I marked the occasion by getting royally drunk, of course, and threw a week-long party at our own place while my wife was in hospital. Visits from friends had been restricted in the final weeks of pregnancy and much lost time was made up for. Unfortunately though, I didn't get around to dealing with the aftermath. The house was knee deep in empty bottles when my wife got home, and a strange new phase in our life began with my spouse sitting on the bed in ominous silence while I feverishly cleared up.

Chapter 5
Karma drama

The whole situation, with our son living a few miles from us, was quite bizarre. It was having some strange effects on me and my wife was struggling with her own demons, and it was not long before we decided to move away to Oxford, which was a place she had a thing about. We drove there in an old van and lived out of it while looking for work and somewhere to stay; and after a couple of days I found a job and we moved into an attic bedsit in the unusually named Divinity Road.

I had the most alcoholic Christmas ever at my parents-in-law's house, for, although in many ways they were a perfectly respectable forces family of officer rank, they took an extremely lively view of the festive season. Things got off to a good start when my father-in-law took me out to walk the dog, misjudged a high-spirited twirl around a lamp post, and dived headfirst into a ditch. Next my mother-in-law dropped the turkey in the kitchen, which was immediately pounced on by the dog. Any remaining illusions about oldies being boring vanished as she got down on her hands and knees and wrestled the turkey back from the dog, each growling at the other with their teeth sunk into opposite ends of the bird.

After this, a night out with my sister-in-law and her new boyfriend ended up in a drunken fight on the front lawn at two o'clock in the morning. Unsurprisingly, it was triggered by my wife's lively view of other people's boyfriends, and it was only afterwards that I realised I had stood by while he slapped my wife and then whacked him when he did the same to my sister-in-law. It was not the end of the story, either, as the conflict spilled over into the boyfriend's family house down the road next day, with my mother-in-law leading the charge.

I awoke from several days of liquid festive cheer with the worst hangover of my life. I opened my eyes and felt so horribly ill that I couldn't bear to lie still, but when I struggled to sit up my head swam and I began to pass out and had to lie down again. I could hear a radio next to my head blaring out the news at full volume that stopped abruptly when I tried to find where it was coming from, and when I looked around the room I could see ghostly animals in garish colours floating in the air. It was like being trapped in hell and seemed to last for an eternity. Things did not get much better when I finally did struggle to my feet as I found myself urinating blood into the toilet. It put me off drinking for a whole three weeks.

I suspect that one of the reasons I didn't kill myself with alcohol was that I couldn't afford to drink spirits very often. I was probably fortunate that their relative cost was so much higher at the time. A full bottle of spirits might have cost the equivalent of a day's unskilled labour at this point, while it would currently be more like one or two hours. I came near to putting an end to myself in Oxford – more than once in fact. I went to a party at a West Indian friend's flat after an evening in the pub and started knocking back tumblers of neat mixed spirits. I apparently passed out while still on my feet and was carried home unconscious, waking up next morning on the floor with my wife kicking me furiously and yelling, 'Wake up, you bastard, and go to work!' Afterwards, I learned that she was entitled to be angry. She had been up most of the night trying to prevent me inhaling my own vomit and could well have saved my life.

Something else that started to calm my alcoholic excesses a little was cannabis, which was becoming more prevalent about this time. It made me happier and more content than alcohol did and helped to calm the reckless boozing. I only smoked it occasionally at first, to begin with valuing it mostly because it was such an excellent hangover cure. Over a number of years, I mixed it with alcohol more and more often, until I eventually abandoned alcohol almost completely.

Oxford was a curious place, a strange mixture of beautiful buildings and mysterious gloom. We lived a somewhat surreal life, acting as if our child did not exist and starting to get to know a whole new group of friends. Actually, these were acquaintances rather than friends, at least to me they were. Many of the people we met were involved in the drug scene, or at least in the fashionable psychedelic side of it, and appeared to be playing elaborate games whose rules I did not understand.

Once the novelty of being permanently surrounded by projected swirling colours and wearing flowery shirts began to wear off, I did not feel particularly attracted to them. I did make one lifelong friend in Oxford, a guy I got to know while selling fish, of all things. He was as out of his element as I was in the fish shop, taking time out from university, and we later both ended up in London.

I suppose my initial antipathy towards the psychedelic scene was somewhat surprising, considering my earlier interest in unusual experiences. I had not really connected with that part of myself much for some time, in fact, having been somewhat sidetracked by the heavy emotional drama of my unusual marriage. I was not particularly happy and spent a lot of time getting drunk and listening to music that reminded me of my first girlfriend. I had also become used to socialising with alcohol, laughing and swapping jokes in noisy pubs and parties. Sitting in stoned silence and listening to weird music while striking poses and exchanging significant looks was quite alien to me.

Also, my wife was an attractive girl; some of our new friends smelt blood in the water where our marriage was concerned, and they made no secret of their ambitions. She loved all the attention and took to this strange new world with great enthusiasm; our relationship became increasingly disconnected, and we drifted through a hazy progression of psychedelic parties towards an inevitable parting of the ways.

My first overtly 'spiritual' experience occurred when the relationship finally hit rock bottom. I was upset and depressed, but not just about the break-up. I had been dumped again, but there had been occasions when I had thought it might be nice to get out of the relationship too. I was still attached to my wife, even though the relationship had become difficult, and I had always had a kind of innate conviction that relationships were for keeps.

I did not feel the shock and disbelief I had experienced the first time around; instead there was a sense of fatalistic desolation, a feeling that everything I had hoped for in life had slipped through my fingers. Now it seemed that the magical land that had always shimmered on the horizon was just a mirage, and if this was all there was to life I did not want it. In a fit of depression, I went out and bought lots of aspirin, spent forever swallowing, them then kissed the world goodbye and lay down to make my exit on the floor of our dingy bed-sit. I had no idea at the time that a lethal dose of aspirin might take days to kill me.

Perhaps I should have taken more notice of the name of the road I lived in. I was beginning to feel a bit strange, when I noticed a small platinum disc spinning in the air near the ceiling, and, idly curious, I watched it start to move down towards me. It grew rapidly in size and became golden, spinning closer and closer until it filled my vision. Then, abruptly, it stopped, and I was startled to see the face of Christ etched within it, glaring fiercely at me. It shocked me out of the growing lassitude that was settling over me, and I jumped up without thinking, gulped down as much salt water as I could and vomited up a lot of aspirin. I felt pretty rough for a few days, with everyone I met seemingly talking to me from the other end of a long tunnel, but I gradually returned to normal.

Strangely enough, I then put the whole episode behind me and got on with my life. I rarely thought about it or questioned it in any depth for years. I suppose I just consigned it to the vault of inexplicable things that I couldn't talk to anyone about, including myself. There were a lot of confused emotions swirling about inside me that overrode everything else; I was not much given to introspection at this point in my life, largely, I imagine, because I was avoiding the emotional minefield surrounding my son. I managed to avoid facing any real spiritual issues over the incident and yet accepted on some level that I was not allowed to jump ship. I knew I had to go on living, but not why, and I did not feel particularly inclined to like it much.

I moved back to my parents in the West Country, got myself a job on a farm and bought a large motorbike. With the basics established, I re-entered my old social scene and proceeded to burn the candle at as many ends as possible. I roared about the countryside in a permanently exhausted, drunken or hung-over condition, getting up very early in the morning, working very hard physically and spending as much time as possible at pubs and parties.

A few weeks after leaving Oxford, I started to feel a deep aching pain in the left side of my chest and to experience heart palpitations, or at least what I assumed were palpitations, lots of irregular skips and jumps. I also became hyper-aware of my heart beating sometimes; it seemed heavy and out of rhythm somehow, like the shuddering vibration set up in a car when the engine tick-over drops too low.

A visit to the doctor produced a total lack of findings. Nothing was wrong with my heart, I was told. The symptoms persisted on and off for years, and I tried a couple more times to get them medically checked out but always with the same result. There was nothing wrong. The only thing I could say with any certainty was that it became more acute after drinking binges, and in the end I just learned to ignore it. It was not until a long time later that I learned what these symptoms meant.

I actually enjoyed working on the farm. Wandering around a dark field at six o'clock in the morning to round up the cows took a certain amount of perseverance, but driving them leisurely back from milking in the morning sun and anticipating a two-hour breakfast break was great. I liked the hard physical work and bombing around the fields and country lanes on tractors. The farm was on fairly high ground and there were some fabulous views of the rolling Somerset hills. I liked the earthy reality of farm life and the natural cycles of the work; it felt good to plant the seeds, harvest the corn and bale the hay and the straw.

The animals were fun. I was fascinated by the individual characters of the cows and how they always went through the gate in the same order; and I had lots of adventures with pigs, mostly of the life-threatening kind. I had no idea pigs could be so aggressive; one jumped clean over the gate to its sty and went for me, barking like a dog. I could only fend it bloodily off with my pitchfork and yell for help until a (large) fellow farm-hand whacked it over the head with a railway sleeper. Another pig knocked me right out through the side of its hut, and the piece de resistance was an escaped boar that turned around and charged us as we chased it in a tractor. It actually burst the front tire with its tusk, and it pranced up and down the road in great satisfaction as we abandoned the tractor and retreated to consider plan B.

In many ways work was a relief from the rest of my life, which I mostly spent drunk, stoned or asleep. I would sometimes arrive for milking on a Sunday morning straight from parties, wearing gaudy clothes and much the worse for wear. It was something the cows tended not to appreciate, and it earned me some well-aimed kicks.

Once again I acquired a girlfriend I was not really interested in, and once again I found that the less affection I showed her, the more she seemed to like me. Outwardly, I worked hard at enjoying myself, which mostly meant drinking like an idiot and doing monumentally stupid things like jumping into the bonfire one night yelling, 'I am the god of hellfire!' and melting my cowboy boots. (I also seem to remember jumping into someone's swimming pool on the way home and arriving dripping wet and extremely tipsy in the middle of 'after-church breakfast'.)

Inside, I was unhappy, even suicidal at times. When I wasn't raving to Led Zeppelin or Black Sabbath, I would listen to Leonard Cohen and brood darkly on the absence of true love in the world. The fact that I could do this while ignoring both the girl I was with and the thicket of conflicting emotions surrounding my son speaks volumes for the idiotic nature of my ego. I was living a totally self-indulgent life at home, behaving like a teenager and treating my son like a younger brother while my long-suffering parents brought him up. Looking back, there was so much pain, confusion and guilt going on inside me that I scarcely knew what I was doing.

A couple of times, though, something different happened. One night, I shared some cannabis at a flat I had gone to after the pub closed and almost immediately felt a powerful surge of energy move up through my body and explode in my head. Everything around me was suddenly changed into wonderland. I was convinced that a funfair had set up in the road outside, complete with music and lights, and that angels were singing in the sky above. I felt ecstatically happy and could not understand why no one else wanted to rush out and enjoy the fun.

A second incident took place on a beach late at night as a crowd of us sat around a bonfire. There were no drugs about, but there had been a fair amount of alcohol consumed. I have always loved staring into fires, but now I felt transfixed by its beauty, and a profound sense of peace and contentment grew inside me. The fire-lit scene took on the appearance of an artistic masterpiece, and the sense of peace deepened into an intense, silent joy. I felt amazingly relaxed and everything about the moment seemed perfect. I tried to communicate what was happening and failed. Anything I said was hopelessly inadequate and was just taken as the drink talking. It was as difficult to explain the next day, and I didn't really try. I didn't understand it myself, but it lingered at the back of my mind, along with the other experience, as a kind of elusive utopian state of being that I vaguely associated with alcohol and cannabis.

Events took a new turn when I fell off my motorbike one night in front of a police car while extremely drunk. Knowing I was going to lose my licence, I decided to move up to London, where it was easier to get around and to find work without needing to drive, and I set off a few weeks later. I knew a number of people who had moved to London, and I crashed on various floors until more friends or friends of friends from the West Country turned up and we got a flat together. For a year or two, life was something of a home from home. I got a job as a despatch clerk in Oxford Street and hung out with a gang of people who mostly went to the same pubs and parties.

My girlfriend remained in the West Country and, although we met up a couple of times, our liaison faded away, which suited me as I no longer really felt capable of or interested in having a relationship. For a while new sights and experiences, and the different scale of everything in London stimulated a certain amount of novelty. But, with an unexciting job and no motorbike to roar about on, drinking increasingly became my centre of attention and, apart from reading science fiction and occasionally daydreaming about joining the merchant navy, I became largely preoccupied with trying to escape a creeping sense of gloom and despair in an increasingly manic alcoholic haze.

An important part of the high that drink gave me was the expectation of the release it would bring from the mundane life I felt stuck in; however, it rarely lived up to its promise. The initial energised exuberance would gradually lose its edge, and I would drink more and more to try and keep it going, but the steady drinking put me into a kind of intense emotional fog where I was fixated on a high I wanted to reach rather than the state I was actually in, and I would routinely spend the first half of a party hiding bottles and the second half trying to find them again. I didn't just want to feel good, I wanted everyone else to feel good too, and I would run around trying to be the life and soul of the party without ever really noticing that the crowning moment never actually arrived; I never reached the perfect joy that always lingered just beyond the next drink.

My drinking became steadily worse, and I got to the point where I could sometimes pour pints of beer straight down my throat without swallowing, and frequently drank throughout the weekend without eating at all. I was off sick so often after the weekend that my boss offered me a pay rise if I guaranteed to come to work on Mondays. I thought this was a creative approach, and I felt morally bound to comply, but some of the states I turned up in beggared belief. My hangovers were awful and often lasted a couple of days. Not only would I feel horribly ill, but the deep aching pain in the left side of my chest could be almost unbearable, my heart would skip and jump, and its heavy, arrhythmic thumping made it impossible to relax. It was often so bad that I would be unable to sleep on Monday nights, and I began to use increasing amounts of cannabis as a hangover cure and a way of reducing alcohol consumption.

Most of the people I knew in London were not really into smoking dope, and for a while it was something that only happened occasionally; however, some of my friends began to show an interest, and with the widespread availability of drugs in London we began using it more and more. I suppose the drinking scene seemed to be acquiring a somewhat jaded air, and mixing alcohol with cannabis reintroduced a sense of novelty and fun. It was a little like discovering alcohol all over again, and we enjoyed it just as friends having a good time, without the kind of studied seriousness I remembered from Oxford.

Nevertheless, just as had been the case with alcohol, getting stoned became more important to me than it was to my friends, and I began to develop an interest in others who seemed likewise inclined. I had steered clear of the drug scene per se up to this point due to the unhappy associations it had for me from Oxford and the eccentric appearance of many of its apostles. The contact I had had with 'druggies' had been fairly arbitrary and had taken place only to obtain cannabis from time to time. We had got to know a few of these types on the periphery of the circles we socialised in, including a group that lived in a flat nearby. Most seemed nice enough, but I still had reservations about them. One we nicknamed 'the cloaked wonder', on account of the purple velvet cloak he wore everywhere. He had a somewhat off-beat theory that one should never pause for traffic when crossing the road; and his sudden disappearance from the neighbourhood one day was put down to either a flaw in his theory or a momentary loss of faith while carrying it out.

A sea change in my attitude to the drug scene occurred when a hippy couple arrived to stay at the French girls' flat below us. (I have never actually met anyone who called themselves a hippy. In the sixties the people in my neck of the woods who took drugs were known as 'heads' for some reason, and those I got to know later referred to themselves as 'freaks'.) Unexpectedly, the said couple (the guy Australian and his girlfriend French) were to become long-term friends.

Chapter 6
For this is all a dream we dreamed

They were an unusual pair, but fun to be around, and I was surprised at how much I enjoyed their company. I felt a strange sense of recognition and affinity that I could not explain, and the more I got to know them, the more interested I became in what they had to say.

I liked the fact that they were more interested in creating a magical, genial environment than in the everyday concerns of material existence. They reawakened a sense of the mystery of life in me, and I became increasingly fascinated by their descriptions of consciousness-altering drugs, such as LSD. Their involvement in the psychedelic scene went back a long way, and they knew a great deal about the states of consciousness such drugs could produce. It did not take them long to convince me – and a startling wake-up call began in my life.

Generally speaking, LSD dissolved or stripped away much of the outer personality in which my sense of self normally dwelt and exposed a deeper, more primal self that felt amazingly alive and aware. All of my senses were greatly magnified: touch, taste, sound and colours were amazingly vivid, and emotions greatly heightened. My experiences varied tremendously, and I found I could penetrate into many different depths of perception of myself and of my environment.

It was a lot of fun to begin with; there was great novelty in having completely new perceptions of everything. I could play around mentally and emotionally, become fascinated by new ideas and perspectives, have wild hallucinations and find childish enjoyment or hysterical amusement in the simplest of things. I remember taking hours to make a hot drink for my flatmates, laboriously lining up all the cups in a row and filling each with hot water with great effort and concentration, only to discover I had filled the sugar bowl as well and collapse helpless with laughter for the rest of the trip.

As well as enjoying myself, I became aware of a deeper, more contemplative self that was unimpressed by superficial games and posturing, and I began to see I was not always true to this self; I was not as honest, open and genuine as I thought I was. At the same time, I felt a deep empathy with people who were 'serious' about taking LSD. They showed me I could enter deeper levels of experience by becoming more introspective instead of playing around with the interesting new manifestations of my psyche, and that I could have superficial, confusing or frightening experiences in situations where I felt psychologically vulnerable. They demonstrated that taking LSD in a peaceful and secure environment with like-minded people could be a very special experience indeed.

It can be understandably difficult for someone without direct experience of LSD to believe that anything real or profound might be attained through its use. Contemporary wisdom holds that such experiences are hallucinations created by the brain and unique to the individual, and crossing the subjective threshold is seen as compromising the power of objective judgement. It is a Catch-22 situation that might seem perfectly sensible to the rational mind but is quite laughable in the face of the sheer magnitude of the experiences that can be achieved.

Nor is it purely a question of impact or intensity but rather an innate recognition of new and self-evident perspectives on the nature of reality, among them the surprising one that these experiences are collective in nature and can be shared by many people at once. Just how a substance like LSD can trigger such powerful psychic events I have no idea. My best guess is that it may mimic chemicals produced naturally in the body in high-energy states and trigger latent processes built into the nervous system. I have certainly found that many of the states of consciousness it initiates can be realised in a much more complete and stable form without any drugs at all.

Any scientific attempt to understand such things is limited to physical observation and mental analysis, and trying to understand altered states of consciousness in terms of physiological processes is a bit like describing a meal in a great restaurant in terms of the chemical interactions taking place in the stomach. It cannot address or even begin to imagine the living experience of the whole being. I certainly dislike the way science has decided to label hallucinogenic drugs 'psychotropic'. It is an attempt to compartmentalise and control something the mind cannot understand, I suppose, but they will always be psychedelic to me.

I imagine that many scientists and the (conventionally) religious-minded have similar problems, in that neither can easily conceive of a goal towards which purposeful intelligence might be working in the universe, or of the scale on which it might be operating. Darwin's evolutionary theory may have originally been an honest attempt to understand the mechanisms at work in nature, but it has been manipulated to suit all kinds of agendas, including the promotion of science itself, and now seems to have congealed in the western brain to turn us into the most pointlessly successful consumers of all time.

To me, Darwinian theory, or at least the popularised account of it, is saying, 'The bicycle went to market because its wheels went round and round,' and is as quaintly absurd in its way as the doctrines of the more extreme Biblical Creationists. It is missing a large chunk of the story. Science cannot easily imagine a 'technology' capable of generating the infinitely vast and complex processes of physics, or why it should do so, and church-goers cannot imagine a God who is not hard at work looking after their relations, physical ailments and employment prospects. Both parties may unite in believing it is impossible to get 'something for nothing' and that the drug experience is a delusion. It's an understandable view and true enough in some ways, but not in the ways that they think. Neither considers the possibility that the instrument designed to reveal the truth about reality has already been evolved by the universe and stares back at them every time they look in a mirror.

LSD is not a 'designer drug', tailored to trigger a particular chemical high. The experience varies widely from the frivolous or frightening to the awesome and profound, depending on the attitude and calibre of the person taking it. I found it to be a powerful catalyst for the exploration of consciousness, albeit a crude one. It could produce spectacular results when used with respect and cause mayhem when it wasn't. There were still plenty of risks involved in taking it, but that did not mean it could not open up consciousness to things that were real.

One of the most important ways in which drug experiences can be misleading is probably that the high-energy states of consciousness they can trigger cannot be sustained. Nor do they reveal how such states can be achieved on a permanent basis. It is a bit like being launched into the sky from a catapult. The view may be similar to that from a jumbo jet, but the intrepid Icarus is going nowhere, has little time to enjoy his flight and can only hope that his parachute works. There are other differences between natural and drug-induced experiences but I think the similarities need to be recognised before the pitfalls.

Attempts to communicate altered states of consciousness to a rational observer are notoriously frustrating. The real difficulty is the unimaginable gulf between everyday human experience and the vastly expanded perspective of high-energy levels of reality. I had little thought of encountering God or divinity when I set out on my personal quest to explore consciousness, though no doubt I should have. Nor did I expect to be confronted by mind-blowing dimensions of reality as far beyond my human understanding as I was beyond the amoeba.

Religion depicts 'Heaven' or the 'Kingdom of God' as a kind of Disney Park for believers and relegates it to a mysterious happening after death. It is a nice, comfortable idea, but bears little resemblance to the stunning reality of the divine; to entering the data stream of a living power that can create a universe. It was not that Heaven did not exist; rather it was an awakening of a level and magnitude incomprehensible to the human mind, of wonders beyond my wildest dreams. The impact of spiritual experience could be quite a shock.

When I learned to surrender myself to the energy LSD released, amazing things started to happen. I could relax and let go of everything as I came up on the trip, feeling strange new energies reverberating throughout my body and vibrating audibly inside my head, building all the time in volume and intensity. My body often became restless and uncomfortable, with deep, aching sensations in all my limbs. It literally felt as if deeply rooted tensions and fears were being burned out of my being; my mind, my whole sense of identity would start to dissolve and fall away, and I would emerge gradually into a completely new world.

The experience could be overwhelming on a sensory level alone, with my senses awash with myriad sensations of subtle intensity, while the natural world was extraordinary, a rich, heady riot of beauty, colour and fragrance overlying a still, pervasive sense of unhurried, ancient sentience. I sat on the living earth in complete astonishment as a thousand new perceptions flooded into my being. The sublime perfection of the natural world was a timeless mystery, a great truth that hovered on the edge of understanding, and a quiet joy filled me as I drank in the wonder of it all.

On another level my mind became amazingly fluid and creative, as if I had entered consciously into realms I had previously experienced only in dreams. I could hallucinate wildly. I remember watching in great delight as a Hollywood movie on TV disgorged a horde of Technicolor pirates into the room, and marvelling as parking meters turned into palm trees while I walked along the pavement. Deeper still, I could enter unexpectedly into astonishingly profound spiritual experiences.

Nothing looked fixed or static on LSD; everything rippled with possibilities, its outline constantly changing as if I were watching it under water. The effect was especially evident when looking at living things, when a tangible life force seemed to emanate from plants, animals or people, often superimposed with somewhat whimsical visual embellishments of their character. This hyper-awareness was imbued with all kinds of subtleties when looking at another human being. It was a bit like having a greatly enhanced sensitivity to body language but at the cost of an equally magnified sense of vulnerability and instability. I felt very exposed to others and hesitant about making eye contact with them.

This, however, was exactly what I was encouraged to do by my new psychedelic friends. I had to learn to surrender the 'defences' that I had supposedly formed to protect myself against fears and insecurities, real or imagined, and to confront the emotional pain stored deep within me that had purportedly caused them. Part of this process involved looking into the eyes of another person sharing the trip and trying to be as open with them as possible. I certainly became aware of a pretty defensive outer layer to my personality in these sessions. I felt awkward and uncomfortable, and experienced stabs of alarm when deeper emotions were touched.

I would hallucinate vividly, witnessing my partner's appearance constantly changing in a rapid succession of positive or negative images that depicted the person concerned as anything from evil, ugly or threatening to kind, serene or extremely beautiful. Sometimes this could become very intense, with a torrent of such visualisations flashing in and out of existence amid sharp stabs of fear and intense emotion. These feelings and visions were shared, projected and received on both sides. Mostly the barriers would gradually fall away and emotions come to the surface, at which point I would often see my partner looking very young, even childlike; then new barriers and a deeper sense of anxiety might surface, and the process would go on.

Someone already experienced in this could often help to reassure and coax another to gradually emerge from their personal cocoon, and lift them into higher states, and the more I let go the more profound and intriguing the visions became. Animals would sometimes appear, and people from past times and places in history; amidst increasing glimpses of an elusive inner self, tantalising images of radiant beauty and power that conjured exotic hints of eastern mythology.

This kind of psychic exploration could also be conducted introspectively by gazing into a mirror. I could watch the reflected images projected by my mind and probe deep into myself with complete candour. Behind the grimaces, ferocious glares and woefully dejected looks, something amazing would begin to appear, and a mixture of high anxiety and excitement would grip me, the vision blazing with light and colour in a rapid-fire sequence of pure creative energy.

My alarm at facing or exposing this mysterious inner self lessened as time went by, and the more I learned to relax and surrender my 'defences', the clearer its nature became. I could not doubt that I carried the seed of something wonderful within me, something of indescribable beauty and timeless origin.

I was astounded to realise that the ultimate frontier of knowledge and discovery had been inside me all along. Only our human perception of ourselves stood between us and the ancient enigma of our existence; and even my first glimpses of the magical beauty concealed within us all triggered an innate recognition that began to make sense of my life at last.

A timeless mystery started to reveal itself, an awakening and remembering in the core of my being that spoke from beyond the genesis of this material creation. As ancient and wondrous as this universe was, there was something older, infinitely older and more awesome; and tantalising visions of the fabulous story of eternity stunned my imagination. I found myself sharing an ancient quest and kinship with like-minded souls, those of the present and the past, and enjoyed the allusions to it in many of the songs of the time. 'Believe it if you need it, or leave it if you dare,' sang one of my new favourite bands in bittersweet longing. 'Maybe it's been seen before through other eyes on other days while going home.'

I had to learn to have complete trust and openness when I took LSD, a new honesty in which I could bare my soul to another and share myself completely with them. Nothing was taboo. There were no inhibitions. Any barrier, no matter how intimate, embarrassing, shameful or foolish, was shared and dissolved in mutual love and compassion. When I shared this with a girl, it could become sexual and lead to lovemaking, but it was not animal passion. We were trying to reach something on another level entirely, and it was as if we were already so close that sex didn't really matter.

Physical intimacy was regarded as an expression of love and reassurance, a chance to help each other dissolve the deepest fears and inadequacies of the ego. It was an imperative that transcended relationships; jealousy and possessiveness were considered un-cool. Love ruled everything, and everything had to be shared. It was not an easy thing to get used to, but it certainly broke down barriers, and I felt profoundly humbled and grateful to those who shared these things with me.

The trail led into increasingly strange territory. Paradoxically, the deeper I probed within myself, the more collective the experience became. The inner self that began to emerge through the layers of dissolving ego had a vital new perception of everything around it, especially people, and communication could be extremely direct and intense. The space between individuals and objects was no longer empty; it was permeated by a kind of tactile viscosity, a vibrant field of living awareness. It was a rich, palpable ambience, something like the first caress of warm sand, sun and sea on the beach, only far more sensual and poignant.

There was literally a tangible connection between everyone and everything, a shared understanding as immediate and vital as physical contact. It was a bit like being in love; each person could be an open book to the other, and it was possible to know and connect with each other intimately and completely. I could literally get inside someone else's skin and share their feelings, even their thoughts. It could become extremely telepathic - in fact, sometimes it was hard to know who was who.

It was gradually brought home to me that I was not a separate being from the rest of the world but an integral part of it. I went through a kind of perceptual sea change, in which my sense of self began to shift from the isolated, thinking being inside my head to a more complete and intuitive being that was far more aware of my body and the world around me. I felt immersed in a primal field of awareness shared by all living things, from the primitive sensitivity of the tiniest insect to the rich, vibrant awareness of the animal kingdom.

I suppose I had always seen people and animals as individual entities that generated their own feelings and perceptions, and it was a strange and wonderful thing to find that collective awareness appeared fundamental to the life process and to all living things. Animals appeared to share this intuitive communication with their own kind and across the species divide, and everything in Nature seemed to cooperate unconsciously within a collective feedback system or interdependence that incorporated all life down to that of plants and bacteria.

All except human beings, that is. We seemed unnaturally isolated from one another and from the world around us, our egos crashing about like bulls in an ecological china shop. The most immediate realisation I had was that reality existed in its own right and my awareness of it was limited to the degree and quality of the experience filtered through my nervous system. In other words, my perception of reality was dependent on what I could feel emotionally, think mentally and physically sense or touch.

LSD showed me that these things limited, not defined, my sense of self and restricted my conscious perception to a narrow band in the existing spectrum of reality. I did not dwell on the idea that the ego might have a role to play in the evolution of human consciousness at this point. I had no idea if it was an interim stage in a purposeful progression of consciousness, a capricious act of nature or an evolutionary survival mechanism.

What did become clear to me was that the faculty most wholly divorced from the rich, vibrant reality that was flooding into me was the mind. It seemed to exist as an entity apart from the world, watching life like an exile from the feast, peering at a banquet it could not savour or consume. It had obviously had a fair bit of time on its hands and whittled this away by setting itself up as the principal arbiter of reality, cataloguing everything it saw and constructing ingenious intellectual explanations for it all.

I didn't pay too much attention to the processes going on in the brain though; I just saw how much thinking isolated me from the rich enjoyment of life shared by other living things. I knew there were many good things about science as far as it went, among them the fact that it works. The 'as far as it went' bit was the problem because, although science recognises limits to its understanding, it sticks stubbornly to the view that only quantifiable scientific process is real and refuses to believe in things it cannot measure, calculate or physically tinker with.

One of the first things my changing perspective brought home to me was the extent to which I had taken my own existence for granted. How improbable it suddenly seemed that such complex and sophisticated beings were wandering about in this world as if it were a perfectly normal, bog standard thing to do. I felt as if I had been immersed in a kind of living dream without ever really waking to question its reality or my role within it; sleepwalking through life with little or no respect for the extraordinary world I found myself in, or the millions of years of evolution that had preceded my existence. It was my first inkling of how stupid the ego could be.

When I was high, I could sometimes see distinctive animal traits in the ego, and life could look comically like a scene out of 'The Wind in the Willows.' People who identified strongly with their ego could look gross and aggressive, sly and cunning, fearful or dull and lifeless, and were typically self-conscious and suspicious of anything outside of their habitual existence. Others looked more open and exuded life and joy, and I caught fleeting glimpses of inner beauty within them. It made the world look like a living fairytale in which people glowed like lamps in a shop window, some beautifully decorative and brightly illuminated and others lit more dimly or barely at all.

I felt a real sense of wonder that this ancient world had given birth to my body and to such a huge abundance of life, and I was eager to explore the magical realms of consciousness that beckoned. I was thrilled by the certainty that something wonderful lay behind the mystery of life and the myths and dogmas of the world's religions, and I threw myself wholeheartedly into the search for it. Anything seemed possible, and I devoured all I could read about drug experience, mysticism and spirituality.

I had lots of LSD trips. Sometimes I experienced vivid images of other times and places, once floating above a soldier sitting by a roadway trying to fix something on his boots, feeling the trouble in the air and the echoes of the disastrous battle he was running from. I often dreamt about flying and of watching beautifully detailed landscapes slowly passing far below me, images that could also appear in my waking mind if I shut my eyes.

Tripping at night in the woods, I wandered through ancient memories of other ages on the earth; when humans seemed to have understood the energy of the planet and lived in harmony with it, and sensed a fall from knowledge, and exile from the living power that permeated the natural world. The more I opened up to new experience, the more aware I became of the long story of spirituality that ran from humanity's earliest days. I was excited to discover that many primitive societies used psychedelic plants to gain spiritual insights, and that even the legendary Rig Veda of ancient India spoke of the magical qualities of the sacred Soma plant. I remembered the shiver of delight I had felt as a boy at pictures of prehistoric man in my school text-book, and I felt as if my life was back on track at last. I was my real self again.

My job as a despatch clerk was undemanding and impinged little on my subjective preoccupations. My performance at work actually improved. My heavy drinking and crippling hangovers were a thing of the past and I felt excited and optimistic about the new direction my life was taking; timekeeping and attention to detail at work were incidental but effortless. I was eating healthier food and exercising, often walking from Shepherds Bush to work and back. The basement stockroom was my own private realm and between weekends I existed there in serene seclusion, reading a lot, venturing out to browse the record stores in Oxford Street, contemplating my last trip and looking forward to the next.

I had complete faith in what I was doing and (looking back) was surprisingly fearless in my quest for deeper and more profound experience. On one trip, my age regressed at a tremendous speed like a rewound movie, carrying me back through my birth and shrinking me in the womb until the nature of reality altered completely and I was launched out across a vast, timeless void. I sailed out into nothingness and landed like a speck of dust on the great feet of an awesome deity that towered off into infinity. To touch its being was to be suffused with ecstasy, but I was propelled away again, back across the void and into the womb where I grew 'forwards' in joyous anticipation of my coming life, riding in the vanguard of a glorious anthem that embraced the whole of creation. But expulsion from the womb was alarming, and the story began to change as knocks and shocks buffeted me from all sides like flak around a plane over enemy territory, and the song of life began to falter.

Even apparently negative experiences produced amazing results. I came up on one trip to find myself immersed in a strange, negative world that was utterly devoid of beauty or joy. The room looked much as it usually did on LSD (i.e. like a gently undulating holographic movie), but now everything looked drab and dull, as if the energy had been sucked out of it. It was a dead world without hope or purpose, and a sense of total despondency permeated everything. I felt trapped in a kind of eternal purgatory where nothing ever happened, but it did not alarm me. I found it quite fascinating and spent a good while just taking it all in. Gradually, though, it began to feel oppressive, and I felt I had had enough and started looking for a way out.

I had learned that the best approach to LSD was to surrender to whatever was happening, so I just let go of everything. At once I became aware of a lighted candle that was burning low as if oppressed by the heavy, lifeless atmosphere in the room. My attention was drawn to the flame, and I saw that despite its burden the light was reaching upwards, its energy constantly renewed and constantly rising, and, in one of those wonderful psychedelic moments of complete surrender, everything just flowed and my being dissolved into a blissful energy that was drawn into the candle flame.

I passed through the flame, which became bright and clear, and was drawn up above it, rising higher and higher until I burst out of the negative space like a cork out of water. A great wash of emotions poured over me, saturated with associations of my (now ex) wife and my son, then drained away leaving me feeling quite transformed, and wonderfully light and clean. Somehow, I realised, the whole experience had burnt away a heavy negative legacy from my marriage. I felt liberated, emotionally alive in a way I hadn't for a long time, and I came out of the trip feeling extremely positive.

A couple of things became immediately obvious to me. I saw how much I had been neglecting my son, making only sporadic visits home to see him because of the guilt and confusion I associated with his existence. Also, as the emotional baggage from my marriage dissipated, I was surprised to find deep feelings emerge for a girl I had known for a while. I knew she liked me, but she did not possess the kind of obvious attractions that appealed to the worst of my nature, and I had thought of her only as a friend. Looking back, I had had little thought of anything other than self-destruction for quite some time.

Now my ego seemed to have been washed clean, and I was surprised at the feelings I had for her. There was nothing otherworldly about it; it was simple and seemed generated in every cell in my body, and carried the subtle fragrance of the earth. It was not high romantic drama but was rich with feeling, and was all about companionship and having someone to laugh at life with.

I found myself in something of a quandary because she was not a member of the chemical exploration fraternity. I did not know how I might explain myself to her, and I could not see her joining me on the path I was following; I did not even know where I was going myself, so I said nothing and waited to see what the future would bring. My son was a different matter, and I began to visit him more often and tried to build a better relationship with him.

My spiritual quest continued to gather pace, and a trip came where my growing collective awareness crystallised suddenly into a state of oneness with everything around me. Time stopped and space froze into one solid mass like a paused movie or a fixed, static hologram.

It was totally stunning, as if I had struck the bedrock of reality and become somehow fused with the molecular structure of the room. My awareness diffused instantly within this frozen tableau and extended throughout its form, all sense of personal perspective transformed into an integral awareness of the whole. Consciousness existed everywhere, in everything. I looked down from the ceiling, in from the walls and up from the floor; then the frozen image of reality shattered into a kaleidoscope of pixel-like fragments to reveal luminous worlds beyond. The familiar psychedelic environment of shifting impermanence and creative profusion stabilised and perception and experience united in a new acuity of vision, an innate recognition of new transcendent realities.

It was a powerful and profound experience, a blissful dissolution of the self into a monolithic ocean of consciousness that permeated everything in existence and enveloped space-time within itself like an eternal, omnipresent womb. Mass, energy and consciousness were all different aspects of the same thing. Everything was the work of an unimaginably awesome primordial power, and to share in this primal consciousness was to stand on the foundation of a higher reality. A new perspective dawned; London looked like Toy Town and vainglorious humanity, like a comically tragic tribe of lost children who remained stubbornly oblivious of their true heritage.

It was the end of the story of space-time and the beginning of the story of eternity, and reality was turned on its head. The weighty matters of human history shrank to a brief, stumbling evolutionary step, and humanity's destiny blossomed into something greater than the material universe; the solidity of matter transcended by an infinite ocean of consciousness manifesting far more potent realms of reality. Space-time was reduced to a nebulous, dreamlike field of pre-existence lapping at the shores of eternity, and the perception of spirituality completely reversed, with the material world ethereal and unreal, and the divine the foundation of reality.

I was stunned by visions of awesome, incomprehensible things happening on an impossible scale, of dimensions way beyond human understanding. Unimaginable realms existed in the depths of eternity, patiently working out an ancient purpose over infinite time, and each new insight into their nature left me more mystified and more enthralled than ever.

We were eternal, multidimensional beings, it seemed, seeded in space-time but destined to grow far, far beyond it. Collective consciousness was not the end of self but the realisation of its true nature; the freedom of the glorious being within to unfold its real potential. It was to walk in a land of living poetry where the greater self of the divine smiled in a thousand different ways, as different from the ego's solitary existence as the outside world from the embryo in the womb. How, the unborn child might wonder, can each being stand on the same ground and breathe the same air? I had experienced elements of it in my childhood, I realised. It began where self-consciousness ended, in simplicity, spontaneity and innocence; in taking such joy in the company of another it was hard to tell where one personality ended and the other began.

There was a wonderful freedom in being part of everything. In the weeks that followed, I was sometimes so relaxed that I was hardly aware of my body at all and existed effortlessly within a rich, luminous sea of consciousness that recognised no barriers between people and material structure. One night I hit a sea of white light, of utter bliss, unexpectedly while taking a pee – and ran up the stairs in ecstasy, shedding sheets of cool, white fire, the 'vibes' becoming so amazing that the mice came out into the room and frolicked happily around with the cat.

Life seemed perfect, and I felt as if a high tide of the spirit was flowing. The world appeared encased in glass, permeated by a crystal-clear essence that made everything sparkle in beauty. I lived a deeply contented existence, enveloped in a rich and full awareness of the present moment.

I had to laugh at the ponderous intrigues of religious and occult mystery that had so fascinated humanity down through the centuries. Secret knowledge and ancient riddles were the stuff of mind and matter; the truth was far more fantastic than we could have imagined, and it had been staring us in the face all the time. I did not think much. The sun shone in my heart and I went around grinning like the Cheshire cat at everyone I met. The atmosphere where I lived felt wonderful; fragrant, deeply relaxing and full of love. The air was thick with vibrations and candles always seemed to burn with huge, still flames.

Chapter 7
The Icarus factor

Sharing this collective sense of self with others was an amazingly rich experience, causing limitless facets of the divine to manifest in beautiful and fascinating ways, but understanding it all on anything other than an instinctual level was another matter. 'The Kingdom of God' could be as bewildering as it was mind-blowing, and at times I felt much as an amoeba might on becoming aware of human civilisation.

There was always something missing, an answer that didn't quite reveal itself or an ambiguity that said everything and nothing. I glimpsed angels, devas, gods and goddesses, but I was really little the wiser. I saw Buddha and Christ, and people in other times and places practicing Yoga, prayer and contemplation, but I received no message from them. I had no doubt, for instance, that Christ existed as a timeless archetype manifesting almost unbearable purity, beauty and power, but whether the historical Jesus Christ was an incarnation of this divine being or a man who had achieved Christ consciousness, I could not say. Certainly a Christ-like state of consciousness existed potentially in everyone.

Nor did I get the impression that the world was full of immensely knowledgeable hippies, although they were certainly aware of a lot of things beyond the experience of ordinary people. As I got to know more people in the drug scene, I was surprised to find that not everyone was seeking with the intensity and commitment my early experiences had led me to expect, and for a while I tended to believe people I met were more profound and aware than they actually were.

People reacted to, and interpreted, their drug experiences in many different ways; according to the depth and quality of their personality, their life history, their social roots and education, and the circumstances in which, and with whom, they took drugs, especially LSD. In the accepted convention, it was all about 'getting off', escaping the everyday tensions of life and feeling good, which could mean anything from being relaxed and happy to experiencing a high, egoless state.

There were plenty of people who just wanted to have a good time and had no thought of facing their demons. I would not be surprised if relatively few people ever succeeded in opening themselves fully to really high states on LSD, despite the fact that rock music was full of references to it. Apart from anything else, it can be difficult to retain the memory of some of the higher states after coming down (and strange to re-enter them at a later date. 'My God,' I would marvel, 'how could I have forgotten this?').

Some enjoyed intense experiences on a sensual level or a rich appreciation of the natural world. Some had deep insights but did not communicate them to others, and some played games, ranging from innocent fun to elaborate role-playing and power games. Others passed through some or all of these things at different times to different degrees.

One thing I became aware of took me back to my younger days, and this was the association of smell with people's characters. Strangely, it appeared to be some kind of subtle manifestation unrelated to body odour. It certainly became more noticeable in high-energy states, and could be delightful or quite horrid. It seemed to happen when people opened themselves up in some way, as if an inner self were exposed, which could be beautifully fragrant or stagnant and putrid.

I experienced the latter sometimes when people confronted negative aspects of themselves they had kept hidden and secret, and it could actually be a positive and cleansing process, in which the unpleasantness dissipated and left the personality fragrant, fresh and renewed. Others seemed quite unaware of these things and identified with these less-than-savoury aspects of their being. I remember a girl I met one night who took some speed and in no time at all was singing and cavorting happily all around the house, but bizarrely trailing an astonishingly foul odour as she did so.

Some individuals were totally wrapped up in their egos and ploughed obliviously through the fringes of psychedelic experience like tanks. My biggest shock was a guy who said, 'OK, now what shall we talk about?' as the acid started to come on and then announced that he didn't believe anything that happened on LSD as it was just his brain making it up. He turned out to be a thief whose main ambition in life was to hoard the proceeds of his nefarious activities until he could book into an expensive West End hotel for a couple of weeks and pretend to be rich.

Most people, in fact, felt the pull towards a more open, compassionate and simple existence, which went hand in hand with the growing sexual freedom of the times, but not so many were prepared to open up to each other completely. Not that 'opening up' was crucial to attaining higher states of consciousness. Sometimes the ego could be shed spontaneously on LSD, but the atmosphere around people with a deeper understanding of psychedelic experience was peaceful and reassuring, and more conducive to achieving an egoless state. They could often steer less adept protégés away from difficulties and into deeper realms.

Sometimes, for instance, people felt they were dying, which could be a terrifyingly intense experience if faced without understanding, but it was usually just the ego's fear of losing control, and often associated with childhood anxieties and emotional trauma. Learning to let go and surrender to one's greater self was a deeply profound revelation. It was also useful to learn how deeply rooted and powerful the psyche's defences could be - the habits and evasions the ego employed to keep the attention distracted, and the lengths to which it would go to avoid facing itself.

There were plenty of risks for psychedelic trailblazers in the multiple mazes of the mind and in the numerous other distractions that LSD could conjure up on many different levels.

But, wow, the heavenly treasures encountered by the fortunate few! Very occasionally, I came across complete strangers who were manifestly radiating really high states of consciousness. I remember one at a Grateful Dead concert and another on the London underground. Both were grinning hugely from ear to ear, and so was everyone else anywhere near them. It was impossible to do anything else.

LSD drove me inexorably through fascinating dimensions of consciousness and revealed fabulous spiritual realities, but I could not hold onto them, and I could run into treacherous eddies and currents of fear and confusion, and experience vulnerability, insecurity and pain. I was entering unknown realms and sometimes unsure of my ground, and doubting or questioning myself or those around me.

Extraordinary, undreamt-of potentials existed within us all, and I had visions of wondrous heights we could aspire to, but they were undermined by deeply rooted problems. Sometimes we got tangled up in each other's pain and destabilised ourselves, triggering frightening and confusing experiences while swept relentlessly on by the energy LSD released. A trip lasted for many hours and, once off balance, it could be like riding a bucking bronco; there was little or no control and one could only hang on and hope for the best. On the whole I regarded this as part of the adventure and, once I discovered the perspective of the collective being, my sense of confidence and detachment grew, which made it easier to ride out these episodes in a witness state, a bit like watching a movie.

Many of my experiences were good, and I believed they could only get better; and I pursued the journey of discovery with a cheerful optimism, sharing my adventures with my brother and youngest sister, who were as enthusiastic as I was. They joined me in my quest, in spirit if not always in company, and their stories were interwoven with mine in many respects. I tackled everything with positive determination and did not doubt I was working towards eventual stability and blissful revelation.

I went to see gurus and various New Age apostles, but they mostly seemed to be just fellow travellers on a well-trodden path. Some gurus did appear to have spiritual powers, but I felt no inclination to follow them. Some were even a little alarming. I had a spectacular trip after going to visit one such protagonist, in which a huge, golden Sphinx appeared in the room and fiery hieroglyphics lined the walls. I thought it was great at the time, although it caused some consternation to a couple of old friends I was tripping with, who shared the experience. I only realised later that it had helped to send me down a rather strange Egyptian cul-de-sac for months.

It was not necessary to reach the top of the tree to recognise that all sorts of wonders existed beyond the confines of ego, and a lot of people were launching themselves on all kinds of trajectories in a glorious psychedelic free-for-all. I came across rumours of chemical casualties among the vanguard of the Aquarian age but airily dismissed them as unavoidable collateral damage in the great awakening of humanity. I assumed these things happened to people who did not really know how to use LSD or who had existing mental problems. I did not believe anything bad could happen to me.

Events, however, were to prove differently, and I was to find that LSD could open doors to hell as well as to heaven. I suppose the first intimation of this was a brief, strange episode during a trip in which I saw a non-human entity inside one of the people I was with. It was a bizarre creature a bit like a human rhinoceros. It was bright red with a single horn on its head, and I felt a strange sense of recognition at the sight of it. It was as if I knew this creature somehow, or rather some part of me recognised the realm of harshness and power it hailed from.

It was not harsh enough, however, and I learned nothing from it, in fact quite the opposite. Although undoubtedly negative, it had also been a powerfully magical being, and I felt I had stumbled across some kind of living mythical creature. I was more intrigued than ever. Then came the trip where everything changed. Its impact astonished me - an unfortunate demonstration of the power of high-energy experience, I suppose. Its memory haunted me for years, and its image remains clear in my mind today. It began perfectly. I was barely aware of the acid coming on, and in no time at all I was feeling amazing, deeply at peace with myself and the world. I knew I had regressed to very early memory; I felt like a baby, my skin delightfully soft and wrinkled, my body profoundly relaxed and light as a feather.

I glanced into the mirror and, sure enough, a wonderfully comfortable, complacent baby returned my gaze; then the image changed and a dazzlingly beautiful cobra was striking out at me, its scales sparkling with beautiful colours like living jewels. A last impediment gave way in my heart, a sense of trepidation at opening out to the world, and I stepped free from the chrysalis of the ego to revel in the ultimate and most precious gift of creation.

The layers of contradictions were gone, the divine revealed. A fabulous eternal being sheltered deep within me from a gross and unfeeling world, and, though battered and bruised by the callous indifference of a material age, still it held the potential to light up the world with the song of the divine. I touched riches beyond the dreams of avarice, treasures infinitely beyond the material trophies of this world – the ecstatic joy of oneness with the divine; power and love beyond imagination, and the wonder of eternal life.

A luminous portal of pure energy appeared, glowing with symbols potent with mystery and power; and through it I glimpsed wondrous realms of fabulous beauty, where glorious high-dimensional beings travelled in magical joy with the power of will. The physical universe shrank into insignificance and I gazed out on a far greater reality; a vast, unimaginably ancient tree of immaculate energy that blossomed in eternity. Its origins were lost in unfathomable mystery, its far-flung limbs great highways carrying the timeless song of creation in all its unbearable beauty and power. I watched Christ carrying his cross as people lined the streets with blind, superstitious eyes, and I saw the power he released in the world. Then, illuminated by joy, I slipped fatally from self-confidence into overconfidence.

An old school friend made one of his unpredictable appearances and, perhaps because of the extraordinary vibes, or his own thirst for unusual experiences, decided he wanted to join in, and I gave him some acid. He was a veteran of the school midnight-loft-exploration team and, no doubt inspired by this taste of high adventure, had joined the army when he left school. He was now part of a certain elite military unit that was mysteriously involved in helping to defend the Sultanate of Oman against armed incursions from Yemen. I did not know exactly what he was up to at the time, of course, just that it was active service abroad, most likely involving deadly force, and he was definitely not someone I should have been tripping with at this point.

All continued to go well until a certain point when I looked at him and a kind of tunnel formed between us. My peripheral vision faded and I felt a connection forming. It was something I had experienced before, and I was quite relaxed about it. Next, however, something happened that I didn't expect. The energy flowing through this 'tunnel' disturbed something in him, and a horrid entity emerged from the back of his head and jumped at me.

It looked like an obscene and predatory slug that I instinctively felt belonged to some low and gross dimension of existence. I was unsure how to react. I hadn't imagined such things existed. Ultimately, I knew, everything was part of one primordial being, and I could not imagine there was anything to fear, so I just faced it without any real idea of what was happening.

A fantastic blast of energy roared through me like a hurricane, striking this thing in mid air, and it began to disintegrate. It kept coming, though, fighting the power that assailed it, like an evil salmon trying to force its way upstream. It fell apart completely just as it reached me, and for a moment I felt the impact of its nature, a foul, thuggish creature with a murderous hatred of life; then it was gone.

I was shocked to the core and found myself spiralling downwards out of the high I had been on; I felt blasted and violated, and my mind was suddenly racing. I came out of the trip feeling numb and confused, literally feeling burnt inside, and there was a sour taste like ashes in my mouth that stayed with me for days afterwards.

Everything was different after that. My confidence, optimism and magical joy had gone, and I was back to pre-LSD days with a vengeance. My emotions cut off so completely that I totally forgot about my recently rediscovered feelings. When I did remember the girl I had felt so much for I wondered if I had imagined it, and I felt an anguished sense of bereavement years later when these emotions bubbled unexpectedly back to the surface.

An iron band of tension clamped around my jaw and temples; even my sense of taste and smell seemed dead for weeks. Worse, I could not get high any more. LSD is a funny drug in that it only really works if a week or two passes between trips, and the strength of the dose doesn't necessarily relate to the intensity of the experience. Now any amount of it just made me feel like a car stuck in the mud, wheels spinning, engines revving, and going nowhere.

The fluid, creative, visual level of perception still manifested to a limited extent, but now it projected alarming visions of writhing serpents and scuttling spiders everywhere; and my reflection in the mirror evoked only grotesque images of pain and madness. My inner being was clearly frightened and distrustful, my mind chattered with endless nonsense, and I felt trapped in my head, unable to let go and relax, and no longer part of the world around me.

It was as if a rug had been pulled out from under me; my old familiar self had disappeared, my positive certainty replaced by anxiety and doubt. I couldn't believe that just one incident on a trip could have this effect on me, but the longer it went on the gloomier the outlook became, and gradually, wearily, I began to resign myself to the long haul. I felt marooned in a remote, material universe, languishing on a mundane world on the shores of an elusive ocean of consciousness, knowledge and bliss.

I had no idea what had happened, I did not know whether the horrid entity had been real and I did not know what I could do about it, but I came across a piece attributed to Shakespeare that seemed uncannily apt:

Have you e'er seen the Phoenix of the Earth,
The Bird of Paradise?
I have; and known her haunts, and where she built
Her spicy Nest; 'till, like a credulous Fool,
I shew'd the Treasure to a Friend in Trust,
And he hath robb'd me of her.

I did not blame my friend, though, only my own stupidity. He was just someone who wanted adventure and challenge in life, and who had been putting his life on the line for his country. In fact I like to think that the episode may have dissipated some of his karma somehow; certainly he landed on his feet after going through a fairly wild and volatile period in his life, and settled down to raise a family.

I, however, had opened the most delicate and subtle part of my being to the impact of the most extreme violence the ego was capable of, and there was a heavy price to pay.

Chapter 8
Broken wings

Things seemed to gradually calm down inside, but I remained 'locked in'; cut off from my real self and imprisoned by anxieties and tensions I could not get to grips with.

I read a lot during this period and periodically took LSD to see if there was any let-up in my psychic constipation. I moved into a new flat in North London with some friends from the West Country and whiled away the time by turning my bedroom wall into an ancient Egyptian mural, complete with hieroglyphics and lots of brightly coloured men walking sideways under many-handed golden suns. I continued to work but it had now become a daily drudgery, there was nothing to look forward to at weekends and my job seemed increasingly irrelevant and disconnected from the problems I was struggling with. My LSD trips were frustrating and mostly boring, with the pain in my head and neck greatly accentuated and hallucinogenic effects extremely muted, but mysterious events continued to happen.

Late one night I was alone in my room on a trip that was going nowhere as usual and listening to Handel's 'Messiah'. I had a large, psychedelic poster of Christ in one part of the room, and I focused on it for a while, trying to forget about myself as the image flowed and melted, but frustratingly never getting to the point where it dissolved into the realms of light and bliss its flowing design hinted at. After a while, I began to feel that there was something nasty lurking inside me; I did not really know what it was, only that I wanted to get rid of it.

Next a cat came into the room, and I found myself thinking

about the Biblical story of Christ putting spirits into pigs. I looked speculatively at the cat, wondering somewhat bizarrely if it would make a suitable pig into which I could rid myself of the 'thing' inside me. The cat stood stock still and I looked into its eyes. It was like peering into a still, bottomless pool of consciousness, and we stared unblinkingly at each other for what seemed a very long time. Finally I felt that trying to offload this thing would not be fair to the cat, and broke eye contact – I never actually considered how such an operation might be carried out.

Next morning I was in the kitchen, 'coming down' after the trip, when one of my flatmates, a girl who shared the room below mine with her boyfriend, came in to get some breakfast. She told me that she had had a nightmare during the night.

'It was terrible,' she said, 'I dreamed I was a cat and you were going to put something evil into me!'

My psychedelic mentors had been away in Morocco for some time, and when they returned they were quite horrified at what had happened. They tried to help, and we had several trips together but, although I got a little higher with them in some ways, I could not escape the sense of numbed inertia that gripped me or the rigid tensions in my neck and head. I could not surrender or open myself up in the way I had been able to before.

There was much talk of defences, hang-ups and the release of primal tension, but eventually it became evident that they did not really have any answers and I was on my own. They did suggest, though, that it might help to 'get out of the rat race' for a while and to branch out from the West Country expat scene to mix with other kindred spirits.

This meant leaving my job and flat and learning to live in one of the squatting communities that had sprung up all around London. Some of my flatmates from Somerset had gone along with the increasing use of cannabis and shared a certain amount of my interest in LSD but, like most people, they were a great deal more down-to-earth than I was, there was a point beyond which they did not want to go.

Only one or two of my friends had really been prepared to jump into the unknown with me and, fond as I was of everyone, I knew there were things we could not really communicate about. I felt some rekindling of excitement at the idea of getting out of the boring routine that work imposed; and, although the idea was pretty alarming, I had no doubt that having to socialise with the free spirits in the squatting scene would break down barriers and force me to be more spontaneous and open to life.

It was the only way forward I could see, although I knew it would not be easy, and my life oscillated between alarm and adventure for months. The squatters were a likeable bunch who lived a bit like a tribe of astral Apaches on the fringes of the materialistic society. Their philosophy was to be free, get high and avoid the greed and stress of the establishment agenda, and their squats seemed to float in a different dimension from the busy streets around them like serene oases of stoned tranquillity.

Acquiring one of these oases of tranquillity was a daunting prospect, though, and I took the mental equivalent of a very deep breath before launching myself into my new life. When it came down to it, the biggest problem I had was the state I was in, for I met with much kindness and hospitality among the squatters. I was only once or twice without anywhere to sleep, and although I often had little money I rarely went hungry.

What happened in the incident with the policeman in the alley? It actually turned out OK – he seemed a decent guy. I was as high as a kite and the turmoil and anguish I felt inside seemed to communicate itself to him. I told him I was upset over an argument with my girlfriend, and he was quite fatherly about it, merely suggesting I found somewhere better to go. I even managed to go back later and retrieve my dope.

Initially I moved in with my psychedelic mentors, who now had their own squat, and kept an eye out for other people who might want to share the task of getting a new place. I was living in a sizeable squatting community that had grown up near Euston in central London, and it was a new and exciting life. The squatters came from a wide range of backgrounds and included travellers from abroad who were just passing through. They were all larger-than-life characters, and life itself seemed to be basically one big party. It was a party I could not join in with much, however, as I was still struggling with the after-effects of my disastrous trip.

Things seemed to be getting worse rather than better. I felt as if my ego had clamped down defensively with an iron grip; and the physical tension I felt in my jaw and head was becoming increasingly acute. I could sometimes take large doses of LSD without experiencing much effect at all. The divine beauty within seemed shattered and peeped out from my reflection in the mirror behind horrific writhing images of fear and pain. My feelings worked in only the most rudimentary way, and I had little confidence in who I was any more.

My sense of spontaneity and fun had largely disappeared, and I frequently got lost in deep ponderings about the symbolic meaning of casual remarks addressed to me, often analysing a number of possible responses to consider which would be the most genuine! I was quite capable of walking into someone's place and sitting for hours without saying a word. I remained determined to free myself from the shackles of my old life, though; as this was the only positive course I could see. Most of my fellow squatters did not really understand my problems – for that matter I did not understand them myself – but they were kind enough and helped me out where they could.

Before long, word came through of a large new squat opening up near Baker Street, and a number of the people I had recently got to know descended upon it. This was not before time as far as I was concerned as I was sharing a room with a gay couple, which was somewhat awkward. I arrived to find a huge building with a classical facade overlooking Regent's Park, its doors wide open and dozens of would-be squatters milling about among the ornate wood-panelled walls and grand staircases inside.

I first bagged a room in the main building and then learned that some of the people I knew had discovered a row of terraced houses, in a service road behind the main block, that were part of the estate. Each property had originally been servants' quarters of two rooms and a bathroom above stables of some sort, now a separate garage on one side and a front door into a sizeable ground floor area on the other, with a second inner door at the foot of the stairs to the flat above.

There was one unit left, the most dilapidated, and I decided to go for it, jumping into a scenario not unlike that of a shanty town in the Wild West, in which many of my neighbours were friends and acquaintances from Euston. A rip-roaring spring and summer followed.

I had a bit of a battle on my hands to begin with as I found I was sharing the stables area at the foot of the stairs with a tramp named Mr Moneypenny. (I learned that these characters frequently went under extraordinary names, and I was later to become acquainted with three winos called 'Concrete', 'Mugs of Water' and 'News at Ten'.) Mr Moneypenny would turn up in the early hours, sometimes with a friend, with a strange assortment of edible goods from mysterious sources and devour them with great relish. One night, I remember, two of them entirely polished off a huge crate of yogurts. I eventually got rid of him by putting a new lock on the outer door and painting it bright blue or red, I forget which.

Giving up my job was a problem because I had no money in the bank and unemployment or social security payments would be cut off for months if I gave up my job without reason. Fate intervened when I met an interesting guy on a train who was involved in the Theosophical Society. I was high on amphetamines and struck up a conversation with him in which he mentioned that his doctor believed people sometimes needed a break from the rat race. This seemed too obvious a cosmic coincidence to ignore, and in no time I had arranged to use his address to sign up with his doctor.

The next step was slightly tricky as I had to turn up at the doctor's surgery and pretend to have a nervous breakdown. I did not feel totally unjustified in this as I was certainly struggling with a deep trauma of some kind, but it still seemed a pretty wild thing to do. I started off by acting weirdly at work, wandering around being vague and confused about everything. All went reasonably well apart from a surreal phone call, when one of my sisters chose that day to ring me. I tried to sound strange for the benefit of work colleagues, while attempting to drop hints that I wasn't mad to my sister; totally mystifying her in the process, but probably contributing greatly to the impression I was trying to make at work. Eventually and thankfully I made it to the end of the day and set off resolutely to see my new doctor.

Everything went swimmingly. It helped to have got into character during the day, but I found to my surprise that it was not entirely necessary to act the part. Confessing something of the inner turmoil I had been struggling with to an authoritative figure was a strange relief, and the doctor was everything my railway companion had promised.

If anything, he was over-helpful. He signed me off work immediately, and over the next few weeks he discussed all sorts of possible options for my future. It dawned on me that if I wanted to I could just hand over responsibility for looking after myself and let various kinds of state apparatus take over; in fact I almost felt I was being encouraged to do so. What surprised me most was a moment when I felt tempted to let this happen.

I was certainly very aware of the toll that the whole situation was taking on me, and one evening I came close to unravelling completely. I was walking under an amazingly vibrant full moon that was reflected everywhere around me, bathing the silent streets with a strangely compelling luminescence. I reached a crossroads and was unsure which way to go, and somehow, no matter which direction I turned, the moon seemed straight in front of me, flooding me in a brilliant radiance that confused and disorientated my senses.

A weirdly intense image formed in my head, and I saw the everyday world as a ponderous building or stage set containing formal rooms in which fixed social roles and duties were played out. They were separated by walls with cavities inside them where a more nebulous existence subsisted, spaces where one could hide and slip between the rooms and their formal responsibilities. I felt I could just let go and flow freely within the walls without a care in the world, and it was strangely tempting to give up and let it happen, but the moment passed; I just felt I could not give up responsibility for myself.

I also knew perfectly well that western psychiatric medical practice did not have a clue about the areas of the psyche I was struggling with. My new doctor, whom I had now nicknamed 'Doctor Cosmic', respected my wish to deal with my problems in my own way and helpfully signed me off with 'depression' for the months I needed. He did make a couple of suitably cosmic attempts to help, which I went along with, one being hormone treatment and the other hypnosis, but, apart from learning that hypnosis did not seem to work on me, nothing came of it.

Chapter 9:

On the road

Life as a squatter was an adventure in itself. I tried to have fun where I could, and derived some satisfaction from putting myself through the rough-and-tumble of life on the streets, which was forcing me to confront my conditionings and making me more confident and self-reliant, at least in a practical sense.

One thing about the drugs scene was that life was always pretty intense. The squatters were a rough-and-ready lot, but they looked out for each other. They were always keen to 'get off' and believed that life was all about love but not necessarily at its deepest level.

I felt a mixture of anxiety and excitement at being without a job or somewhere secure to live, and great delight at the new freedom I had. I liked to laugh at the commuters speed-walking out of Baker Street tube station each morning as I headed home for bed, and I revelled in long, stoned afternoons in Regent's Park. There were not-so-great times, too, such as having to confront other would-be squatters who kicked the door in during the night, or thinking I had blinded myself in the gigantic flash when we reconnected the mains electricity cables, although it was still kind of fun.

I was learning to get high again in the sense that I was finding ways of getting out of the box – of breaking out of my frustrating re-confinement as an isolated mental being stuck inside my head. The experiences were very different now, though, and missing the wonderful inner illumination from my heart. Without the rich, vibrant flow of love, psychedelic life could be a bit like living in a war zone. I felt vulnerable and adrift, never quite knowing what was going on, and struggling with turbulence both within myself and in the world around me.

I fought to claw back the inner being I had lost in every way I could. I took up Hatha Yoga, visited New Age groups and tried different meditation techniques. If I got stoned enough, I could still become aware of love in a detached, abstract kind of way, as it existed everywhere in the fundamental nature of reality, and sometimes I could feel vibrations flowing like an electro-magnetic current through my body and resonating everywhere around me. This ubiquitous collective presence, while shifting in quality and expression, formed a kind of universal constant that encompassed the fauna and flora of an endlessly changing psychedelic landscape.

At times I seemed to experience two distinct aspects of divinity, one a timeless, omnipresent witness that watched the cosmic drama in serene detachment and the other an inner, more passionate being, potent with beauty and power that seemed trapped behind the pain and insanity of the ego. I felt that the two aspects should become united, but I had no idea how this might be achieved, and I struggled back and forth chasing endlessly mysterious, shifting images of the divine that constantly slipped through my fingers.

I knew that the gateway to the divine lay in the power to remain focused in the present without thinking. Well, pretty much everyone did as Richard Alpert's 'Be Here Now' was practically required reading at the time. I took drugs to reduce my thinking and expand my awareness of the present as much as possible. Different drugs initiated different qualities of perception and experience, and life was not unlike a mystical treasure hunt in a vaguely anaesthetic fog, with the sun breaking through weakly every once in a while to illuminate a mysterious succession of strange and magical lands.

My adventures in the squatting community continued apace. There was always something going on, some of it a great deal more than I had bargained for. One night I opted out of a bum LSD trip with some barbiturates and went to sleep, and the next thing I knew I was staring in dazed bemusement at a mass of beautiful, dancing flames. I knew there was something important about this vision, but I just could not think what it was, and it seemed to take an age before I realised that it was a fire and it was in my room.

I had left a candle burning on the resin and plastic top of a coffee table, and it had burned down and set the table on fire. It was a miracle I had woken up at all. A moment after I recognised what was happening, a wickedly viscous cloud of dense, filthy smoke came down and obscured everything. Only the flames showed through as a dull, red, flickering glow.

I knew I had only seconds to act, even though the combination of LSD, barbiturates and sleep had spaced me out in a very strange way. I grabbed a blanket and managed to smother the fire, then staggered towards what I thought was the door. I could feel the smoke pouring into my lungs like an oily liquid, and I felt oddly detached from what was happening. It seemed almost too much trouble to try and save myself.

I touched an object I recognised, and realised I was in a completely different part of the room to where I thought I was, and some distance from the door. I dived across the room to where I thought the door should be, lurched through it and half fell; half stumbled down the stairs, landing in a heap at the bottom. I lay there coughing and spluttering with everything spinning around me, and had barely taken a couple of breaths of clean air when I heard an awful 'whoomph' and realised that the fire had re-ignited itself.

In complete disbelief I dragged myself back up the stairs and went through the whole thing all over again. I had a squat-mate at the time whose existence I had completely forgotten about, and he woke up in the other room at this point, half asphyxiated and not best pleased. I flung open the window and let out huge clouds of smoke, which would have attracted a lot of unwelcome attention had it not been the middle of the night.

I was still coughing up soot a day or two later when my old friend from the fish shop in Oxford came round to visit. He was suitably horrified and obviously concerned at this latest incident in the bizarre direction my life was taking; but I was surprisingly unfazed by my brush with mortality; and, after a considerable amount of cleaning and painting to make my room habitable again, I pressed on with my agenda.

Some things about squatting I enjoyed and others I endured. I disliked the unwritten rule that we did not pay to travel on the tube; we were supposed to blank out the ticket collectors and walk past them at each end of the journey. True, I had little money, and I looked upon it as a confidence-building exercise, but I found it nerve-wracking and did not enjoy it.

Something else I disliked was bathing. My squat did not have hot water, and I had to go to the public baths to keep clean. I had no idea that such things existed, but discovered I could buy a ticket and queue up for one of a row of cubicles to be vacated and have its bath cleaned and filled for me. The baths were great, huge with tons of hot water, but there was a demeaning and institutional air about the whole process that did not endear itself to me.

Life went on, and I passed through a leisurely surreal tableau of events, awake much of the night and asleep much of the day, often while sunbathing in Regent's Park. I hitchhiked about the country and visited Wales, where I encountered New Age groups and rode a horse. I remember half a dozen of us standing in the pouring rain with our heads stuck through a large plastic sheet, watching the light show as 'Yes' performed on stage at the Reading festival. In another image, a gang of us is running around Regent's Park at three in the morning, all stark naked and out of our heads on speed, inspired to practice 'power running' by Carlos Castaneda's dodgy books.

Memories from the past often surfaced. Sometimes I felt I was a schoolboy again, feeling just as I used to, complete with the simple freedom of shorts, muddy legs and a snotty nose. I began to experience past lives, or other existences, again, now more subjectively and more vividly. Once I was an Indian practicing yoga postures with great dedication and prowess, enjoying the consummate mastery of my movements and the power embodied in the archetypal animal forms I was expressing in the postures.

Sometimes I inhabited the personalities of animals and birds themselves, on one occasion becoming so completely immersed in a lion's animal nature that I found I could growl and roar with an astonishingly deep and powerful force that reverberated back at me from the walls of the room I was in. I revelled in the sense of power it gave me, but felt a strange desolation afterwards, as if I was lost and wandering down a track leading into wilderness and desolation.

Sometimes, strange things happened that I did not understand at all. On one trip a massive serpent unfolded itself from the shadows around a camp-fire on a Sussex beach and loomed over me. I did not find it frightening, despite the great power I sensed in it, as it radiated a kind of maternal benevolence. I felt it kiss me on the wrist with its great, blunt snout, sending a current flowing through my body. All sorts of things happened throughout the night that I cannot really put into words, but at one point I felt I was encased in an egg, with a soft shell like that of a snake, that had been ripped open, leaving ragged and torn inner linings exposed in forlorn disarray.

At times I saw strange entities. I also saw what appeared to be damaged *chakras*, or energy centres, and distorted images of divinity reflected within me, but I could not understand or resolve the problems they represented. I was moving into deeper realms of existence, but I was travelling without a map and I had no real idea of where I was or where I was going. I was becoming increasingly engrossed in the abstract, collective nature of existence and less aware of the everyday practical circumstances of my life.

I could often hear the collective being expressing itself through the unconscious everyday remarks of people around me. Conversation could be understood on two levels if one was attuned to it, with spontaneous conversations among groups of individuals often reflecting wry comments and humorous symbolic references by the collective mind about the abysmal level of human enlightenment.

It was not that the collective being boasted a witty repartee in English; it permeated everything and was aware of everything; it knew the human race through and through, and to be part of that awareness was to share in a myriad simultaneous connections and associations. Every image, every smell, every sound was laden with unconscious significance. Even the way people coughed or blew their nose said all kinds of things about them. Everything was connected, everything woven into a revealing tapestry of primal fear and desire, and played out within an age-old drama of purpose and meaning.

This kind of background collective theme manifested everywhere, on advertisements, shop signs and magazines, even on radio and television. Everything had its origin in the unconscious mind, and it played out on many levels of reality. Political wrangling, natural disasters, and human hopes, dreams and tragedies were all symbolic dramas expressing humanity's slow, faltering steps towards enlightenment.

It was difficult to walk the line between this kind of awareness and a paranoid suspicion that everyone knew my innermost secrets. The border between my ego and the collective being was unclear, and it often seemed difficult to separate my personal struggle from humanity's collective journey towards spiritual awakening.

It was extremely disconcerting to feel that people around me were, if not reading my mind, at least aware of my problems on some level, and the events and circumstances of the world around me persisted in poking fun at my failings as I plodded determinedly on. It was all amazingly confusing, and I had to struggle to maintain a sense of humour and optimism as I tried to steer my way through it.

Looking back, it seems extraordinary that I kept going at all, and yet I do not remember being wholly despondent or depressed. I think rather I was numb, my life lived wholly in depression, and I pushed myself through it by fixating on the memory of the divine's transcendent beauty and witnessing my struggle to regain it with a kind of grim detachment. I also think that the horizons of my perception were shrinking around me as the quality of life deteriorated, and I could not see how far I was falling. Things could easily have turned out very badly indeed.

I made repeated attempts to break out of my spiritual prison, experimenting with various techniques and using different combinations of drugs to focus and intensify my attention. I learned to watch the world with a non-specific gaze that did not focus on individual objects or three-dimensional depth but looked on reality as if it were an image reflected in a mirror.

Over time this perception built up to the point where I could watch without reacting and reality would look right back at me, with perceived and perceiver exactly reflecting one another. The image of the world would gradually change into a dancing pattern of energy, a superficial veil of shimmering pixels masking a limitless depth of consciousness; and, with the passing of time, on an LSD trip I could stitch my consciousness deep into this fabric of existence until I became part of everything around me.

If I got it just right, with the reflection perfect, I could sometimes read people's minds. Their thoughts would just pop up into my head. If I delved more deeply into their psyches, I became aware of the thought processes themselves, watching impressions form into ideas and ideas into words. On one occasion I became so impatient at seeing the next three responses in various laborious stages of construction deep within the mind of the guy I was talking to that I irritably and stupidly said them for him, much to his confusion.

The hedonistic ethos of the rock-and-roll movement was very much a reflection of LSD experience, which saw the divine being within as repressed by sexual guilt at a very deep level. Certainly the inability to be unselfconscious about sexuality seemed to be at the heart of the schism between humanity and nature. Anger, aggression and hatred seemed to be expressions of the agony created by chronically repressed sexuality on a primal level, expressed in the curses and swearing that exploded in episodes of rage and pain.

To say that psychedelic lore held uninhibited sex to be the solution to all humanity's woes would be an oversimplification, but something along these lines did seem to trickle down through the ranks. It was not really about sex in itself but the release of the tensions and restraints of the ego and the liberation of the whole being. Unsurprisingly, as a philosophy it had a few flaws, but these were not necessarily obvious at the time. The fear, anguish and tension encountered at the inner core of the being were frighteningly intense, and the astonishing store of love and beauty dammed up behind them such an overwhelming revelation, that anything seemed possible.

I could certainly see that sex had been perverted in many destructive ways and that few people were able to enjoy sexual experience with the whole of their being. To me, it was all about reaching a state of completion where sex regained its natural place in the scheme of things and became just a beautiful and special expression of love.

Not that there was much chance of this in the state I was in. The squatters had a more Darwinian attitude to sex than my first psychedelic friends and some of the girls could be quite predatory, occasionally alarmingly so. I actually found it difficult to relate to women at this time unless I sensed a connection on a spiritual level, which is something a little tricky to put into words. Everyday social interaction was generally problematic for me during this period as I often felt self-conscious, introverted and tongue-tied in casual conversation. It was far worse with females because I felt unsure and confused by unclear nuances and connotations around them, which made it difficult for me (and them) to behave naturally.

However, things could be different with women who were 'awake' on certain levels of consciousness as I could communicate with them on a different level. If I took enough of the right kinds of drugs, I could sometimes get past my 'block' to some degree and interact with them in a place where love and compassion were more unconditional.

This occurred with unexpected intensity on a visit to the West Country, that came about because an Italian girl staying locally had taken a shine to one of the guys from 'the terrace', as everyone referred to the houses we were squatting in, and began to fret when he failed to return from a short trip to Cornwall. She wanted to go down to see him but was unwilling to hitchhike on her own, so I volunteered to accompany her.

We enjoyed a delightfully aimless journey across the west of England, with our route following the lifts we were offered, and once there we tracked him down at a friend's house where a visiting couple were also staying, an English guy and a remarkable young lady from Caracas. She was on holiday with her boyfriend and had alighted temporarily from a jet-set lifestyle worlds apart from that of the urban squatter, yet the moment we met there was an instant rapport.

During an LSD trip a powerful telepathic experience manifested between us, and I recognised an unusual spiritual depth in her. It was unexpected and intense, and I was overwhelmed by the feeling that I had met a close friend from another time and place, perhaps from another dimension of existence.

She may not have had the same kind of conscious knowledge or experience I had, but she made up for it with an irrepressible exuberance and a fearless and intuitive grasp of things that few people were even aware of. The interaction became increasingly powerful as the days went by, and I felt a deep awakening taking place within each of us. We seemed to be acting as catalysts to each other on a very deep level, and a mutual recognition was causing us to open out as if to our mirror images.

At times there were so many colours shining above her head she was like a beacon from a higher world, and so much was going on between us, it was as if no one else existed. I could see that something spectacular was likely to happen and that it would have the power to sweep all before it, but I also had misgivings about the consequences should this occur.

Everything was wrong on the human level; we were on completely different paths in life. She was largely unaware of the true depth of her spiritual nature, despite trading on its power for her childlike enjoyment of extravagance and beauty. She was used to money and the good things in life, and the material world was a playground for her, and I was just a rootless seeker struggling with problems I didn't understand.

There were other things, too. She had the power to reach deep into my being and awaken part of me that had been dead for a long time, and I welcomed these signs of life, but felt a little uneasy about it too, wondering if I might be compromising my spiritual being with more selfish ambitions.

I suspected I might open myself up again in a blaze of glory only to crash and burn in a different way, and I couldn't help questioning whether encouraging her to do the same was a good idea, either, considering the problems I had run into. She was also rather attractive. Her boyfriend was a nice guy and had been hospitable, and I was reminded too well of what it was like to have a woman that everyone wanted. On the last morning we walked and talked a little, and I felt a deep, poignant ache growing in my heart.

'I have pain here,' she said, touching her own heart.

'Me too,' I replied, and had the extraordinary feeling that I was starting to physically dissolve into her being.

'Something is going to happen,' she said.

'The children of the divine are going to wake up,' I wanted to say.

Instead I told her I was going back to London.

'I'll come with you,' she said, and I smiled and shook my head. She felt the impulse, but she didn't really mean it, not yet anyway.

So I took my leave of the psychedelic partner of my dreams with a farewell kiss that cost me a real pang, and hit the road with a heavy heart. It took a couple of days to hitchhike back to London, and I slept that night in a field, but only after gazing up for a long time at my old friends the stars.

Still, I learned a couple of things during this sojourn in Cornwall. During one trip I walked past a sizeable mirror in the hall with the guy from the terrace, and we both glanced into it.

His reflection was a nicely spaced-out, fluid image of dancing pixel-like cells of energy, of oneness with everything, as was mine; but something was open within me from which luminous depths of beauty were shining. There was a succession of openings stretching inward, like open doors along a corridor, with each doorway revealing deeper dimensions of splendour.

'How come I don't have that?' he asked, and it was obvious he was seeing it too.

I felt quite embarrassed. I had no idea what the answer was and could only say that I didn't know. Afterwards it occurred to me that if he could see it he must have had the same potential himself, but at the time it was just one more puzzle in a world full of mystery.

I also joined the UFO fraternity in an unexpected way. We were sitting outside in the garden one evening, smoking dope and taking in the night sky, when the conversation turned to flying saucers. As usual I was deep in a state of stoned collective awareness, not joining in the conversation much and contemplating the scene in an absent, abstract way.

I wondered about UFOs and felt curious about the different things people believed. I wanted to experiment, without really knowing how, and I thought I would try to affirm a belief in UFOs deep down inside myself. Much to my surprise, a UFO appeared right on cue high in the sky above us, a small moving luminous globe, and I was even more surprised when everyone else saw it too. I found this slightly alarming, reluctant to believe I had somehow made it happen, and listened to the excited commentary around me in some bemusement.

Then I realised that an obvious next step would be to see what happened if I stopped believing in it. So I did, and it vanished, to cries of consternation. So I appeared to have an answer, although not one I really understood or felt I could share at that moment. I could only presume that the whole flying saucer thing was something to do with the collective mind and the mythology of the times.

I supposed that in other eras people might have seen fairies or fiery chariots. The inner being appeared layered like an onion; with each step inward opening out into subtle strata of consciousness that permeated everything that existed at progressively more fundamental levels. Flying saucers and aliens, it seemed, were some kind of high-level diversion that the mind projected outward, instead of facing the divinity within.

I could see that western science was restricted to focusing outwards onto the physical universe and perceiving it in a limited dimensional plane, which left it struggling to comprehend the superficial manifestations of a multidimensional reality.

From a human perspective, it made no sense at all to create such a mind-bogglingly extravagant universe, even though we saw evidence of nature's extravagance everywhere. Perhaps a power that could create a universe was of such a fantastic order of magnitude that it could not help but be extravagant – and this glorious universe was but a dim reflection of its true potential.

It was clear to me that consciousness permeated everything in existence, and that planets, suns and galaxies were material facets of multidimensional realities in which microcosm and macrocosm were intricately linked, as were we with everything around us. In some extraordinary way, life on this planet seemed unique; whatever science told us about our insignificant position in the material universe. The wonders of the night sky were transcended by far more incredible dimensions of light and power, and the human mind was incapable of imagining the impossibly sophisticated juggling act that spun the material illusion.

The early thinkers may have been wrong in their reasoning, but they were right in their instincts, for everything did revolve around us. Deep within, within consciousness itself, something ancient and immutable witnessed the ages pass, and watched us climb with pre-nascent self-absorption towards our ultimate destiny.

The purpose and culmination of that destiny, however, if not the fact of its existence, remained a mystery. From the perspective of the uninitiated, the drug scene looked a mess, and so it was, but from the perspective of the drug scene the uninitiated looked equally pitiable, shallow husks of people who were barely aware they were alive.

They glowed fitfully like lamps on indifferent batteries, never dreaming they could shine like the sun with a million volts coursing through their being. At the very least, drugs could conjure thrilling emotional intensity, while to awaken to the wonders of the divine even for a moment was an experience worth more than all the material treasures this world had to offer. It certainly felt worth the risks of seeking such knowledge through drugs. Things had to get really bad before I could accept that I could not grasp the wonders that drugs revealed, and that the path I was on was leading nowhere.

Chapter 10
End game

Back in London, things were becoming quite crazy as our tenure in the terrace began to draw to a close. Someone had died jumping out of a window in the main building thinking he could fly, and there seemed to be police cars permanently circling the area. We had to peer out of our front doors before going out because the police routinely stopped and searched the 'locals'.

One night I left a friend's place further along the terrace with a young lady who instantly flaked out in the fresh air, a delayed reaction to a rather potent Thai stick we had just smoked. The inevitable police car appeared and bore relentlessly down on us, and I had to hold her up with one arm and bang urgently on the door with the other, getting back inside just as the car screeched to a halt outside.

The friendly local drug dealer was becoming something of an endangered species and being supplanted by much more hardnosed characters. Our local supplier, who lived at the opposite end of the row to me, was visited through the back window one night by some unpleasant guys who waved a gun around and cut him up a bit in pursuit of their business plan.

This inspired him to go into hiding and to offer me the chance to look after the place for a while, for which I could help myself to any drugs lying about in exchange. I was like a kid in a candy shop, finding pills and crystalline powders strewn about everywhere, and I passed a surreal couple of days in an amazingly spaced-out state, with much music by the Doors played at high volume.

It was a candy shop under siege, however, with the police watching the front of the place, punters knocking on the door wanting to score and the bad guys an ever-present threat around the back. It was great fun, with a lot of adrenaline flowing in my bloodstream along with everything else, but I was beginning to feel that events were spinning out of control.

I was aware that my drug-taking was becoming increasingly reckless, but saw it as a justifiable assault on the 'block' caused by the trauma of my bad trip, which I remained stubbornly determined to break out of. I would take three or four acid 'tabs' at a time and snort cocaine while the trip came on, but nothing really worked. I would start to take off, but rapidly lose stability and direction and struggle for hours with chaotic energies, deep-rooted tensions and bizarre perceptions of reality before I could regain control of the trip and ride it through into some sort of stable high.

An additional boost of amyl nitrite seemed set to solve my problems permanently one night, when my heart gave the most horrendous bang followed by absolutely nothing for what seemed like forever. An eternity afterwards there was another huge bang, a bone-jarring 'ka-boom', and a lot of agitated palpitations before my heart returned to normal.

On a few occasions, I seemed to hit the right combination of drugs in the right state of mind at the right time, and a really powerful experience would start to build, but even this would not manifest fully; at some point its stability and momentum would falter, and I would fall back into writhing uncertainty.

I became increasingly desperate, obsessively pursuing the perfect balance between relaxation and energy with barbiturates and amphetamines; sometimes escalating the quantities to the point where I was so spaced out I scarcely knew what I was doing. It seemed that nothing could unlock the tensions deep within me. On a good day I believed I would make it, and on a bad day I felt I was justified in cushioning the pain with drugs. Sometimes the iron band gripping my head and jaw was so painful and tiresome, I just wanted to blot it out, and went on barbiturate binges for days. There were long periods about which I remember very little, and others where I got up to all kinds of crazy things that were pretty off the wall, even for us.

I remember 'star trekking' one day, where, one by one, we would squat down and hyperventilate, take a long 'blow-back' from a joint then stand bolt upright and tense all the muscles in our bodies. This caused us to go out like a light, falling backwards onto a mattress, before slowly returning to consciousness with a fast-receding memory of a long moment in a totally amazing space.

We all stood around in a circle to take our turn, falling down, coming round, staring uncomprehendingly at the ceiling and then staggering off to the back of the queue. It was incredibly stupid and was, I suppose, symptomatic of the degeneration of the whole ethos of drug experience for me. At one time LSD and cannabis were regarded almost as sacred, and people would not have dreamed of using anything else, but now cocaine, amphetamines, barbiturates and even heroin were becoming commonplace, and the quality of drug experience had not increased with quantity and variety.

Somehow, though, I could not lose the belief that I would find what I was looking for, even though part of me could see how crazy this was. There was nothing I could really pin it on, but every so often things happened that seemed to suggest something momentous in the future.

The first experience in this vein actually happened quite early on, before everything went wrong, and at the time I assumed it was a symbolic representation of the spiritual awakening that LSD had triggered. It happened right at the end of a trip, after dawn, when I was preparing to go to sleep. I closed my eyes as I was listening to the finale of Beethoven's Ninth Symphony and had a stunning vision.

The vast dome of a brilliant blue sky shone high above me, a huge hole at its apex, and descending from this opening was a great spiral of pure white doves. It was totally unexpected and I opened my eyes in surprise, then felt annoyed with myself, thinking I had lost the vision. I closed my eyes again and was overjoyed to find it was still there, and went to sleep with my mind filled with its beauty.

I had no defined sense that it was a vision of the future, or a vision of something that would affect my future, but it left me with the conviction that some fundamental truth inspired the seeking I saw everywhere around me, and that there must be some resolution to it.

Then there was a visit I made to my ex-wife during the time I was squatting. I forget why I went, but she had become heavily involved in the Wicca 'white witchcraft' scene, and at one point she looked rather puzzled and announced that I had a wonderful future ahead of me. The puzzled look was not just because I had long hair and looked like a tramp; I was puzzled myself when she explained that she had seen a vision of hundreds of women throwing flowers over me! It was quite inexplicable at the time (although I came to understand its symbolism later), but it did add to the sense that something remarkable lay ahead.

The final event occurred while I was in Oxford Street in central London one day and had a sudden vision of a dark-haired woman with divine love pouring out of her eyes. None of these things made much sense, but they helped to give me faith that I was not searching in vain.

In the meantime, things were looking increasingly grim. Calling at a place a few doors along the terrace one day, I came across a girl sitting and crying, with an enormous pile of amphetamine powder on the coffee table in front of her and long dark rivulets of blood running down her arm. She had been fixing herself with the speed and was crying desperately, sobbing that the speed was no good and she could not get off on it. The failed high was not her only problem, as she had made a big investment in what she believed was a worthless heap of powder.

I offered to give her a second opinion and extracted a generous line to snort, and the next thing I knew I was totally spaced out and absolutely flying for 24 hours. I told her its quality was really good, which relieved her financial worries, but left her shocked that she had built up such a massive tolerance.

It gave me pause for thought, too. It was incredible that it had not affected her, even when injected directly into the bloodstream. She seemed a nice person, and it was frightening to see her in such a state. The implications worried me and did not bode well for the future.

I was unhappy that there seemed little ambition in the people around me to move beyond drug experience, or that, if there had been, it had largely dissipated. I was starting to feel that the drug scene was chasing its own tail, its intensity and camaraderie attracting free spirits repelled by a cruel and stifling material establishment, but its carefree horizons inexorably shrinking within a deteriorating quality of life, with more and more drugs producing less and less effect.

The exploration of consciousness seemed increasingly on the back burner, and the positive optimism of the sixties was turning into despondency and cynicism. 'All you need is love' was becoming 'whatever gets you through the night', and people were beginning to talk about life as a bad joke and the divine as an elusive trickster that had abandoned us to our fate. Many people seemed to have run into trouble of some sort on LSD, even if it was not on a par with my nemesis trip, and it was not uncommon to find those who would not take it any longer.

People were on many different levels, and each approached the question of drug experience in their own way. My experience was that few enough of those I met were really seeking in its deepest sense, and I was beginning to see that even those who were did not necessarily expect to pursue this beyond the drug scene. It was becoming clear to me that my original LSD mentor had been up and down for years, and on and off heroin at different times, and now seemed to be slipping into another down period. He would always be looking for answers, I realised, but he did not really believe he would ever escape the drug scene completely, and regarded it as a price worth paying for the experience gained.

I could understand this well enough because to awaken into the realm of the divine is a rare and precious privilege. It is rather an exclusive club to join, and I could see it would be easy to revel in this hidden knowledge and drift into a sort of perversely romantic role as a martyred warrior of the heart, prepared to risk everything for one more taste of the love of the divine.

Heroin users had gone even further, regarding the modern world as an abomination and their habit as the only thing that made it bearable. Some said it made them feel close to God, but I could not settle for a predictable and addictive chemical high. I did try heroin a couple of times, and its euphoria offered instant relief from frustration and pain, but its cloying embrace felt alien to me; it meant opting out of the quest and giving up responsibility for myself, and I was not ready to do that. I did not like the idea that we were the helpless victims of a cruel and pointless life, and I did not want to believe it was impossible to reach the divine without drugs.

I couldn't help feeling that a certain amount of hedonistic self-justification was going on, and that the relentless revelry of the drug scene was acquiring a rather tired and cheerless air. It was all very different from the colourful, vibrant immediacy of early drug experience, and I sometimes had to shake off a weird feeling that the spaced-out highs we lived in were starting to turn us into ghosts haunting the backstage of life.

I also noticed that people with no notion or interest in seeking were starting to appear on the scene, and heading straight for the intense and guaranteed highs of the more hardcore drugs. Life was becoming more about breaking into chemist's shops, and grapevine calls to swell the ranks of picket lines for violent confrontations with the police than love-ins in the park, and at times I felt I was turning into some kind of urban guerrilla. It was all very different from the deep and loving nature of my early experiences in the drug scene.

I was not taking care of my body at all by this time, I was so locked into trying to get high that I paid it little or no attention at all. I often lived on little more than Mars bars and speed, and the goals and values of the life I was leading had considerably declined.

I suspect it would not have been long before I quit my body for good if things had not changed. Some years later, my eldest sister told me that she had had a series of dreams about me at about this time in which she had seen me lying in a coffin, and in each successive dream she had drawn closer, until finally she was looking directly down at my body. I guess it doesn't need much interpretation. It was as if I were pursuing two futures; one mysterious and wonderful and the other stark and disastrous, and which had the greater claim on me hung in the balance.

In the meantime, I had plenty to occupy me in the day-to-day dramas of life on the streets. The final chapter of life in the terrace involved a typically surreal legal case in which a bunch of us signed up for legal aid with names like 'D. Duck' and appeared in court looking like something out of the Muppet show. It was really just a gesture to mark the end of a memorable chapter in squatting folklore, but we managed to get an eviction notice postponed for a month, and

I set about looking for another squat. When the eviction was finally enforced, surprisingly large numbers of police had the satisfaction of finally overrunning the enemy trenches, but, apart from a few die-hards letting off fireworks on the roof, the enemy was long gone.

Acquiring a squat meant becoming a de facto occupant of a property and being in possession of a key for the front door. The law was relatively unconcerned about how this state of affairs came about unless there was blatant evidence of a break in, so the trick was to get into the property as unobtrusively as possible, preferably without breaking and entering, and change the lock.

The onus was then on the owners to prove their right to the property and apply for an eviction order, with legal proceedings taking months and allowing plenty of time to look for a new squat and start all over again. Actually, it often took quite a while for eviction proceedings to begin as the owners might live anywhere, even abroad, and if they owned a lot of properties it could be some time before they even became aware that the property had squatters in it.

The absent-landlord syndrome was so prevalent that I felt no guilt about making use of these empty buildings. We generally targeted places that had obviously been vacant for some time, often for many years. The getting-in part could be fairly nerve wracking, though, and I remember a few heart-stopping moments. One night I clambered up onto a roof with a couple of other would-be squatters to check the rear windows of a house after drawing a blank on easy points of entry at the front. The first two we tried were locked up as tight as the rest, and we were beginning to think about giving up.

I was determined to get in, though, and steeled myself to break the glass on the final window with my torch. It was two in the morning, and we froze in horror as the diabolical noise this created echoed all round the neighbourhood; then, after a long nervous wait, I felt inside for the catch and discovered, ironically, that the window had been open all the time. This squat did not last long, though, as renovation works had been planned by the owners. The builders turned up one day and beat us at our own game, kicking the door in and filling the place with lots of nasty, rough men and equipment before we could call for reinforcements.

One of the easiest ways of getting into the big, three-storey terraced London houses around Baker Street was to climb up onto the roof and move along the row to enter through the roof hatch of the desired dwelling. The outer coverings of these hatches were basically just shallow upturned boxes resting over the wooden sides of the protruding hatchway and could be lifted off without difficulty. We could then drop down through the loft into the top floor of the house.

Getting out again was not so easy, however, and when I mistakenly dropped down into an occupied house with a friend we had great difficulty getting back up into the loft again. There were a couple of reasons for this, one being that there was no loft ladder and the other that it was my companion's birthday and he had eaten a generous portion of hash (cannabis) birthday cake before setting out.

The mission became more impossible by the minute as he dissolved into a giggling jelly, and even when we did climb out I thought I would never get him off the roof. We eventually secured the house we were after, which was great apart from its proximity to the Balcome Street siege, which led to it attracting a raid by armed police.

Chapter 11
Fortune smiles

Life continued, with the only apparent choice being to follow Bob Dylan's ironic advice and 'keep on keeping on'. New developments were on the horizon, however, the first hint of which had appeared at an open-air Pink Floyd concert at Knebworth some time earlier.

I spent much of the night prior to the concert trying to sneak in over the perimeter fence, which was quite daft because I had been given a ticket by a friend. Two of the people I was with were ticketless, though; one a friend from the terrace and the other an enterprising English girl we had met up with who had just hitchhiked back from Afghanistan.

The first time we got over the fence, we were run down by security guys in Land Rovers; we hugged the ground in the long grass, but the bouncing headlights closed in on us like safari hunters chasing their prey, and we were hauled aboard and ferried back out through the gate. Later we found someone from the terrace working as a security guard who let us in, and we set off in search of a suitable tree to hide in until the gates officially opened in the morning, where we passed the time drinking tequila.

Two remarkable things happened up in this tree. One was that I received a postcard from my youngest sister, who was en route to India. As the night wore on, various other enterprising souls joined us in our hiding place, and among them was someone we knew from the terrace. He had come via my place and picked up my mail, although how he had expected to find me in that huge mass of people I couldn't imagine.

The other remarkable thing was that I learned my original

psychedelic mentors had gone to see an Indian yogi lady instead of coming to Knebworth. Missing a Pink Floyd concert was unusual enough, but gurus had been off the agenda for quite a while, and this seemed completely out of character. The general consensus was that gurus were money-grabbing frauds, who did not know any more than we did.

There was something unusual going on, and I asked about it when I saw them, but found them surprisingly reticent on the subject. I received the impression that they were a little embarrassed and wanted more time to evaluate what they were doing before talking about it. This awakened my interest even more, of course, and I resolved to find out all about it when I got the chance.

The chance came one Sunday afternoon when I learned that one of this erudite pair had set off to see the mysterious 'yogi lady'. I chased after her and, after some persuasion, accompanied her by bus to Euston with my youngest sister, who had just returned from her trip to India. It turned out we were going to the flat of an Indian Hatha Yoga teacher I knew who had been giving free Hatha Yoga classes to the squatters in the Euston area; but when I walked into his flat I encountered something very different from my expectations and quite unlike anything I had known before.

My first feeling was one of surprise. I had anticipated a hushed, mystical atmosphere and was confronted instead by an extraordinary Indian lady, who seemed ten times more alive than anyone I had met before, telling off an elderly Sikh gentleman in an extremely forceful manner. My surprise quickly grew into astonishment as I realised that everything around me seemed full of light, and I sensed tremendous spiritual power being commanded in the room.

I felt as if I had stumbled out of a jungle path onto a broad, royal highway, and I had the oddest sensation of having somehow walked inside the pages of a Bible – as if a scene from a biblical epic was taking place all around me. 'This is what it must have been like to come across Christ teaching in the market place,' I found myself thinking in confusion, torn between the fascinating immediacy of the experience and alarm at the religious references my mind appeared to be making. It all seemed on a different level from anything I had experienced before, although I could not say why.

As I tried to figure out what was happening, the 'yogi lady' asked me to come forward, and placed her hands on my body. Her manner was cheerful and forthright, but I sensed compassion and concern in her.

'This one's sick,' she announced, rather spoiling my dramatic entrance, and then, after a pause, 'Don't worry, you will be all right.'

I felt a surge of relief and realised, to my surprise, that I believed her. Next she asked for some water, and someone gave her a glass bottle that had been filled from a tap. As I watched, she turned and appeared to open a door in the air behind her, revealing a kind of 'atomic furnace' that blazed with a stunningly beautiful, blindingly bright light, and held the bottle in this naked energy for a moment before closing the door again and handing it to me.

I was dazzled by the wonder of it all and did not really question this, but I have since wondered if the physical sequence of events I witnessed actually took place, or if I was interpreting something I experienced on a higher level.

I spent the remainder of the meeting standing with one hand out of the window, 'clearing out' my subtle system, but there was a final element to my first encounter with this most unexpected 'yogi lady'. As she left the flat, she turned and blew me a kiss in a gesture of amused, playful mockery, with a certain flair in its execution that exactly captured the style of a particular young lady from Caracas.

Actually, there were two final elements; the water she gave me had a remarkable effect – I drank some when I got back to my squat and its potency was immediately apparent. I felt what I can only describe as the presence of a powerful celestial horse manifesting within me, and an equally powerful urge to make haste to the toilet. There the grand finale of this most unexpected day proved to be the inexplicable but powerfully cleansing experience of defecating like a horse!

I felt wonderful for a couple of days and then took some LSD to try and gain a higher perspective on it all, as was my habit. I had a strange trip that began with feelings similar to those I had had in the yogi lady's presence. I again sensed the presence of a powerful spiritual authority with Christ-like, biblical associations and wondered if this was some new depth of my being that had been affected by Christian conditioning when I was very young. I became aware of a vast power that pervaded everything in existence and drove a fundamental process of change and transformation at every level, and I had a stunning vision of a great cosmic machine at work. It was made out of vibrations of many beautiful colours and processed matter in a constant, unrelenting process, like some kind of awesome, divine combine harvester.

I saw myself basking in a state of golden, utopian bliss, then being flung violently across a matrix of steadily degraded images of reality, into a stratum of existence far removed from its idyllic centre. The eye of God appeared over the horizon in the shape of an all-seeing, all-knowing orb, which rolled around the circumference of the earth against the direction of the planet's rotation and processed all that passed under it. The story of my life was laid out below me like a distant landscape, with good and bad juxtaposed like coloured countries on a map, and some parts were blasted, dark and ugly.

I felt I had made a real mess of my life and came out of the trip feeling quite despondent. I consulted the *I Ching*, the ancient Chinese 'Book of Changes', as was my habit, and it seemed to urge me to go back to see the extraordinary Indian lady. There was another meeting scheduled to take place the following week, and I intended to go, but I became distracted by various things that were happening and did not make it.

Afterwards, however, I was touched to learn that she had asked after me, and I resolved to go at the next opportunity, which came along a week or so later. Once again I walked into a room awash with light and power, and once again I felt a strange sense of familiarity and recognition. Shri Mataji, for that was the lady's name, spent the entire time 'working' on people; placing her hands on different parts of their bodies and asking them to participate in various ways, by placing their own hands on their body or towards the floor or the ceiling, and sometimes by asking questions within themselves or 'taking the name' of various spiritual personalities.

It was strange to hear references to different religions being related to different parts of the body, but there was a powerful resonance to it that silenced my scepticism, at least for the time being.

A lively conversation interspersed these activities, with questions, answers and a robust commentary from Shri Mataji, which varied from high good humour to profound solemnity. The unexpected combination of cheerful eastern mysticism and biblical gravitas encompassed a dynamic spirituality that was strangely both magical and religious at the same time – elements that had led very separate lives in my understanding for a long while.

It was easy to enjoy it, but the experience was also new and strange, and I was sometimes perturbed and confused by things Shri Mataji said. I struggled to maintain a suitably irreverent and cynical perspective on it all, but there was undeniably something reassuring and familiar about being in her presence, and I was thrilled to feel enveloped by high experience again, even if the experience was different in quality from much that I had known before.

I had encountered people previously who seemed able to penetrate, interact with, or manipulate the vibrational fabric of reality; I had even done a certain amount of it myself, but, whenever I was with Shri Mataji, it was as if the fabric of reality itself was being rewoven all around me. I felt immersed in a rich tapestry of living energy that was being constantly reworked by dancing vibrations of multiple densities and frequencies, and that grew in quality and excellence with every passing moment.

It put me in mind of the matrix of possibilities I had glimpsed on my recent LSD trip; as if in Shri Mataji's presence multiple alternative realities were being realigned, reintegrated and drawn back into their optimum potential. A fundamental sense of well-being crept over me, a sense of clarity, relaxation and contentment. I found it almost embarrassing at first, as if I had been scrubbed clean and given a new set of clothes to wear.

It felt extremely satisfying, though, and could become quite blissful; and the longer I spent in Shri Mataji's company, the deeper this state became. I experienced a kind of childlike purity growing within me, and at one point memorably felt as if I was a golden child sitting at the foot of an ancient tree.

It was a bit like living in Wonderland, all the more so because it was happening without drugs. At one point, entirely without warning, I saw bright, multicoloured streams of light shooting out from Shri

Mataji's forehead, the colours vividly luminescent and indescribably beautiful. This was high-energy experience indeed, thrilling but alarming too, as if I were witnessing some kind of super-advanced technology in action. Rapid bursts of this fantastic energy shot out each time she looked at someone, then slowed abruptly at the last moment to sink gently into their body. Shri Mataji quickly turned to me and said, '[A word I did not recognise] is open. You have no authority,' and the vision ceased.

I did not question the fact that I had these high experiences in Shri Mataji's presence without the use of drugs (other than my regular intake of cannabis, of course). It felt entirely natural, somehow, although I had never encountered anything like it before. After this second meeting I realised that I had lost the high from my first encounter without really noticing it, and had now regained it. I suddenly felt optimistic again. I knew I had a mountain to climb, but I felt capable of tackling it, even that it would be fun to do so, and I was surprised at how quickly my mood had changed.

Everything was fine when I was with Shri Mataji, but, when I left the intense field of vibrations that enveloped me in her presence, things could become rather different. I felt as if I had been filled with some kind of spiritual elixir that gradually drained away once back in my usual haunts in the squatting scene.

At first I regarded this as just another come-down from a high, although less obvious than with a drug experience. I noticed a distinct difference between the clean, silky-smooth quality of ease that I felt in this state and the frenetic energy of speed, or the stoned dispassion of cannabis or barbiturates. I also noticed a strange lack of focus when I first took these things after being with Shri Mataji, a kind of dullness or loss of sensitivity in my awareness, but this passed, or I ceased to be conscious of it.

Something that did change permanently from the time of my first encounter with Shri Mataji was my awareness of a subtle electromagnetic energy flowing through my body. I had experienced something similar at times during drug experiences, but now it had become a permanent feature in my being, flowing sometimes faintly and sometimes more strongly, but always present.

The other people around Shri Mataji also appeared to be feeling vibrations in their body, although they seemed aware of a much subtler range of sensations than I was. My sister spoke of a strong, steady flow of cool vibrations, like a wind or a cool breeze. Shri Mataji called this 'vibratory awareness' and said the flow of vibrations could feel cool or hot, and that positive or negative indications from energy centres in the body registered in specific fingers and parts of the hands (and feet), but I could not distinguish these things.

I could observe the reactions of people around me, however, including those of my intrepid sister, and they certainly appeared to be feeling these things to some degree. They described them not in terms of a learned or cultivated sensitivity but as a whole new set of sensations that seemed to have sprung into being of their own volition.

I did feel pain and tension in various places inside my body at times, which Shri Mataji said were indications from the chakras on a deeper level. She told me that my insensitivity to the subtle variations of vibratory awareness was largely due to damage to the chakra at the base of my neck, which seemed entirely possible judging by the heavy aching tension I often felt in my shoulders, neck and jaw.

At the other end of the spectrum, I continued to have profound experiences that I greatly treasured, feeling sometimes like a faulty light bulb that flashed on and off at random moments. One minute I would be sitting there feeling uncomfortably numb, and the next moment the floor would become as transparent as glass and I would find myself floating in a delicate lotus on a crystal ocean while a great wind rushed through the room.

Shri Mataji encouraged us to 'use' the vibrations to bring about positive changes in ourselves, in each other and in our environment, but the only way I could experiment with this was to put my attention on – or direct my hands towards – people or objects and allow the subtle current to flow through me while hoping for the best.

I did find that some people could become aware of a subtle energy flow themselves when I did this, but I did not really know what was going on. I had actually tried something like this before when I had felt energy flowing through me on LSD trips, but I had been unable to achieve any noticeable effect – apart from a friend jokingly accusing me of trying to electrocute him – or to draw any real conclusion about it.

For the time being, I remained cut off from the subtle kind of sensitivity that Shri Mataji talked about, and contented myself with vibrating my (cannabis) joints before smoking them!

I visited Shri Mataji again a week later, and this time there were quite a lot of people present. The meetings had moved from the Hatha Yoga teacher's flat near King's Cross to a maisonette above an office and a barber's shop in a fairly compact town house near Euston.

It was right in the middle of the squatting community I had first moved into, and a substantial number of the local squatters were present. In this meeting, a discussion about the validity of drug experience became rather heated and the 'locals' became quite vocal in their assertion that drugs were good and got you high.

Shri Mataji's position was basically that drugs damaged the subtle energy system within us, and that no one serious about their spiritual ascent could keep taking them. This struck a chord with me as I had always regarded drugs as something I would leave behind one day, at least in theory, but only one person in the room was actively taking Shri Mataji's side, a seeker from Switzerland who had appeared on the scene, and a number of people were becoming quite aggressive.

At one point Shri Mataji sat back and wrapped her arms about herself in a striking gesture of concern and despair, and I glimpsed a surprising incongruity between the stunning power I had seen her wield and the helpless distress she now displayed. It was as if her power were neutralised by boundaries of individual freedom that she could or would not cross. She looked like a mother surrounded by naughty children, and I made an impulsive decision. I would give it six months and see what happened.

'OK, I'll stop,' I said, sailing forth into an abrupt and reproachful silence.

I felt quite indignant at the glares I received from some of those around me. I felt I had every right to do whatever I wanted. So off I went feeling virtuous and keen about this new phase of my life, and reasonably consoled by the fact that, in my book, cigarettes and alcohol didn't count as drugs.

A week passed and Shri Mataji invited everyone to visit her at her house in Surrey, but somehow or other I volunteered to meet up with a guy from Nigeria who wanted to come with us, and when he did not appear I waited too long and missed everyone at Victoria Station. They had given up on me and caught a train, and I could not follow as, impractical as ever, I had no address or phone number, so was left high and dry.

This was obviously an instance of great cosmic unfairness, and I took revenge on the cosmos by going round to a friend's place and consuming every available chemical substance I could get hold of. Indulging myself in this way gave me little satisfaction, however; the buzz I experienced seemed somehow crude and oppressive, and its intensity oddly joyless. Something had changed, and I realised I was no longer comfortable with my old life. Shri Mataji had brought to a head the doubts and dissatisfaction that had lurked at the back of my mind for some time, and I knew I could no longer believe in the wisdom of taking drugs in the way that I used to.

I passed a week or two in a kind of limbo, smoking dope without feeling I particularly wanted to. We were invited to Shri Mataji's house again, and this time I made sure I got there. We arrived at the small rural station of Hurst Green and walked for fifteen minutes or so along country lanes. It all seemed very ordinary and English, although the suitably named 'Godstone' was not far off. The detached house was in a comfortably appointed cul-de-sac, and I was conscious of how outlandish some of us must appear in these salubrious surroundings, wondering what the inevitable watchers behind the net curtains would be making of it.

Arriving at the house, I realised that I felt different to the way I had on my previous encounters with Shri Mataji. I was again enveloped by a powerful atmosphere of vibrating energy, but the smooth, serene high eluded me. Instead I felt tension and anxiety in my chest, and my heart began to beat erratically. It set off a familiar churning feeling that I had struggled with only too often; of being frustratingly unable to be still and engage with myself properly, of constantly striving to relax enough to gain a stable purchase on reality. Shri Mataji picked up on this in no time at all, and announced that my heart chakra was 'catching' and she wanted to work on it. The next thing I knew, I was sitting on the floor in front of her and she had asked me to hold my breath for a few seconds, then closed her eyes.

What happened next I shall put into italics to highlight that for me it marks a clear watershed between past drug-associations and the beginning of spontaneous high experience of a different order. I prefer to describe it in the present tense; as such experiences always unfold in a kind of eternal, timeless present:

Almost immediately I see a subtle figure rise from her being and move forward as though to stand over me. It is the form of a woman wearing a kind of Arabic garment, with her hair covered, but the whole image has a classic style to it that does not seem to belong to any specific race or period of history.

The cloth is not of any recognisable material but appears to be made, as does the lady herself, entirely of vibrations, rather like a picture made up of silver or platinum pixels on a TV screen. I find myself looking at an absolutely pure, primordial image of womanhood that radiates immense power as well as great compassion and holiness.

I feel totally overwhelmed. I know I am confronted by some kind of archetype, and one I feel I recognise, but the vision is so powerful I cannot face it for more than a moment. 'My God,' I think, 'she's not human,' and I look down at Shri Mataji's feet instead. There is no escape here, either, as I appear to be seeing an X-ray of her feet, somehow.

I can see the bones of her feet, which look hollow and have a kind of atomic energy flowing through them. I experience a sense that I am existing inside a biblical story again and find myself thinking, for no apparent reason, 'This is how Christ's feet must have looked when he walked the earth.'

Shri Mataji's feet begin to grow in size, becoming huge. I feel myself drawn down into them, entering into the hollow bones of her feet, which become vast tunnels filled with love that stretch away into infinity. I feel absolutely secure and relaxed, and slowly become aware of myself sitting in front of Shri Mataji again. Her eyes are open and she is smiling.

Now I feel an impossible joy awakening in me and a wildly burgeoning recognition and knowledge. There is an overwhelming

95

sense of déjà vu, of cosmic completion; a primordial awakening from a cosmic sleep of millions of years. My sister, who is watching, tells me afterwards that I look like a flower opening out to the sun.

Suddenly I feel Shri Mataji halt the process. I literally feel her push me back down with a regretful smile. Immediately my joy turns to anguish. I am so near to something so wonderful! Yet I know I am in no shape to sustain great spiritual heights and, more to the point, I realise that the anxiety and tension in my chest has completely disappeared; I am back down to earth, but I am again enjoying that elusive, silky-smooth ease of being.

It was incredible; something I would have struggled with for hours on an LSD trip had vanished in no time at all and left me feeling great – and the experience I had gone through was awesome. There were still many things I wanted to know and understand about Shri Mataji, but I was quite sure of one thing, I was going to stick around and find out.

I realised that she had extricated me from old problems I had fallen back into during the drug binge I had indulged in, and I had no difficulty in reaffirming my intentions to abandon chemical assistance in my spiritual journey. I knew this was easy to do in her presence and a challenge back on the streets, but I really felt there was no going back. I felt a reawakening of the optimism I had experienced when I first started seeking, and I set forth on this new path with as much enthusiasm and determination as I could muster.

The next few weeks were a fascinating mixture of confusion, astonishment, disconcertion and wonder; of unexpected experience, new information, conflicting ideas and new perceptions. Despite not always being certain what was going on, I greatly enjoyed Shri Mataji's company and that of the handful of seekers with whom I shared it, pleasantly surprised that the profound nature of much of the conversation left so much time for humour.

A constant dynamic was maintained, with Shri Mataji 'working' on each of us and demonstrating subtle changes in 'vibratory awareness' while answering questions and proposing novel spiritual perspectives on the history of religion and the purpose of evolution.

The vibrations would build up until we all seemed to swim in a golden haze of dancing energy. Sometimes I initially felt tense, self-conscious, or 'blocked up' by the emotional, mental and physical junk I seemed to accumulate in the outside world; but this would begin to dissipate almost as soon as it was highlighted by Shri Mataji's presence, and I would soon find myself participating in events with an exuberance that surprised me.

It was not that I was floating about in bliss, but I did feel put back together enough to function in this unique environment at a basic level at least. I could feel a strong flow of vibrations and a reassuring sense of stability, but behind this welcome footing in reality I often felt intense, aching pains and pressure in various parts of my body; these were sometimes quite painful, especially in my head and neck. At times it felt a little as if I were being held together by a giant Band-Aid, but any discomfort was amply compensated for by the humour, knowledge and compassion that enveloped me.

We were really spoiled by Shri Mataji, were fed sumptuous meals, took long siestas and enjoyed fascinating conversations late into the night. On one occasion she gave me the world's most amazing head massage with oil. She spent a lot of time discussing our backgrounds, the story of our seeking and the more improbable aspects of western culture, and often expressed surprise, horror and concern at the experiences we related.

Chapter 12
Wind of change

The story of creation that Shri Mataji was putting together was quite different from anything I had come across before. Pieces of the jigsaw I had been struggling with for years would slip unexpectedly into place and become suddenly obvious, yet the surprising nature of some of her statements could trigger doubt and confusion in my mind, too.

The scale of her vision and the concepts she described were quite breathtaking, and it could take a real effort of will to consider them in an objective manner, while at other times her words clashed with ideas and concepts I had formed, and triggered resistance and resentment.

Books I had read and past drug experiences would sometimes pop into my head as Shri Mataji spoke, and create doubts and puzzlement as I tried to match them all together. Sometimes I would try to discuss these sticking points with Shri Mataji and sometimes I would just shelve them for future consideration, as I could see it was going to take a while to grasp the big picture.

It is difficult to recall exactly the progression of events that took place with Shri Mataji and the small group of seekers who were with her at that time, and in trying to retrace this journey I have described her words as I remember them. It was long ago, however, and I was certainly not taking notes, so I am not quoting her directly.

Shri Mataji consistently related any spiritual subject to a subtle energy system within each human being and maintained that a high spiritual state depended on the condition of this system or, more correctly, on our ability to maintain and develop it. She spent much of her time working on this subtle system and showing us how to experience this for ourselves.

It was actually quite unusual for someone apparently on a high spiritual level to emphasise this kind of practical working knowledge. Gurus had always seemed somewhat enigmatic figures to me, tending to retain power and knowledge as their own preserve while dispensing cryptic comments and mysterious allusions, or demonstrating unearthly powers. This kind of 'hands on' approach and the open sharing of knowledge seemed very different.

Still, its significance eluded me to begin with, partly because of the difficulty I had in understanding Shri Mataji's declaration that the 'vibratory awareness' she was demonstrating was 'self-realisation'. For me, this term meant the be-all and end-all of everything; it was nirvana, liberation, oneness with God; it was not feeling quite nice and experiencing unusual physical sensations in various parts of the body.

I already knew a bit about the energy system - the chakras and the kundalini power - that Shri Mataji spoke about. *Chakra* is a Sanskrit word meaning 'wheel' and refers to subtle energy centres situated at specific points in the spine. *Kundalini* is another Sanskrit word that is feminine and means 'coiled'. The primordial power of the divine is recognised as a feminine force in Hindu tradition, and 'coiled' indicates that the power is potential; *kundalini* therefore describes a residual or potential power of the divine that is latent in human beings. (The feminine aspect of the divine, I knew, had been conspicuously absent from the mythology of many cultures for a long time. It appeared to have been widely prevalent in prehistoric times, but to have become increasingly marginalised with the development of male-dominated materialistic societies. It tended to be associated with inner, subjective spiritual experience as opposed to collective religious organisation and control.)

I had had some high-level experience of this energy system on LSD trips, but, although such events were fantastic, they had tended to manifest mysteriously and unexpectedly, and remained essentially elusive and ungovernable. I associated the kundalini and the chakras with the powerfully magical and the miraculous; it seemed almost mundane to be relating them to subtle physical sensations in the body, particularly as I found my sensitivity to such things was not good at all.

However, I could not dispute that magical things kept happening:

Shri Mataji demonstrates a technique she calls 'shoe-beating', explaining that it can help to separate our attention from people we feel are affecting us in a negative way. She takes one of her shoes, traces a name on the carpet with her finger and then strikes the spot repeatedly with the sole of the shoe. Just as I am wondering if such symbolic acting-out is really necessary, the floor becomes suddenly transparent, and I find myself staring at a beautiful image of the planet Earth, which shines brilliantly against the vast blackness of space beneath Shri Mataji's shoe.

Such stunning experiences occurred sporadically for no apparent reason. Less dramatically, many things that Shri Mataji spoke of conjured strikingly beautiful images in my mind's eye, putting into context, or sparking recognition of, things I had experienced on LSD.

However, such visions fell far short of fully manifesting the states of consciousness that inspired them, especially as they were accompanied by all kinds of tensions and aches and pains. I felt as if I had discovered a castle full of treasure and tried to get in through the back door, only to be sent packing with a lump on my head; then struggled to construct a rickety scaffold up the outside walls to find I could only peer impotently in through the windows. I suspected I was going to have to climb back down, dismantle the scaffold and go a little more humbly around to the front door.

I could not deny that even in a high, positive LSD experience I had little real control of what was going on, and even less understanding of the problems I could run into, and it was increasingly brought home to me that I had learned little from drug experiences other than that higher states of consciousness existed. Long conversations, debates and experience with Shri Mataji were making it clear that I had been somewhat naive in my pursuit of 'spiritual truth', and that the heights I had reached for required strong and stable foundations and a far more comprehensive approach than anything I had imagined.

Shri Mataji was quite blunt in her assertion that it made no difference how 'high' my drug experiences may have been; if I had not mastered the subtle system, I was nowhere. I had not established and maintained my self-realisation, she said, and I had no understanding of the subtle infrastructure that underlay it. She pointed out that I had not even considered something as basic as the physical effects on my liver and kidneys of the drugs I had been taking, or realised that the liver played a vital role in the quality of awareness, which was an important factor in the spiritual ascent.

She said that drugs could open up realms of experience not meant for human beings, however intriguing they might appear. Once she likened it to venturing behind the scenes in a power plant where dangerous forces were at work, instead of tapping the energy at its intended point of use.

At other times she spoke of the attention being drawn away from the centre into past collective memory or visions of the future, and warned us that there were many subtle realms or dimensions where the souls of the dead existed between physical incarnations. She said that not all of these were high astral levels; there were lower strata, too, where negative and dissatisfied souls lurked. We could get lost, she said, enticed by things that could appear fascinating but did not help our evolution, in fact quite the reverse.

The spiritual ascent had nothing to do with the mind, communicating with spirits or seeing auras and visions, she told us. The centre path was one of pure awareness, of expanding the depth and quality of consciousness in the here and now; it was the thoughtless awareness of the meditative state and direct vibratory experience of the chakras. Not until the ascent was complete would we be able to see into all of the dimensions of existence, she said, for then they would be part of our being, and we would have transcended their separate realities. To seek them out before this was to move away from the centre into illusion, confusion and disintegration.

The point Shri Mataji was making, I realised, was that the human subtle system replicated the topography of the collective unconscious mind and had the potential to resonate with any part of it. The attention could open human consciousness up to other dimensions of the collective being, but the collective being was a single integrated whole and the human being was not. The drop had to become one with the ocean, but first it had to become a drop, and I began to see how the awakened kundalini had to weave all of these dimensions of our being together into a complete image of the whole.

The subtle system, the physical, mental, emotional and spiritual being, all had to be integrated and transformed into something that transcended their separate functions. The third eye of legend did open, according to Shri Mataji, but not onto the past or the future; the fully integrated subtle system was its lens and it looked upon the land of the divine.

She said that our confusion about spiritual reality was compounded by something she called 'mental projection', which was the remarkable ability of the ego to convince itself that anything it believed in was true, real and effective. From her point of view, this was a belief system based on an imaginary concept, an authentic spiritual truth or a subjective experience; which was embellished or superimposed with mental interpretations and assumptions that had no independent means of verification, or active connection with the subtle system.

It operated in much the same way in an eccentric individual as in a society or a religion, and each 'mental projection' could happily contradict any number of others, as each simply believed it was right and all the others were wrong. It was all quite crazy, of course, but I was beginning to see that I had been doing much the same in the drug scene. Although the new states of consciousness I had discovered had been stunning revelations in themselves, I had still imposed my own ideas on them, and had been influenced by books I had read and the views of those around me. I had assumed I was learning everything there was to know, and it had not really occurred to me that my own chosen field of interest might have been holding out on me.

Those who have had some experience of the divine will know that fabulous visual beauty is an integral part of its wonder. It is, however, an awakening into a higher reality in which perception and experience are one and the same. All of the faculties are assimilated and transcended by oneness; the transformation is complete, and it is both the beginning of a higher phase of existence and a final escape from the perils of *maya*, and of the embryonic struggles of the soul in the physical universe (*maya*: in Hinduism, the material world, considered in reality to be an illusion).

I began to see that Shri Mataji was taking us step by step through a process I had attempted to jump clean over on LSD. From the perspective of eternity, the drama on the human level seems relatively insignificant, the shedding of the ego and the flowering of the divine a simple and natural progression. It is an important but brief and inevitable process in the greater scheme of things, something like the birth of a child. Shri Mataji explained that the integration and transformation process could take place instantly if the chakras were in perfect condition, such as had happened in the case of Buddha, but emphasised that he was an exceptional person with a long and illustrious spiritual history.

Something similar seemed to happen to seekers of a certain calibre on LSD, and although such experiences were totally mind-blowing I began to realise that they might not be particularly helpful in the long run. It may be that LSD functioned as an artificial chemical key and initiated spontaneous processes that occur naturally in high-energy states. It certainly seemed to dissolve the ego and allow deeper aspects of the spiritual being to manifest; but, however it worked, I suspect that much of the depth and quality of experience depended on the degree to which the subtle system had developed in previous lives.

Shri Mataji told us that some souls were born realised, having achieved their self-realisation in previous incarnations, and that they could have achieved various spiritual heights. She also said souls could be born with their kundalini awakened through previous seeking, which meant that this energy was active and could rise quite high in certain conditions, but that the process was not yet complete and self-realisation had yet to be established. She said that this could drive a strong desire to seek because such awakened souls were sensitive to both the divine and to negativity, but did not have the stability and confidence of a realised soul.

As well as this, or in relation to this, she spoke of human evolution as entering a final phase in which many souls were close to awakening to their spiritual destiny; and all of these things, I began to see, could have played a part in the psychedelic era and its legacy. I think a large part of the problem was the effortless way in which the divine being within us could sometimes awaken and unfold in a powerful LSD experience. From the divine side of things, it seemed deceptively easy as the process occurred so spontaneously, but little was learned from it; the ascent remained a mystery and the descent inevitable.

Also, paradoxically, the power of drug experience and the ease with which it was achieved seemed to undermine the whole ethos of spiritual aspiration. Seekers were overwhelmed by the wonders they were propelled into rather than being inspired to reach them, and the experience itself was devalued by the ego's tendency to see it as an easily accessible and given right, to be enjoyed at will.

The knowledge that love hides in molecular structure did not preclude the development of a number of self-destructive attitudes. When reasserting itself after an LSD experience of omnipresence, the ego could identify itself with the collective being and effectively believe that it was God, with the right to do as it pleased. Stealing from shops, for instance, would not be regarded as wrong because everything belonged to everybody. The impact of unexpected and undreamed-of high-energy experience tended to belittle the mundane requirements of everyday life, and could lead to a lack of interest in, and unconcern with, its practicalities.

I started to see lots of reasons why the idealism and optimism of the psychedelic era might have foundered. There was a fundamental lack of knowledge, an ignorance of the principles that sustained the subtle system and a casual assumption that our temporal perceptions were universally valid.

There was also little awareness of how vulnerable we were in high states and of the damage we were potentially opening ourselves up to; and scant consideration given to the long-term effects of the drugs we took on the subtle and physical being. There was certainly no understanding at all of the primeval battlefield we were venturing out onto. I remember a young lady I got to know on an interior design course at Chelsea School of Art some years later telling me how she had experienced thoughtless awareness and the cool breeze blowing strongly for hours on an LSD trip, but had had no idea where to go with it, and had eventually got bored and looked for something more interesting to do.

She also told me that she had once had an experience very like I had had, in that a horrible entity had jumped at her from someone else she was tripping with. However, she had been unable to fight it off. 'It got me,' she said (she was a truthful soul). She did not elaborate (not that truthful) but said that by the end of the trip she felt as if she had been raped.

There could be a very human attachment to drug experience. I found that my identification with the driven state of psychedelic drugs was a surprisingly strong one, despite the temporary highs and inevitable lows that they delivered. Years later, when I started to experience high states spontaneously, I actually found it strange to feel I was sustaining them from within myself. When that happened, I could feel the kundalini standing within the whole length of my spine, and I could increase its power simply by desiring it, like accelerating a car.

Shri Mataji said that a chemical similar to LSD manifested naturally in the brain when the kundalini rose in great force. She agreed that comparable substances had been experimented with at different times in ancient India, but in a very different environment and with a very different attitude from the careless 'free for all' of recent times. She said that seeking had taken many forms across the millennia and that these things belonged to the distant past, whereas all down through time the evolutionary process had been working towards the stage where all humanity would be ready for a collective evolutionary jump in consciousness.

According to her, real spiritual knowledge had been known to very few up to the present time, with living knowledge of the subtle system kept secret in India and communicated directly from guru to disciple for thousands of years. She said that, in modern times, the wider availability of Sanskrit scriptures and the disreputable activities of failed or rejected disciples had helped to create the hotchpotch of tradition and ritual that is the Hindu religion today.

She was concerned that western seekers were taking spiritual pundits, yogis and gurus at face value. 'You are just going from a Christian sermon to a Hindu sermon or an Islamic sermon,' she would say, and warned that some gurus were only interested in amassing money and influence, and were manipulating their disciples for their own purposes. She said that many seekers had drifted or been manoeuvred away from the centre and had gained unusual experiences, powers and perceptions that could seem exciting but were actually evolutionary dead ends.

In my own case, I could see how I had forced the pace of experience and attempted to break through the layers of ego into the core of my being with the introspective technique of a battering ram. I had even partially succeeded, but I had opened myself up to unknown dimensions of reality without any understanding or protection, and had paid a heavy price for it.

There was a whole mythology surrounding the subject of kundalini that seemed to originate mainly from certain kinds of *sadhus*, or gurus, and their followers. The legend was that it was a dangerous and unpredictable force that could manifest in a violent and harmful manner, and few people could approach it without fear. It was something I had been puzzled by, in fact, as I had never experienced anything like this in apparent encounters with the kundalini on LSD.

Negative or frightening experiences had come from personal fears, other people or weird and unpleasant entities, but manifestations I associated with the mysterious kundalini were always absolutely wonderful, magical and beautiful. It felt, in fact, as if I were encountering my real, innermost self, and the effect of negative situations was to drive it away and bury it out of reach somewhere deep inside me.

Shri Mataji herself was quite adamant that there was nothing dangerous or harmful about the kundalini at all, and said emphatically that such stories had come from people without real knowledge or experience of the matter. There was actually more to it than that, and she went into the subject more deeply later on, but meanwhile there were certainly no dramatic repercussions either in me or in the people around me.

I was beginning to realise how little I really knew about the kundalini other than the fact that it existed. I believed I had experienced some of its manifestations, but I had not known its innermost secrets. It occurred to me that I had even seen the kundalini trying to warn me of my peril on my nemesis LSD trip; I had marvelled at the divine beauty of the royal cobra striking out at me from the mirror without realising its meaning. It had triggered powerful events, but they had not remained anchored in the centre; even my highest experiences seemed to have occurred mostly around the periphery of the central channel. Certainly my subtle system had not been stable and my attention not wholly detached from a human agenda.

Shri Mataji said that kundalini awakening should occur effortlessly and spontaneously from the deepest part of our being; it could not be stimulated through outward mental, physical or emotional exertion. She described the kundalini as rising through the innermost of a subtle cluster of inner pathways in the central channel of the subtle system and threading its way through the centre of each chakra up to the crown of the head.

There it connected human consciousness with the all-pervading power of the divine, manifesting a spontaneous meditative or witness state that she called 'thoughtless awareness' and a flow of cool vibrations experienced as a 'wind' or subtle current of cool energy flowing in the body, together with a new sensory awareness of the subtle centres in the central nervous system. She said that this experience grew and intensified as the first strands of kundalini expanded within the central channel and the chakras began to open out more and more, allowing it to flow with a steadily increasing force.

The kundalini itself is described in Sanskrit literature as an aspect of the primordial mother that exists innately within each human being as the potential for its spiritual rebirth. Shri Mataji spoke of it as the power that manifests the spirit, described in many spiritual traditions as the 'breath of life' or the 'breath of the divine'; the 'Ruh' of Islam, the 'Holy Spirit' of Christianity or the 'Ganga', the holy river pouring from the head of Shiva, in Hinduism. 'It is the power of pure desire,' she said. 'It awakens when you forget all other desires and seek only the spirit.'

She said that the kundalini and the chakras in our subtle system set the whole tone of our personality, of our entire life in fact; and explained that those who longed for the divine grew spiritually through the power of their desire in a process unfolding over many lifetimes. She described the human personality as a reflection of the underlying quality and condition of this subtle system – in which the kundalini and the chakras made up the essential core of the soul

– which survived physical death to reincarnate over and over again, gradually awakening to its divine nature.

Shri Mataji portrayed the subtle system as a kind of living blueprint in which the energy centres had the potential to resonate with specific attributes of the divine that the evolving consciousness needed to assimilate in its spiritual ascent.

What little I knew about chakras was largely theoretical, having come from books and fairly random experiences on LSD trips, but under her tutelage a new perspective began to form. Instead of individual energy centres, I started to see a system at work, as if a higher state of reality had been transmuted into the essential principles an awakening soul needed to imbibe and establish, something like light separated down into the spectrum of colours in the rainbow.

Shri Mataji said that there were seven aspects of the divine reflected in seven chakras, and elaborated on their fundamental principles in considerable detail. She spoke of each chakra as potentially manifesting a different quality of consciousness and a different kind of bliss, with the topmost chakra at the crown of the head manifesting all of these qualities in an integrated form that transcended them all. 'At the Sahasrara chakra there is nothing but bliss,' she said.

Her descriptions of these seven heavens put me in mind of some of the LSD experiences I had had, and her explanations of the qualities of the chakras conjured up subtle visions of beauty as though from multifaceted jewels. I could see how these myriad forms of loveliness might manifest through the soul in limitless permutations, making each uniquely beautiful; with each human being shining more brightly in proportion to their quality and containing the potential for infinitely greater wonders to unfold.

Shri Mataji told us that the energy principles of the chakras existed on both a microcosmic and macrocosmic level and played complementary roles in the evolutionary ascent. On a microcosmic level they worked out the individual awakening and transformation of the soul, while on a macrocosmic level they drove the evolutionary process itself. She explained that the primordial forces expressed in the chakras manifested everything from the creation and organisation of matter to the evolution of life, and were not abstract energies but self-aware archetypical processes functioning in the collective unconscious mind, a bit like programs running in a computer.

She described these archetypes as specific aspects of the divine, whose images of divine perfection were reflected in the chakras; and which had entered human consciousness in a variety of ways at different times and places throughout history. They had been represented in tradition, folklore and mythology with various degrees of accuracy, she said, and had incarnated to play key roles in the unfolding of the evolutionary process, establishing fundamental milestones in the spiritual ascent by awakening the chakras one by one in the collective human psyche.

I was quite fascinated by Shri Mataji's story of creation as a sequential progression of evolutionary stages designed to unfold the subtle energy system within us. In the same way that each cell in our being is imprinted with the DNA of the whole body, she depicted each human soul as an individual cell in the body of the primordial being, with the entire history and potential of creation encoded within it. The scale of the whole thing was amazing, and the sense of purpose Shri Mataji's words instilled into the sprawling mystery of existence, and the tremendous confidence she radiated about the future, were hugely inspirational.

It had gradually dawned on me that the vibratory awareness Shri Mataji was teaching us about might be a tad more significant than I had first thought. She talked about the subtle system as a functional instrument hardwired into the evolutionary process with the potential to fine-tune the human psyche into the evolutionary 'program' of the collective unconscious mind. This, of course, implied an extremely sophisticated process at work, in which the evolution of matter unfolded in the image of a universal template that allowed the consciousness of nascent divine beings to develop in successive incarnations. I actually had no doubt that some of the mysterious goings-on I had experienced in higher dimensions of consciousness had the potential for this level of 'technology', but it took a while to accept that the system Shri Mataji was demonstrating might actually be the elusive key to high-energy experience.

This was partly due to the condition I was in, as my sensitivity to vibratory awareness varied from slight to abysmal and I could jump from feeling clear and positive to down and doubt-ridden in the blink of an eye. There was also the natural inclination to question something that seemed too good to be true. However, I could see that, in theory at least, it could provide both tangible evidence of ultimate purpose in life and a practical means of completing the ascent to the divine. It just might, I slowly came to realise, be a stairway to heaven after all.

It certainly offered different possibilities to the unsustainable highs and disastrous lows of psychedelic experience. I realised it might mean going back to square one in a way, but I would be starting at the bottom of the escalator and going up rather than at the top going down, which would be a welcome change from my experience up until this point.

According to Shri Mataji, the vibratory awareness of the subtle system manifested initially within the innermost and subtlest channel of the nervous system; and only gradually spread outwards to enrich the emotional, mental and physical senses, and to unfold the greater dimensions of the divine. She described the subtle system as an instrument programmed to trigger this process when the kundalini was awakened, and which adjusted itself to the calibre and condition of the individual. The kundalini had the potential to open out everything completely if the subtle system was perfect, she said, or to initiate a process of growth, integration and transformation that worked more slowly towards the same goal.

She was quite adamant that kundalini awakening and vibratory awareness initiated an experimentally verifiable dialogue with the collective unconscious, and that we had only to improve the quality of the instrument to see if this was true.

I felt I had no choice but to check this all out, and started to pay more attention to the vibratory sensations I felt in my body. I tried to absorb the flow of energy, information and explanation pouring from Shri Mataji and to relate it to my own inner experience, and to that described by the people around me; and I was fortunate in this respect to have my sister as a fair witness as I knew I could trust her. She was also in much better shape than I was, and felt the vibratory sensations far more clearly than I did.

Shri Mataji told us that the hands were particularly sensitive to the vibrations, although vibrations could also be felt at chakra points in the feet or directly in the location of the chakras in the body; and we set about experimenting with 'vibratory awareness' by putting our attention onto people, places and objects and holding our hands out to see what we could feel.

Each finger, the thumb and particular parts of the hands had been identified by Shri Mataji as related to specific chakras, and she said that a cool breeze or a flow of cool vibrations could be felt flowing in the hands and the body if the vibrations were positive and a variety of negative sensations would register if there were problems. She also showed us that the kundalini could be seen physically pulsating in the body on occasion, sometimes quite dramatically, where its ascent was obstructed at a particular chakra.

The cool breeze was particularly elusive in my case; I did feel a flow of energy that varied in intensity, but it was usually hot or lukewarm. My sister could often feel a gale of cool breeze on her hands, and sometimes even that one hand was hot and the other cool. This, according to Shri Mataji, was because the left hand registered the left-side energy (emotional) and the right hand, the right-side energy (mental and physical), and these channels heated up if they became blocked or overactive.

Shri Mataji explained that the primary emotional, mental and physical energies of the left and right channels were evolved and refined by the qualities of the chakras at their respective levels, while the chakras themselves were sustained by the evolutionary power of the central channel.

In this way, she said, the unfolding of the subtle system developed new subtleties in evolving humanity, enriched and enlightened human consciousness and drove the spiritual ascent. A negative indication in a specific part of the left or right hand would signal a problem with left- or right-side energy in relation to the qualities of the relevant chakra. Feeling these 'catches', as Shri Mataji called them, was an odd experience. At various times my sister reported feeling heat, tingling, numbness and sudden stabs of pain that she described as quite definitely localised in specific fingers and parts of her hands.

I also felt this sometimes, and it is difficult to convey the electrical immediacy of the experience, how specific and insistent it could be.

111

Sometimes I felt as if there were a thimble on the end of one of my fingers, or an unpleasant ache would develop in a finger deep in the bone all the way to the knuckle; at other times I would feel a sudden tingling or stabbing pain in my fingers or the palm of my hand that was distinctly emphatic in nature. Another effect was an involuntary twitching in one or more fingers, which sometimes took on a life of their own to the extent that they would jerk back towards the palm, or even appeared to pivot or rotate slightly around the knuckle. Occasionally the whole hand would tremble or shake.

It was not just the physical sensations that hit home but a real sense that my own being was poking me with attitude and saying, 'Hey, what's this, I don't like it!' I also felt a delightful creeping, prickling sensation on the crown of my head on occasion, as if delicate nerve endings were releasing and opening up. Some people felt this quite intensely, and even reported that it felt like a small animal moving about on their scalp.

Although, due to my poor sensitivity, much of my early experience with 'vibratory awareness' was restricted to observing the reactions of others, I was somewhat bemused to find that other people I attempted to 'work' on sometimes felt the cool vibrations and the sensations in their chakras too, including people unrelated to the group of seekers with Shri Mataji.

This was intriguing as it meant that some kind of collective manifestation was at work that acted on the consciousness of others, although it took me a while to be clear about this. I had by no means attained the stability or sensitivity needed to be certain what was happening, and on a number of occasions I found myself 'awakening the kundalini' of people who could feel much more than I could, which was quite embarrassing.

In time, I found that, once what Shri Mataji called 'self-realisation' had taken place, it could communicate itself spontaneously between subtle systems on a level fundamentally independent of the ego, and that sometimes even quite badly damaged systems could 'pass the experience on' and initiate the process in others.

Shri Mataji spent a lot of time teaching us how to 'work' on the subtle system, both our own and those of other people. There were many ways of doing this, the simplest being to feel which chakras were hot, painful or tingling and to direct the flow of cool vibrations through the hands towards their location in the body.

One technique was to use the elements, to sit with the feet in water, for instance, or hold a candle flame in the vicinity of a chakra that was 'catching', until the system cooled down. She explained that the subtle system had to be sustained by respecting the subtle principles of the chakras, and taught us how to use mantras to awaken the divine qualities within them.

All of these things had a tangible effect on the quality of our awareness and sense of well-being, and 'working' on the chakras of someone else or being 'worked' on by them seemed to strengthen the experience, presumably because the process operated on a collective level and increased the participation of the collective unconscious.

Something as simple as coming in from a difficult day and sitting with my feet in a bowl of water, while someone worked on my subtle system, could create considerable changes in my mood and state of mind. Even I could feel heat, tensions and fatigue flowing down into the water, and I would often jump up after twenty minutes or so feeling quite different.

Chapter 13
From little acorns

Feeling vibratory sensations in the chakras was one thing, but recognising the subtle complexities they related to was another. 'Vibratory awareness', and a comprehensive understanding of the processes underlying it, would eventually mushroom into a truly vast subject.

It was not intellectual knowledge as such; it was more like a kind of cultural understanding of the functions and values of the collective unconscious mind, that was absorbed and accumulated as our living experience of the subtle system grew. We were able to match the things Shri Mataji taught us with the reactions we felt in our own beings and the effects we observed in each other, and the whole edifice gradually built itself up in a natural, organic way. It was actually quite possible to grow and deepen in inner knowledge purely through meditation, but few people seemed to possess that kind of humility and simplicity. We wanted to know everything.

Shri Mataji called what she was teaching us 'Sahaja Yoga', although the term little suggests its potential or its universal nature. *Sahaja* means 'inborn' or 'born with you', and implies something that is innate and spontaneous, and *yoga* means 'union'. *Sahaja yoga* therefore means 'inborn or spontaneous union with the spirit or the divine'. The word 'yoga' has become synonymous in the west with beaming ladies in leotards doing complicated exercises, and it is easy to miss the significance of Sahaja Yoga amidst the plethora of health and fitness techniques that have allied themselves to yoga's mystique.

There was another term that Shri Mataji sometimes used for her work; *Vishwa Nirmala Dharma*, 'the universal pure religion', which was far more evocative of its true nature, but she was unimpressed with social perceptions and fashionable ideas. Kundalini awakening was 'sahaja', and self-realisation was 'yoga' as far as she was concerned, and that is what she called it.

A huge amount could be written about the 'background' knowledge of Sahaja Yoga, but I prefer not to get too involved in this here as, before anything else, self-realisation is about direct experience, and a comprehensive understanding of the big picture can come later. Nevertheless, over time a vast array of interrelated knowledge came into play when the vibratory sensations registered in the chakras, and a brief overview would go something like this:

According to Shri Mataji, there were three principal energies operating in human beings:

(1) The left-side energy (*Left Channel - see diagram*) rose from the left side of the Mooladhara chakra at the base of the spine and crossed over to the right side of the brain at the Agnya chakra in the forehead. It sustained the feminine, emotional sense of self, was past-oriented and stored memory as our conditioning. This sense of identity, born of our subconscious mind, Shri Mataji called the superego.

(2) The right-side energy (*Right Channel - see diagram*) rose from the right side of the Swadhisthan chakra (at a higher point than the left channel, therefore) and crossed over to the left side of the brain at the Agnya chakra in the forehead. It sustained the masculine, physical and mental being, was future-oriented and created the rational mind that plans and organises. This sense of identity, born of what Shri Mataji called the 'supraconscious mind' was located in the left side of the brain, and was defined by her as the ego.

(3) The central energy (*Central Channel - see diagram*) evolved, balanced, and replenished the energies of the left and the right, and was our connection with the collective unconscious mind. It functioned spontaneously, beyond conscious control or awareness.

This subtle system was contained within the spine, she said, with the chakras connecting to the physical, mental and emotional processes through the relevant plexus in the spine. According to Shri Mataji, the systems were actually sheathed one within the other, with the central channel innermost, the left-side channel overlying this and the right-side channel outermost. She described the feminine, emotional energy as springing from a deeper and more intuitive level of the subtle system than the masculine energy; with the energy principle of the Mooladhara chakra that supplied the left-side energy being innocence or egoless awareness, while the creative energy of the Swadhisthan chakra supplying the right side was more mentally and physically orientated.

She explained how the actions and reactions of the ego and superego built up the personality, creating a unique cocoon of identity that enclosed human consciousness and enabled self-awareness to develop. From a spiritual perspective, it effectively formed the shell of a cosmic egg that sheltered the evolving being until the time came for its germination and transformation by the kundalini.

Shri Mataji defined spiritual enlightenment at its simplest as the process of becoming conscious of all that was unconscious – she said that everything in existence derived from, and remained part of, a living primordial being that had constructed successive stages of energetic and material form to evolve a completely new being in its own image. It was something I could accept on an intuitive, subjective level following some of my own experiences. I knew that consciousness could literally shine brightly enough to reveal its place in an astounding divine realm filled with wonders, much as an electric light illuminates a dark room more brilliantly than a candle. The origins, processes and practical implications of such experiences had remained a mystery, however. There was nothing abstract or mysterious about these things as far as Shri Mataji was concerned, though, and she spoke about them at great length.

Just why such an unimaginably awesome being might want to reproduce itself, or some part of itself, in this way is pretty pointless to debate as the process would have to be complete before such questions could really be answered. I suppose there is no explanation at all on a human level, other than the wonder and revelation of self-realisation itself. There seem to be no upper limits to the levels of reality, just as

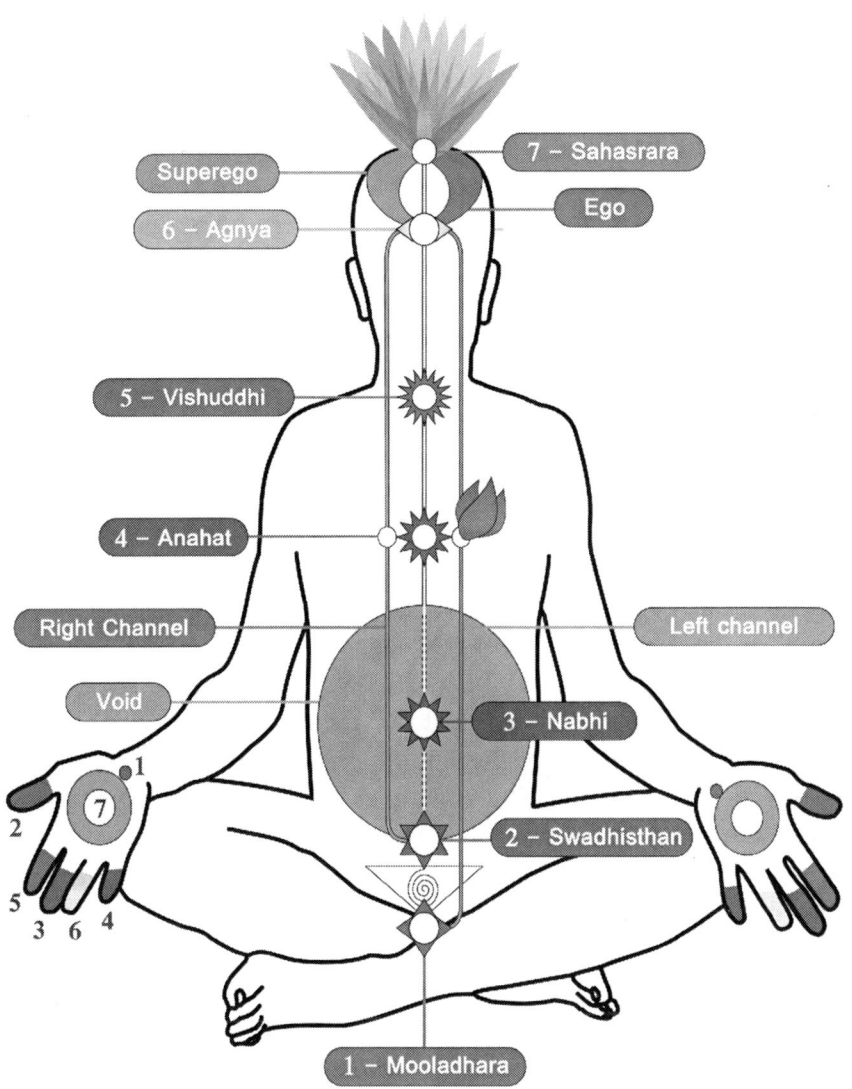

Diagram of the Subtle System

there seem to be no limits to the quality and intensity of bliss that can be experienced, and I have no doubt that the answers are way beyond human comprehension. Certainly my own experience of coming anywhere near the divine is that it engenders only astonishment, awe, wonder, gratitude and bliss. All other concerns vanish like mist before the morning sun.

Shri Mataji portrayed the human nervous system as a microcosm evolved in the image of a vast primordial being that encompassed everything that existed and formed the collective unconscious mind. It was, she said, an energy-processing structure operating on many levels that was brought into being in the earliest stages of creation. She described the fundamental dynamic of creation itself as initiated by the separation of the oneness of God into two fundamental principles; the primordial power, or feminine principle, the quintessence of God's love that created the cosmic drama, and the masculine principle, the detached primordial witness of the play his power created. Creation itself became their child.

Next, Shri Mataji told us, the primordial power separated into three great powers that created, sustained and evolved everything that followed. (This, she said, was the manifestation of the 'Creative Word' or the 'Unstruck Chord', the legendary 'Om', which actually has three syllables; 'AUM', in which 'A' manifests the sustaining power, 'U' the creative power and 'M' the evolving power.) On the fundamental framework of these three great powers, she explained, the seven specialised energy principles of the primordial chakras were established. These were specific aspects of the divine controlled by archetypes, or ideal primordial 'programs', that managed and refined the process of creating and evolving new divine souls in the image of the primordial being.

There was much more to it than this, of course, and I have greatly simplified Shri Mataji's account of the foundation of the collective unconscious mind. She spoke, for instance, of key chakras with overall control of the left- and right-side energies, and of chakras above the *Sahasrara* chakra at the top of the head, but she did not encourage us to concern ourselves with these things, saying that we had to establish the basics first.

She said that the collective being, or the collective unconscious mind, was named the *Virata* in Sanskrit, a term that means something along the lines of 'the vast man' or 'that which is so vast you cannot see the end of it'. According to her, it formed a macrocosmic entity that contained the physical universe within itself and much, much more, an unimaginably vast multidimensional entity of energy-awareness that related directly to its microcosmic reflection in the human subtle system.

Of course, this kind of thing is impossible to think about. The mind is naturally unenthusiastic about hypothetical other-dimensional realities, such concepts being confined to the more exotic realms of theoretical maths and physics, never mind the existence of archetypical entities or universal structures on abstract high-energy levels of awareness. But the mind is looking through the wrong end of the telescope and conditioned by the static, 'locked-in' nature of energy in space-time. High-energy realities can only really be grasped by transcendent experience; in fact all knowledge of higher levels of existence will be experiential in nature if this is the goal of the evolutionary process. Once I had taken the time to consider the matter, it seemed entirely logical that we would have evolved with the potential for the subtle system to signal its presence through the physiological processes of the central nervous system.

What was more, Shri Mataji said, the universal nature of self-realisation meant that the vibratory awareness of the realised soul interacted not only with the Virata, but through that connection, with everything else in existence as well. Self-realisation was like being connected to a computer, she told us – and it was quite some computer. We became collectively conscious, able for the first time to know the absolute values of the collective unconscious; and anyone or anything on which we put our attention registered this vibratory information on our subtle systems. According to her, once we had established our self-realisation, we could know the condition of the subtle system of anyone near or far in real time, and work on their chakras as if they were our own. We could even discover the 'vibrations' of people that lived in the past. All we had to do was clear out our own system and see for ourselves.

Shri Mataji went on to describe the Virata something like this:

(1) Corresponding to the left-side energy in human beings was the mood of the primordial being that loved and sustained creation, known as the *Tamo Guna* in Sanskrit. It contained many dimensions and strata of existence, astral planes, etc, and formed the collective subconscious mind of the Virata, containing the memory of everything that has taken place in the history of creation.

(2) Corresponding to the right-side energy was the mood of the primordial being that created, organised and energised, known as the *Rajah Guna* in Sanskrit. It also contained many dimensions and strata of existence, and formed the collective supraconscious mind of the Virata, imbued with the program or vision of the potential future of creation.

(3) Corresponding to the energy of the central channel was the mood of the primordial being that evolved creation, known as *Satya Guna* in Sanskrit. It contained the seven primordial energy centres or chakras governed by archetypes or deities in the collective unconscious mind, which were the ideal expressions of the energy principles each chakra manifested.

In its entirety, Shri Mataji said, it was a multilayered, fully integrated, autonomous being that created, sustained and evolved living energy, steadily refining its quality from the rudimentary and gross to the subtle and pure. Each of its levels and dimensions of reality operated within its own parameters while remaining fully integrated with the whole. These presented an impenetrable mirror of filtered consciousness, or cascading dimensions of reality, from the perspective of space/time; while this physical reality remained an open book to perception from more subtle levels. The integrated awareness of the collective unconscious mind was the essence of simplicity and was cognisant of everything; while, on each successive level of separation and complexity, perception and enlightenment became progressively less subtle and comprehensive.

In Sahaja Yoga, to recapitulate, the kundalini is awakened in the sacrum bone at the base of the spine and rises through the chakras in the central channel, awakening subtle qualities within each of them.

As the kundalini passes through the Agnya chakra in the forehead, the attention is separated from the ego and superego and enters into a spontaneous meditative state, becoming thoughtlessly aware and a detached witness of the present moment in time.

When the kundalini pierces the Sahasrara chakra at the crown of the head, a connection is established with the all-pervading power of the collective unconscious mind, and vibratory awareness and collective consciousness begin to manifest in the central nervous system. Simultaneously, an inner process of growth, integration and transformation is initiated, the pace and completion of which is dependent on the calibre and condition of the subject.

Many other related subjects were addressed; Shri Mataji spoke about the qualities of the chakras being associated with specific elements, rare metals and precious stones, locations on the Earth, planets, parts of the year, even days of the week (which in English are still named after heavenly bodies or gods). She went to immense depths in her discourses about the nature of reality. Each of the chakras has a specific number of 'petals' or energy functions, with the same number of physical sub-plexuses situated in their corresponding locations in the central nervous system; and she spoke authoritatively and in great detail about the qualities and functions of every chakra on both the physical and the subtle level.

Ancient Sanskrit literature describes one thousand subtle qualities or powers manifested by each of the different deities or archetypes within the chakras, and all of these things added up to a vast storehouse of knowledge and experience. The amount of information was overwhelming, but Shri Mataji did not set about explaining it all in any structured way. Subjects came up when circumstances required it and, to begin with at least, much of what she said had to be accepted on an intuitive level and fitted into the overall picture as time and developments allowed. Nevertheless, the authority and knowledge with which she spoke carried its own gravity and resonated with ancient truth and wisdom; it seemed to echo from the very bones of the earth.

I realised increasingly that the spiritual knowledge of India's ancient scriptures was far deeper and more profound than much of the superficial offerings popularised in New Age culture, and I began to see that I had been trying to achieve something very great in a hopelessly small-minded way. Shri Mataji laughed at the idea that a *mantra* could be purchased from a guru, and roundly condemned a number of other techniques that were common practice at the time. She cited the ancient *Yoga Sutras of Patanjali*, the 'Father of Yoga', saying that the traditional spiritual ascent was an intense, single-minded and extremely disciplined effort to cleanse and master the subtle system, which had been achieved by very few individuals of exceptional calibre. Even under the guidance of an enlightened guru the ascent was a daunting proposition, according to her, and she described the conditions faced by the traditional aspirant something like this:

A would-be disciple had to apply to a guru and have the strength of his (or occasionally her) desire and determination severely tested before the guru would accept him. The disciple would then be put through a long and rigorous 'apprenticeship' intended to detach the attention from worldly desires and ambitions and to establish control over the underlying energy system that drove them.

The aspiring yogi's disciplines were designed to balance the subtle system and tune the attention into the energy principles of the chakras. Mental, physical and emotional weaknesses had to be addressed, their root causes identified and the defects weeded out. Yoga, meditation, austerities, diet, mantras and devotional rituals all played their part, but their employment had to be directed by a self-realised guru with direct vibratory knowledge of the disciple's subtle system.

The guru managed the ascent by assigning practices to cleanse and strengthen the chakras in a regime that had to be tailored to the disciple's needs. Mantras, etc. could be used to stimulate specific chakras, but their use had to be adapted as the ascent progressed and different energy centres required attention.

A flood of vibrations flowed constantly from the guru's kundalini into the disciple's subtle system, inviting the sleeping kundalini within to awaken, and the guru would assist its ascent and help to establish the principles of the chakras until it passed through the Sahasrara chakra at the crown of the head, and self-realisation was established.

Even this remained an interim stage in all but the highest calibre of seeker, according to Shri Mataji, who explained that the embryonic divine being remained enclosed in the cosmic egg after germination while a process of growth and transformation took place. Only when this was complete did a new divine being emerge and awaken into a transcendent realm of bliss and wonder.

This, she said, occurred when all of the chakras became fully integrated in the Sahasrara chakra, the 'thousand-petal lotus' in the crown of the head. She agreed that this could be described as 'God-realisation' but said it did not mean becoming God; it was rather an awakening into a higher world where consciousness was one with the divine and God was everywhere apparent.

For a seeker of the quality of Buddha, she said, kundalini awakening meant instant God-realisation, but for most aspirants it meant establishing the connection with the all-pervading power and nurturing the subtle system until it developed its full potential. She explained that Buddha taught his followers not to believe in God because he wanted them to achieve direct experience of the divine rather than construct mental concepts about it. Similarly, she said, Mohammed taught his followers to shun the idols that were prevalent in the society he lived in and to believe in the oneness of God. According to her, much of the way in which a spiritual being taught had to be adjusted to the mentality of the people around him and to the times that they lived in.

It was a depiction of spirituality that made me feel rather like an uneducated country hick coming to the city and discovering I needed a university degree to get a job. I could feel the power and authority in Shri Mataji's words, and could sense the levels of purity and self-mastery from which she spoke, and it was a perspective that made my Aquarian-age antics look decidedly amateurish. The prognosis seemed pretty hopeless, but Shri Mataji was totally positive that all real seekers would ultimately achieve their goal. There was a reason why seekers were present on the Earth in such unprecedented numbers, she said; a big evolutionary jump was imminent and everyone sensed it on some level. 'There have been few flowers on the tree of life,' she would say, 'but now the blossom time has come.'

She spoke of humanity's journey through a collective evolutionary process, with chakra after chakra awakening in the unconscious mind. Now, she said, the Sahasrara chakra at the crown of the head was beginning to open, which signalled the advent of en-mass self-realisation and the start of a whole new spiritual era.

I looked upon such pronouncements with mixed feelings. There was no doubt I felt wonderful in Shri Mataji's presence, and a deep part of my being seized on the profound store of knowledge that flowed from her with great, almost gleeful satisfaction. It was exhilarating to find elusive pieces of the jigsaw coming together, but I still felt pretty shell-shocked from everything I had been through, and there were times when I was not sure I could handle all this truth overflowing around me.

There was more to it than mere exhaustion, of course. The elation I felt as Shri Mataji resolved spiritual contradictions in delightfully unexpected ways was clouded by the knowledge that there would be entrenched beliefs, stubborn minds and vested interests that would not welcome it. A part of me recognised that the price for this kind of knowledge would be responsibility, and I was not sure I wanted it. Despite everything I had been through, I felt at home with the myth of the quest and the quixotic ideal of the spiritual journey towards enlightenment. I liked the freedom I had achieved from the relentless demands of the material establishment, and I valued the time I had gained to stop and contemplate the mystery of existence.

I have said little about the parts played by my brother and youngest sister in all of the things I had been through because both still have fairly young children, and they will no doubt wish to choose for themselves what to say about it.

However, my brother, as the youngest in the family, was in the process of leaving home permanently for the first time when we met Shri Mataji. He had just secured his first squat and was all fired up for adventure rather than a period of deep introspection. He came to see Shri Mataji and agreed she was amazing, but was a little put out when she asked him what he was about to do that was making him feel so insecure. Eventually he decided that, as he put it, he wanted to 'enjoy chewing leaves for a while before becoming a butterfly'.

I could understand this because I felt rather the same myself, although I was well aware that I had been living on the edge and spiralling downwards into disillusionment and adversity. I had been looking for a miracle and I had found one, and I told myself that I could not really complain if it made some demands of me. I felt a bit like a small boy who had gone fishing in a rowing boat only to find a whale surfacing beneath him. I had found a lot more than I had bargained for, but I could not turn away from it; I felt I had to check out Sahaja Yoga and see if it was everything that Shri Mataji said it was.

There was no doubt it was very different from anything else I had come across, and I could see how arduously Shri Mataji worked with any seekers she met. She would talk to them, listen to them, find out their problems, answer their questions and explain things to them while constantly working on their chakras with unfailing good humour. Also, after quite a long time, it occurred to me that no one had asked me for any money.

Chapter 14
Reflected dreams

Finally, Shri Mataji went to India for six months. At first I felt a bit like a passenger in a plane that had run out of fuel. The dynamic force that had been driving events was suddenly absent, but its momentum sent me sailing on into the unknown, uncertain what the future would hold.

At the back of my mind lurked the doubt that I would be able to maintain my drugless state on my own for any length of time. I was not actually alone because I had my sister for company, but the power and depth of experience generated by Shri Mataji's presence had filled the hole in my life left by the absent drugs, and I could easily imagine that days would come when I would miss them a lot.

I was still squatting, but not socialising much as most of the people I knew took drugs, and many did not approve of the fact that I was no longer doing so, or understand why. There was a certain amount of muttering about 'guru trips', which I found rather irritating. I could understand the caution and scepticism about gurus, but to dismiss something out of hand without investigation and experimentation seemed silly to me, and I was disappointed to find that 'freaks' were just as capable of becoming conditioned by superficial ideas as anyone else.

Spending time with them meant putting myself in temptation's way and could make for awkward conversation, and I began to notice that my subtle system did not seem to like this kind of environment at all.

As the days passed however, I was pleasantly surprised to find that I was not nose-diving after all; I felt buoyed up by an invisible, illusive 'something' that had remained after Shri Mataji had left. The 'electromagnetic' flow of vibrations hummed faintly in my body, and although I did not feel particularly high I felt reasonably stable and centred, and surprisingly optimistic. I was still rather fragile, however, and sometimes felt as if I were tip-toeing along a narrow pathway between towering, frozen seas of desire for everything I had given up that remained poised to rush in and overwhelm me if I faltered. I avoided thinking about this as best I could, and kept my attention carefully in the present, concentrating on getting through one day at a time.

Shri Mataji had encouraged the small group of seekers that had been spending time with her to keep in contact while she was away, and we agreed to meet up once a week. We had all been on very different paths as seekers before meeting her and had very different personalities. In fact, we were such an unlikely bunch that I found it surprising and amusing we could relate to each other at all, but our get-togethers were unexpectedly enjoyable and helped to remind me of the way I had felt in Shri Mataji's presence.

Something else that made a big difference was a black and white photograph I had of Shri Mataji. It had been taken at a *puja* ceremony in India and showed her seated in a meditative pose, with the left hand held forward horizontally, with the palm facing upwards, and the right held vertically, with the palm facing forwards.

In the language of the unconscious, this meant 'I will protect you and give sustenance to your spirit.' She had given one to each of us, saying that we should meditate in front of it as it had strong vibrations. It was something I had experimented with but had been unaccountably reluctant to practice, due, I suppose, to a certain amount of ego, conditioning and embarrassment, particularly when friends and acquaintances were around.

I knew that meditating in front of this photograph had a noticeable effect. I could not feel the 'cool breeze' flowing from it as my sister did, but I did notice an increase in the energy flowing in my body, a subtly heightened sensitivity to various tingles, aches and pains, and a relatively improved sense of depth and peace. I had sometimes asked other people to put their hands towards this photo, too, and several had admitted to feeling tingling sensations, with one or two having stronger experiences, especially children. I assumed this was yet another aspect of collective consciousness, but it was not really something I thought about much. As with many things about Shri Mataji, it baffled the mind, but it worked.

She told us we wouldn't need the photograph after a while, but it would help to meditate on it to begin with, and after she left it certainly did. A long time afterwards, funnily enough, my first sustained experience of a higher state of consciousness was triggered by a casual glance at a photo of Shri Mataji. However, alone in my squat on New Year's Eve, 1975, I sat in silence in front of the black and white photo as midnight approached, my room lit only by candlelight, and wondered what the future would bring.

It was not easy to give up the instant intensity of being that drugs initiated, not to mention the ability to peek behind the scenes of life. I felt I was disempowering myself in a way, abandoning a vantage point in perception and experience, and I had to constantly remind myself that I was aiming to regain everything and more one day, and on a permanent basis.

As the weeks went by, I felt myself slowly 'coming down to earth'. I had cut my hair and got a job, and was spending as much time as I could at my parents' house with my son. I meditated, went to the cinema a lot and hung out with my sister. There was a big change in perspective. It was the difference between looking down at a city from a plane and walking in its streets dwarfed by skyscrapers. Everyday activities grew in importance, or rather in the amount of attention they demanded, and abstract metaphysical contemplation withdrew into the background.

Nevertheless, I was surprised to find how well I was coping with my new drugless existence; I had even stopped smoking and drinking, and I felt that something had changed in me that was sustaining my will. Shri Mataji had maintained from the start, in fact, that self-realisation manifested a strength and detachment that made it easier to discard habits and addictions, but I found it surprising all the same.

That is not to say that it was all plain sailing. I had to remain relatively balanced and clear to feel the support of the collective being, and I was sometimes dragged back into old moods and states of mind and had to fight to get out of them. The important thing was that I now could get out of them, to a state of relative stability at least, and I began to feel that some of these negative states were not really part of me at all but something alien that was polluting my subtle system. It sometimes felt as if I were wearing someone else's old clothes, while unpleasant vibratory sensations protested in my hands and body, and the difference between how I felt when struggling with this kind of thing and how I felt when I was clear was quite amazing.

I also had one positive experience that encouraged me greatly:

Lighting a fire in the lounge fireplace at my parents' house, the flames seem to take on a benevolent, elemental purity that cleanses and sharpens my awareness. It seems to suck everything negative out of my body and leave me feeling keen and alert, content but very aware, as if perception has been quickened and granted a new lucidity. There is a dreamlike sense of timelessness, a rich, almost luxuriant detachment, and the fire becomes the only real thing in the room, the TV relegated to a distant, chattering irrelevance.

The magical vision of natural simplicity from my childhood returns, and the perception of a wonderfully vibrant and powerful archetype overwhelms me. I know little about Hindu mythology at this time, yet I feel sure this is Rama, whom Shri Mataji described as an aspect of the divine existing at the level of the Anahat (heart) chakra. In the Ramayana, *which tells the story of his incarnation, he plays out a drama as a noble prince who honours a promise tricked out of his father and accepts banishment into the forest for fourteen years.*

It lasted only moments but has stayed with me ever since, a treasured reminder that something magical and mysterious lurks in the subtle nature of fire.

The six months that Shri Mataji was away passed slowly, and I eagerly awaited her return, but my expectations were somewhat confounded as she was quite unimpressed with the condition of our chakras and gave us quite a ticking-off. It brought home to me that she regarded self-realisation as a responsibility that had to be lived up to.

She had spoken of a trip to India as a possibility in the coming year, and I had been saving money towards it; however, when she told us our subtle systems were in no condition for us to meet up with our counterparts in India, I assumed the trip was off, and went out and bought a big stereo system, probably the only material thing in life I really wanted. If I had had the experience I have now, I would have just watched the situation play out as, after several weeks of working on our chakras, Shri Mataji announced that we were now all right and the trip to India could go ahead, and I had to start saving all over again.

We were plunged back into the same intensive sessions as before, working with vibrations, questions, answers and long discussions. I noticed that I wasn't having the really high experiences that I had enjoyed when I first met her, but the impact of her presence was still immense. I often felt a great sense of space in her company; she could make even a small room seem cavernous, and a vibrant sense of energy and optimism would always envelop me whenever I was near her.

It felt as if a bright light were penetrating into every corner of my being which managed somehow to both highlight my shortcomings and radiate reassurance and benevolence. There was also an elusive fragrance that I would sometimes notice in her presence, an exotic perfume as though from a living flower that energised and enchanted.

Typically, Shri Mataji would help to dispel self-consciousness with a cheerful greeting when we arrived, and I would immediately feel energies at work within me, with all manner of subtle aches and pains retreating before a mysterious pressure that pushed its way steadily up through the centre of my body. Usually, within thirty minutes or so in her company, I would feel quite transformed, my body light, clear and relaxed, and I would bask in a childlike, golden contentment. As time went on, deeper parts of my being would start to open up, and I would sometimes feel less comfortable as deep-rooted problems began clearing out, but I would always end up feeling relaxed and full of vibrations after time spent in her presence. 'It is like making butter,' she said on one occasion; 'the churning goes on and sometimes you are at the bottom, sometimes at the top. Just be patient and the transformation will take place.'

I still experienced interesting things from time to time, sometimes in Shri Mataji's presence and sometimes not, including an episode that lasted for a couple of weeks, in which I became vividly aware of past times and places:

I am clothed in the styles of different cultures and periods of history, and I can feel the texture and the quality of the clothing, jewellery or weapons on my body. An intense episode brings the world of Chinese antiquity vividly to life for days. I can even feel the Sahasrara chakra on top of my head opening out like a Chinese paper umbrella, complete with a tar-like fragrance. Everything around me looks Chinese, and Shri Mataji looks like a beautiful Chinese deity. When I tell her this, she smiles and says, 'Sometimes you look Chinese to me, too.'

She told us that these were memories from past lives stored in the subtle system, and that we might experience many different things as the kundalini worked out the problems in the chakras. She said we should neither fear nor seek such experiences but remain in the centre and witness them if they happened.

Other experiences were brief and unexpected:

I am sitting with Shri Mataji at the dining table in her house, when I see a beautiful expression of primordial motherhood shining within her. I glimpse elegant simplicity and royal dignity, and something else that intrigues me greatly; an exquisite array of potent powers, or attributes, that have been neatly 'tied off', as if unwanted for the work in hand and put to one side.

I am sitting on the floor a short distance in front of Shri Mataji with a number of other people when I glance at her and am instantly transported into a completely different state of consciousness. I become a mirror image of Shri Mataji, who regards her reflection with perfect equanimity. I feel utterly pure and simultaneously register an absence, a sense of liberation, and I realise the material world has always held an implied threat to my physical being that has now disappeared. A moment later I float within a beautiful golden light in a blissful, formless state before returning, somewhat startled, to find myself sitting in front of Shri Mataji again. She smiles at me. 'Very good,' she says.

I had some amazing dreams around this time. In one dream, my sister and I were given the keys to Atlantis and set out to find it. We entered the foyer of a large building that was filled with a huge crowd of people all arguing with each other. 'We have the keys to Atlantis!' we called out, waving them about, but no one took any notice, and we made our way through the crowd to the centre of the building where an atomic-powered lift stood.

The keys opened the doors, and as soon as we entered the doors closed and the lift began to ascend. It stopped at the next floor, and the doors opened to reveal a kind of control centre something like an airport control tower. Shockingly, it was occupied by an alien being, a creature very like the red-horned 'rhinoceros man' I had seen on an LSD trip, and we fought violently with it. The outcome was indecisive, and the lift continued up to the next floor where another strange being occupied another control centre, and we fought with this, too. The process repeated itself through further floors with the lift moving faster all the time until I started to feel dizzy. My nose started to bleed and everything started to turn white, and I lost consciousness.

'That is your Vishuddhi,' said Shri Mataji when I told her about the dream, referring to the chakra at the base of the neck. I remembered this months later in India, when she worked on this same chakra. I was in a room with her and a number of other Sahaja Yogis, when she asked me to come over and placed her hand on my neck.

After a short while I felt something pushing upwards between my heart and my throat, and I began to feel a strange, light-headed dizziness. The room started to turn yellow and then white, and I felt I was going to faint. I was standing in front of Shri Mataji, who was seated on a bed, and I sank down on the bed beside her for a few moments before recovering and struggling back to my feet in embarrassment. 'I cannot take it out; you cannot bear it,' she said, and told me I would have to wait until I was stronger before the problem could be dealt with.

Another powerful dream with a similar impact to the 'atomic-lift drama' occurred much later. In this dream, I was hiding in a cave under the ground, and my mother was calling me to come outside. I looked up to the cave entrance and saw a huge, dark shape silhouetted by the daylight, which began to move slowly past the opening.

It continued moving past for a seemingly endless time until at last its bulk began to lessen and I realised it was an enormous serpent.

I wriggled out of the opening to discover I was a serpent too, albeit a fraction of the size of the behemoth ahead of me, and out with me wriggled a happy throng of other little snakes. When I looked back at the hole we had been hiding in, I saw it was below the roots of an ancient tree that had been blasted to a stump, and I marvelled at our deliverance from such desolation.

In one of the nicest dreams, I arrived at Shri Mataji's house with some other guests, and she invited us all into her back garden, which was full of trees and plants of beautiful, striking colours and seemed to extend for miles. The next day we actually did visit Shri Mataji, and she suggested it would be nice to go out for a drive, so off we went through the Sussex countryside with the glowing colours of autumn creating magical views all around us, and I experienced a strong sense of déjà vu from the dream of the night before.

We continued to spend time with Shri Mataji through the months that followed, mainly at her home in Sussex and in a house a couple amongst us were renting in Euston, but we travelled to other places as well, including Weston Super Mare where Shri Mataji's niece lived. Wherever we were, sitting on the seafront, travelling by train or on the underground, or having cucumber sandwiches in the Grosvenor Hotel at Victoria Station, Shri Mataji continued to speak and act as she always did, with little regard for her surroundings, and often started conversations with passers-by.

Although there was a lot of laughter in Shri Mataji's company, the atmosphere never lacked depth and profundity, and she worked steadily to awaken us to our frivolous ways and instil a sense of gravity and humility. On one occasion she took us out into her garden and washed our feet in an impromptu ceremony that instilled both of these things to an almost unbearable degree.

She continued to be extremely practical in the things that she taught us, and much of what she said related to interactions between the subtle system, the sympathetic and parasympathetic nervous systems, and the physiological processes and physical organs of the body. She said that many physical diseases, or vulnerability to diseases, were symptoms of problems in the subtle system and could be cured accordingly, or better still, diagnosed in their early stages and prevented. The treatment of physical, emotional and mental problems in Sahaja Yoga was a sizable subject in itself, and quite different from the mysterious 'energy channelling' of spiritual healing.

In a way healing was a natural side effect of kundalini awakening, in that the kundalini automatically began to repair damage and weaknesses in the instrument so that it could function at its optimum level. Realised souls were effectively able to heal themselves in a holistic and comprehensive process that they participated in through the vibratory awareness of their subtle system.

Shri Mataji went into a lot of detail about physical ailments, suggesting various treatments, herbs and meditative techniques for particular problems. Later on, she went as far as describing how the chakras not only programmed the genes but also changed their functions and even created new ones when the subtle system functioned at a high enough level. Ironically, 'healing' was not something that interested me much, despite the fact that I was the most in need of it. My attention was still in the stratosphere in many ways, and I was much more interested in the big picture.

Much of the time, Shri Mataji talked about things that could go wrong with the subtle system; how its processes could be weakened or damaged, and how it could be attacked by negative forces. This I was interested in and discovered it to be as subtle, complex and important a subject as everything else she spoke about. In a way there were two perspectives to consider, since the things she defined as important to sustain the subtle system were very much related to the ways in which it could be harmed.

Basically, it was all about keeping the attention tuned into the evolutionary 'program' of the Virata, which in turn meant respecting and maintaining the energy principles of the chakras. This, she said, required an understanding of *dharma*, which she described as the innate morality of the spirit.

'Morality' sounded a little alarming and somewhat religious, something I associated with hypocrisy and the suppression of spontaneity, but as time went by I realised that the dharma, or 'right action', she was describing was very different from the fire and brimstone I had grown up with. Another meaning of dharma is 'that which sustains', and, rather than guilt and future damnation, it was all about improving the quality of consciousness in the present.

I suppose it could be equated in some ways to the Christian idea of righteousness, but the life style Shri Mataji expanded upon was far more intuitive, subtle and comprehensive. It included such things as diet and was principally about learning to focus the attention inwards on the chakras and the subtleties of life instead of outwards on the distractions of the ego.

It took a while, but I did begin to see how some of my attitudes and behaviour affected my state of mind and the quality of my awareness, and I learned through a process of trial and error to adjust my behaviour accordingly. In time, I came to see it as a natural protocol of the spirit, a way of living life in an honourable and balanced manner that had nothing to do with ritual or dogma.

Generally speaking, dharmic behaviour stabilised the attention in the central channel and established boundaries to individual and social behaviour that prevented the ambitions of the right side or the desires of the left side from overwhelming the ego and superego. More specifically, it related to the subtle qualities of the chakras and the kundalini, with each chakra manifesting an ideal expression of its essential principle, such as the innocence of the Mooladhara chakra at the base of the spine, the creativity of the Swadhisthan chakra in the abdomen or the detachment and collectivity of the Vishuddhi chakra in the neck. Shri Mataji did not describe dharmic behaviour as fixed but as having different styles and expressions in relation to the qualities of each chakra and as being sensitive to variables in any given situation that could change its parameters.

She emphasised that an important part of dharma was the cultivation of a sense of auspiciousness, a quality that she said was innate in a balanced and subtle person, but that we would have to learn by experience. It was an affinity for the centre path, she said, a sense of the succour and support of the divine emanating from the chakras in the central channel. It was to know when a situation was beneficial to the spirit rather than attractive to the ego; to be repelled by *adharmic* (against dharma, or negative) things, however enticing or grand, and to be attracted to what was nurturing and sustaining to the spirit, however humble or simple.

In Sahaja Yoga terms, auspiciousness was indicated by a powerful flow of cool vibrations and a sense of purity, positivity and optimism. It was a vital faculty, Shri Mataji impressed on us, the key to recognising and being accepted by the subtle principles of the chakras in the course of our spiritual ascent.

Mantras were a powerful tool where the establishment of auspiciousness was concerned as they invoked the powers of the deities in the chakras. However, they could only really be effective after the kundalini had opened the Sahasrara chakra, according to Shri Mataji, when a connection had been established between the realised soul and the Virata through the all-pervading power. Energy was released by the deities in the collective unconscious mind when the qualities of the divine were invoked by a realised soul, she said, and these vibrations purified and opened out the chakras.

The art of using mantras, she told us, was to know which chakras needed stimulation and when, and which specific aspects of the divine needed to be awakened for this to happen. Basically she showed us that mantras fortified weaknesses in the subtle system; protecting and strengthening the chakras and increasing the manifestation of the divine, which held negativity at bay and deepened our inner growth.

Shri Mataji explained that there were basically two kinds of mantras and that each stimulated the subtle system in particular ways. There were *bija* mantras, which consisted of pure sounds resonating with the vibrational attributes of specific divine qualities. 'Aum' is a bija mantra, for instance. Then there were Sanskrit mantras, which operated on a less abstract level, invoking the powers of specific deities in the chakras, although the sounds of the Sanskrit alphabet itself were based on the same principles as the bija mantras.

The subtle system could respond to stimuli other than Sanskrit mantras, too. Some prayers were effective; the Lord's Prayer, for instance, worked powerfully on the Agnya chakra in the forehead, where it helped to separate the attention from the ego and superego. Something else that worked in a similar fashion, although perhaps less intensely, was using what Shri Mataji called 'affirmations'. This meant asking for, or affirming, the presence of the subtle spiritual principles in the chakras in one's native tongue while directing the attention to the relevant part of the subtle system. All of these things, like everything else in Sahaja Yoga, could be experienced in vibratory awareness and used to increase the depth and quality of meditation.

Chapter 15
Ghosts in the machine

The aforementioned were all deep and subtle matters and alien territory to my western ego. Something I was much more familiar with, unfortunately, was inauspiciousness, although with little sensitivity as to its real nature. I suppose our entanglement with it is inevitable as our materialistic culture thrives on the exploitation of human weakness, but Shri Mataji was concerned about darker deeds than these.

I had learned that karma was an intractable problem for the ego and a relative and temporary impediment for the divine, and that confusion between the two in drug experience led to neither being understood nor respected. Now I began to see that dangers we had not suspected lurked in the shadowy region between the two perspectives and that we had been splashing our toes in a pond with some pretty murky depths indeed.

Normally, Shri Mataji told us, the evolving human consciousness was enclosed within the confines of the ego and superego, and the psyche was pretty well protected as long as one led a reasonably balanced life.

She warned, however, that this protective cocoon could be broken down by such things as drugs, trauma, extreme behaviour, spiritualism and negative conditionings, which could create openings into various strata of the collective subconscious or supraconscious mind that made the psyche vulnerable to intrusions by negative spirits. We had plenty of questions about this, of course. Did spirits really exist? What were they? Why negative spirits? What about good spirits? What about astral planes?

Shri Mataji described the process that takes place after death something like this:

The soul (containing the subtle system and the kundalini, with the imprint of the recent and previous lives stored within it) separated from its physical elements and remained present for some time to witness the winding up of its physical life, the disposal of its body and its gradual detachment from the environment in which it had lived.

The *atman*, or reflection of the spirit, left the heart and separated from the soul at the point of death. This was the detached, masculine aspect of the primordial being, the father aspect of God, described by Shri Mataji as Sada Shiva in the Hindu pantheon. It was the all-seeing, all-knowing witness of all that existed, and the vital spark of life and consciousness in all living things.

At the human level, this principle seemed to be present in a specifically complete form, a perfect microcosmic reflection of the *Paramatman*, or primordial form of Sada Shiva, which reanimated the soul at each physical incarnation. Self-realisation itself, Shri Mataji said, was a process that was triggered by the union of the kundalini with the atman in the heart.

After death the soul receded into a more passive state, attracted towards the dimensions of existence in the collective subconscious or supraconscious realms of the Virata compatible with its vibratory condition. These planes of existence varied from the low and the gross to the high and the subtle, and here the soul remained for a while, reflecting on its spiritual journey or tormented by its desires, before being drawn back into taking birth again according to its karma.

This process was not without risk, Shri Mataji explained, as the ego phase of evolution was a tricky one. She agreed it was essential for the soul to have complete freedom to choose its destiny but admitted wryly that the human ego was capable of mutating into almost anything. 'Only human beings can turn light into darkness,' she said once.

She told us that if the soul was excessively identified with, or attached to, the life it had left behind it could linger on the fringes of human consciousness, and desire to interact with the living. She also spoke of dissatisfied souls who did much the same, those who had suffered in life, or had become identified with all manner of human failings and remained tormented by them after death, although she portrayed the manifestation of such 'possessions' in the psyches of living people as a relatively mundane phenomenon for the most part – more to do with everyday habits, desires and fixations than dramatic psychic intrusions.

The barriers between the living and the dead were less clearly defined in primitive times, it seemed, and human beings had long existed with the spirits of the dead lingering on the borders of their lives. It was something Shri Mataji depicted as a kind of drag or dead weight on the progress of human development, and one that was still with us today, translated into the addictions, phobias, obsessions and compulsions that plagued society.

Ironically, I did not find it easy to accept her insistence that negative spirits were behind a great many human problems. This was despite my own experience of such things and the fact that on one occasion she had even described a spirit with a single horn on its head just like the one I had once seen. Logically, the jump from accepting that each of us had a subtle inner being that survived death and could reincarnate, to the existence of disembodied souls that could disturb the living was not great, so I'm not sure why I had so many doubts about it to begin with.

I suppose it was again part of the confusion on my part between the absolute, transcendental nature of the primordial being and the relative, illusory existence of the ego. Knowing a brick wall was an illusion did not prevent me feeling pain if I bumped into it, and it took me a while to accept that spirits might be as real as I was in a relative sense, and capable of affecting me until the pitfalls of maya had been successfully navigated.

A large part of the difficulty I had in accepting this lay in my deeply entrenched conviction that humanity's estrangement from the divine had been caused by suppressed emotional trauma on a primal level. It had appeared a self-evident truth during introspective drug experiences, and seemed supported by the fabulous beauty and profound simplicity of being that could unfold when deeply locked tensions were released on LSD.

I had continued to accept this even when I knew positive

experience was becoming more elusive and efforts to liberate repressed feelings, increasingly frustrating. I suppose it seemed an obvious, uncomplicated explanation in keeping with the essential simplicity of the divine and appeared to have the potential to heal the schism between humanity and nature that lay at the root of so many human problems.

Only slowly did a new perspective begin to develop as I spent time with Shri Mataji. I liked the repressed-feelings scenario because it was simple and meant that the problem and the solution lay with me. I also knew there was at least some truth in it and that when I felt whole again only the oneness of the primordial being prevailed. Having mischief-making psychic entities flitting about seemed unnecessarily complicated and relatively mundane, more akin to the goings-on in charismatic Christian gatherings or spiritualist churches.

Gradually, though, my perspective changed, and I began to feel that my attempts to constantly regurgitate my past had led me into an impossible struggle with myself; that despite dramatic initial breakthroughs I had been drawn into an endless wrestling match in a self-imposed straightjacket of ego from which I could not break free (ego in a general sense that is; the entire sense of identity inclusive of ego and superego).

Shri Mataji approached the situation in a completely different way. There were physical, emotional and mental tensions stored in the psyche, sure enough, deeply rooted primal shocks to the chakras - but she viewed these as the negative consequences of the prevailing ignorance of the times; gross habits, attitudes and behaviour in social interaction that harmed and desensitised the subtle being without conscious knowledge or intent.

It was not about personal drama but about learning how to cope with an unsympathetic environment and how to bring numbed and deadened sensitivities back to life. She said that the subtle system was equipped with mechanisms and responses that could throw off the negative effects of its surroundings and quicken its development into maturity.

This meant that problems could be dealt with in a detached way in the witness state, utilising the all-pervading energy of the divine to purify and stimulate the chakras. Effectively, the collective being took the load instead of the ego, something Shri Mataji illustrated with one of her favourite jokes about nervous passengers on a plane trying to reduce its weight by holding their luggage on their heads. By this she meant that we remained attached to our ego and assumed responsibility for solving its problems, when ultimately the only solution was to surrender the ego to the collective being. This also stopped personal identification with negativity and did away with self-centred obsessions. It was a bit like taking off dirty clothes and washing them in the river instead of trying to scrub them on the body, and was a considerable advantage in dealing with emotional and egotistical problems.

The downside was accepting that we were vulnerable to subtle intrusions by destructive psychic entities, and that we were on the firing line of a conflict between positive evolutionary forces and everything that was stale and outdated in nature. Shri Mataji portrayed the *Kali Yuga* – the 'age of spiritual darkness' of Hindu tradition – as a long twilight in the quality of consciousness, in which the ingrained habits of the past cast their shadows over each bright new generation, deadening and shrouding its subtleties.

It was within this ancient landscape that she portrayed the activities of these spirits, dissatisfied shades of the past perpetuating the status quo by seeking to prolong their desires and obsessions through the psyches of the living.

Only slowly did I come to consider that much of the pain and insanity I had experienced on LSD might have been symptomatic of encounters with negative psychic entities rather than evidence of my own suffering. This was something that Shri Mataji called 'misidentification', in which the ego experienced the personality of an entity entering the psyche as its own, and if she was right it meant I had been digging myself deeper and deeper into a bottomless pit of misery.

On the bright side, I no longer had to reconcile myself with all of the negative traits I had identified within myself, and I was cheered by the thought that the evolutionary forces of the divine continued to push and struggle against the weight of history through successive generations. Now all I had to do was clear out the chakras and get rid of the baggage of the past.

There was more to it than just sloughing off old skin, though. Psychic gremlins came in all shapes and sizes, according to Shri Mataji, and could vary from the relatively innocuous to the destructive and depraved; with their activities ranging from the occasional opportunistic invasion of the psyche to a deep penetration of the ego that dominated the entire personality.

She reassured us that we were generally well protected from the more extreme psychic entities, but warned that dubious spiritual practices and psychedelic drugs were opening us up to the attentions of spirits in all kinds obscure dimensions of existence. The spirits themselves could generate extreme ideas and extrasensory experiences, she said, and the seeker could become lost or sidetracked by encounters with them.

I could see that, if spirits were identified with the elemental nature of the realms they inhabited, they might be difficult for the exploring - or inadvertently exposed - human psyche to recognise, especially in the unfamiliar territory of strange, new dimensions of experience. There would not necessarily be any way to differentiate between one's own perceptions and those of an intruding spirit; in fact the encroachment of a psychic entity might be perceived as enlightening or empowering, or as producing a more exotic sense of identity.

During the spiritual adventuring of the 60s, the psyche would have been exposed to a whole new range of clientele; malcontent spirits from across the hoary depths of time with a partiality to substance satisfactions or quirky spiritual practices who would have felt right at home among the avant-garde of the day. For some, hopeful confusion imbued the mystery of life with supraconscious imagery, projecting chakras outwards into the material realm as flying saucers, and their archetypes or invading psychic entities as interstellar saviours or aliens, exotic or menacing. It was an image that could be viewed with a certain amount of amusement from a detached point of view, but if everything that Shri Mataji said was true it was really quite tragic, for it meant nothing less than the disillusionment and broken dreams of many and the obstruction and subversion of the spiritual ascent as a whole.

The inclination of disturbed souls was mostly to avoid incarnating and facing life, Shri Mataji told us, although sooner or later they were obliged to take birth and face at least some of their karma through innate processes at work in the Virata. Despite this, she said, many souls continued to go to extremes and eventually mutated out of the evolutionary process altogether; and she described these grotesque mutations of the ego and superego as being symbolised in the horns of the devil in human mythology.

In a way it was the ultimate testimony to the freedom of the ego phase of evolution, but Shri Mataji described such beings as seeking only to indulge their desires and ambitions and to pull humanity down to share in their ultimate doom. She said, in fact, that the most powerful demonic personalities could incarnate deliberately to create chaos and destruction in the world, as was the case with Hitler.

The seekers were under attack in all sorts of ways, she told us, for they formed the spearhead of the evolving consciousness of the human race, and much negative inertia had accumulated over the long evolutionary process that did not welcome it. She explained that our spiritual ascent was not just an individual affair, each realised soul represented a cell in the body of the primordial being, and its personal journey formed part of the jigsaw of humanity's collective emancipation.

It was our egos' misidentifications that made the negativity we struggled with seem so personal, she said. We had to detach from our problems and work on them in an objective, dispassionate way. A release from negative traits was often experienced as a sense of separation, in fact, of a realisation that 'it is not me'; and in time I came to realise that I did not have to plough through my subconscious mind at all. I had simply to clear and balance my subtle system and rise through the central channel in thoughtless awareness, in the present.

It took a while for me to take all this in, and I suppose my initial resistance showed that I hadn't been as successful at eradicating my western rationality as I thought I had. All this talk about spirits could sometimes appear simplistic and naive, and the fact that Shri Mataji often spoke with little regard for the grand scholarly manner of western intellectuals (although quite capable of doing so when she chose) made it easier for doubts to rise in my mind. Nevertheless, it was important to keep a sense of humour where these things were concerned, especially as it was one quality such entities seemed to lack.

Some people did seem to become aware of the presence of negative spirits, and could feel vulnerable, confused and threatened, especially if left to face the situation alone without knowledge or understanding. Others might self-righteously denounce spiritual entities as evil and claim to cast them out, usually with high drama and a sizeable fee, but were themselves possessed by power-hungry shades of a different kind.

Certain people, of course, were actively involved in seeking out spirits, looking for reassurance of life after death, or trying to gain psychic powers or knowledge of the past or the future. Shri Mataji roundly condemned this practice and maintained that we had nothing to gain and much to lose by interacting with them. She insisted that highly evolved souls would never enter the psyches of the living because they respected the boundaries of human freedom.

We should realise that spirits wanted something from us, she said, even if not always sinister, there were plenty of exhibitionists and busybodies that just wanted to show off. She pointed out that these spirits had the same subtle system as we did, at their point of origin at any rate, and explained that the problems on their chakras interacted with those of their host, effectively imposing the load of their karma onto the system they intruded upon.

She warned us that as they were disembodied these entities existed in a more subtle state than the living and could enter our psyche through the back door, manipulating the ego/superego for their own purposes, and sometimes dominating the psyches of their host completely, pushing them into increasingly extreme behaviour.

In the practice of Sahaja Yoga, the activities of these psychic entities were signalled by negative sensations in the chakras, and in some chakras more than others. Most common was the left Swadhisthan chakra, indicated on the left thumb and often with a particularly horrid and painful tingling sensation. The divine principle operating on the left of this chakra was pure knowledge, according to Shri Mataji, the inner knowledge of vibrational awareness, and she explained that this centre was particularly sensitive to spirits.

Their presence represented a perversion of the Swadhisthan's creative essence, twisted into illusion, fantasy and deception. For the most part they were not something to be feared though; in fact they generally appeared rather stupid. They were just something to be aware of and avoided, a bit like dog faeces on the pavement.

In the grand scheme of things, I suppose such psychic flotsam and jetsam represented the collective karma of humanity that drags at the heels of our ascent to the divine. It was the individual scheme of things we had to be concerned about, and Shri Mataji repeatedly warned us that we could be vulnerable to the attentions of these dissatisfied souls.

Any adharmic behaviour risked attracting the notice of negative spirits, she told us, and the more extreme the behaviour the greater the risk. Pretty well anything the ego got up to could attract like-minded ghosts from the past, it seemed, and taking drugs and seeking for spiritual knowledge was no exception.

Very few had preserved the true depths of spiritual knowledge in this Kali Yuga, or 'age of ignorance', she said, and many seekers had tried to reach God or escape the trials of human existence simply by retreating into the detachment of the witness state. This basically meant withdrawing the attention from involvement in the outside world to introspect deep into the innermost nature of cognisant perception; to reach back into the omniscient consciousness of the primordial being that watched life from deep within us all.

Through intense discipline and stubborn perseverance, it seemed, it was possible to withdraw the attention from the senses and anchor it in this essential spirit, gradually extracting consciousness from material existence and escaping into the eternal, watchful silence that looked in on the teeming fish bowl of life. Shri Mataji did not have much time for such practices, though; she did not seem to think the interests of the collective being were being served in this way and sometimes referred to such people as 'useless fellows hanging in the air'.

She portrayed it as an extreme and pointless strategy in which the soul risked becoming lost in the shifting sands of the collective subconscious, not to mention acquiring lots of new psychic friends. This was certainly easy to see in the lower categories of such seekers, such as the cannabis-smoking sadhus of India, and I could see how this kind of 'escape mentality' might well amount to an evolutionary dead end, something like jumping out of a train before it reached its destination.

Chapter 16
To walk with the gods

Shri Mataji was adamant that the full potential of the evolving divine being could only be realised through the union of the masculine principle of spirit with the feminine principle of power within the child principle of innocence, and that this was a potential way off the scale of human imagination. According to her, the only purpose of creation was to conceive this fabulous being through the evolution of the subtle system, and to accept anything less was to betray our birthright and destiny.

The true goal of religion was not to look after the poor, she said, although it did encompass the solution to all such problems; it was to awaken to the infinite riches of the divine and share them with humanity. It was for each realised soul to take flight into eternity leaving an era of universal joy and fulfilment as their legacy, an idyllic earth from which many would follow them, and the ills of this age would not even be a memory.

According to Shri Mataji, the most fundamental quality of dharma was innocence, which was the aspect of the divine manifested by the Mooladhara chakra at the base of the spine. The word *mooladhara* means 'the support of the root', and she defined this chakra as forming the foundation of the subtle system, which she said was the true 'tree of life'.

She spoke of innocence as a powerful, positive force in its own right, something I found difficult to understand initially as it was rather regarded as a negative attribute in the west, as naivety or a lack of knowledge and experience. It was equally difficult to understand Shri Mataji's assertion that innocence could be regained if the Mooladhara chakra was cleansed. It was hard to imagine that the heavy imprints of the past could be dissolved and forgotten so easily, and yet sure enough I would repeatedly find myself feeling like a child in Shri Mataji's presence, as light as a feather and filled with a sense of subtle, golden purity.

I could see how we could be born into this world egoless with our innocence completely intact; and in an ideal, dharmic society grow and develop within a protective vibrational cocoon, with our quality of consciousness sustained and protected by the chakras. Eventually I was to discover that innocence could remain even in adulthood, for it is very different from ignorance.

Many qualities have to mature in the adult personality, but as my understanding of the Mooladhara chakra grew I found innocence to be a friend that could accompany me anywhere. It was like a Teflon coating that separated the attention from ego, simple awareness untainted by motive or design, but it was no passive detachment - it was the oil that lubricated the wheels of the subtle system, and the oxygen that made the light burn bright.

Struggling to understand an abstract quality such as innocence helped me to realise how important a role the archetypes, or deities, of the collective unconscious played. They acted both as universal benchmarks of fundamental divine principles and as powerful instruments for their implementation, able to communicate directly with the psyche on levels beyond rational understanding.

We could transcend mental concepts by experiencing an archetype's essential nature; instead of, 'Hmm, I must be projecting an imaginary construct derived from a childish interpretation of XYZ,' it is, 'Wow! How can such power and beauty exist? How can I know all this? How can something so awesome be so overwhelmingly familiar?'

This was fortunate because the archetype Shri Mataji named as the power and gate-keeper of the Mooladhara chakra could hardly be more difficult for the western mind to relate to. It represents a divine state of eternal childhood, of egolessness, and is worshipped as Ganesha in Hindu tradition, where he is depicted as a human child with the head of an elephant.

This is a powerfully symbolic image, but the educated mind

will obviously be at a loss here and is obliged to take the mental, linear view; humanity is projecting its ideas onto the cosmos, etc, etc. Eternity is not linear, however; past, present and future all meet in the same place, and many things in nature reflect truths from higher realities. Perhaps we can allow that such iconic imagery may represent the conceptual language of a collective unconscious mind capable of the dazzling creativity we see in the kaleidoscope of life forms in nature.

According to Shri Mataji, the elephant symbolised the majesty and wisdom of the spirit, and the elephant's head expressed the eternal innocence of the child principle, which does not develop a human ego. Impossible or not, the archetype of Ganesha exists, and to experience his nature can be to know purity and auspiciousness so powerfully intense it can scarcely be borne.

I learned the hard way that the importance of innocence cannot be overstated in the realm of the divine. There was no instant transformation into 'holiness'; my subtle system was damaged and fragile, the process still continues, and I have tripped and fallen often along the way. There have been plenty of hard knocks, more than enough to show me that any attempt to reach the higher worlds without the sanction of the Mooladhara chakra must ultimately fail.

Looking at organised religion, on the other hand, it was not surprising that we had been put off ideas about God and purity. According to Shri Mataji, humanity was fashioned after the pattern of Ganesha, and this innocent archetype of the primordial child manifested in a more evolved form as Christ at the penultimate stage of humanity's collective evolutionary ascent. She said that Christ's incarnation signalled the awakening of the sixth chakra in the forehead of the Virata, and that his crucifixion symbolised the death of the ego and the spiritual transcendence of material human existence.

She explained that the ego and superego retracted as this chakra opened out, subduing mental and emotional activity and establishing a foothold in the pure awareness of the central channel; thus unlocking the route to the Sahasrara chakra at the crown of the head, where the soul was united with the divine. It was a subtle mechanism of which I was to have profound experience later on:

'I find myself looking at the Agnya chakra in the centre of Shri Mataji's forehead. It has become beautiful and golden, and my attention seems somehow to roll or be drawn effortlessly upwards in a blissful sensation of surrender and release. Awe fills me as Shri Mataji's face becomes that of a divine patriarch; timeless and golden, the essence of authority, nobility, dignity, beauty and love itself. Is this the reflection of Shiva? - Of the divinity within my own soul? I do not know. I know only that I have entered the kingdom of God.'

This would make Christ's message a simple one, his advent promising deliverance from karma and the ultimate ascent to the divine, but in the short-lived perspective of humanity it became a rallying call for a kingdom of a far more temporal kind. Christ embodied the innocence of the Ganesha principle, Shri Mataji said, and as such was beyond sexuality, but attempting to enforce this on a human level was a mistake.

It was clear enough, looking back at my own Catholic upbringing, that the neutered abstinence of imposed celibacy was not innocence. I could feel some sympathy for those who genuinely tried to remain pure in this way, but the redundancy of sex at a high spiritual level was a spontaneous happening that could not be artificially contrived. At a human level, it was extreme behaviour that had all too often led to secret vice and religious organisations more preoccupied with human manipulation than spiritual enlightenment. Christianity seemed to have been effectively hijacked by politics, the Gnostics put down, and Christ's message of deliverance from the wheel of karma made unrecognisable to the custodians of ancient Hindu knowledge.

According to Shri Mataji, personalities such as Christ or Krishna were primordial archetypes manifesting fundamental evolutionary principles, which had incarnated to play key roles in the unfolding of the subtle system in the evolutionary process. Unsurprisingly, she portrayed the comprehension of the human ego as lagging far behind the patient progress of the divine; and she lamented that these compassionate divine beings were not well understood, mostly treated badly while alive and accepted with little understanding when they were dead (such beings were eternal, of course, but incarnated temporarily in human form for a specific purpose).

She also spoke of archetypes that manifested qualities or 'moods' of the Virata other than those of the central evolutionary path, such as the sustaining power of the collective subconscious and the creative power of the supraconscious mind. There was Kali, who ruled the subconscious, for instance, whose ferocity knew no bounds when her divine children were threatened, but whose love for them was boundless. The image we have of her in the west is of the destructive form in which she confronts negativity, but many of her 1000 names praise her as the source of joy in life, the life force that nurtures all living things, and the essence of fragrance and beauty in nature. Another was Brahma, the aspect of the divine that manifested the physical creation, repeatedly so according to Hindu tradition, which describes the cyclical rhythm of his breath in terms of the successive creation, expansion and contraction of the universe, of many universes in fact. This quality of the divine, according to Shri Mataji, manifested through the Swadhisthan chakra and acted as the creator at the level of the macrocosm and as the creative force in nature, as well as inspiring creative expression in human beings.

Shri Mataji explained that the functions of many chakras were governed by both male and female archetypes. She had already said that the masculine principle remained detached at the highest level while the primordial power acted, but she described these roles as being reversed in a way at more relative levels, with the feminine principle becoming the source of power and the masculine principle, the instrument of its expression.

These feminine incarnations took birth at the same time as their male counterparts at important evolutionary junctures, she said, but mostly remained in the background to sustain the power manifested by the male archetype. She described them as adopting various relationships to the male incarnations, such as wife, mother, sister or daughter, and discussed in some detail many of the roles they played, such as Mary, the mother of Christ, or Radha, Krishna's childhood playmate.

The outwardly passive roles of these evolutionary feminine incarnations stood in sharp contrast to direct interventions by the Primordial Mother in confronting powerful negative mutations, Shri Mataji said. This had happened on a number of occasions in ancient times, she told us, for there had been some serious challenges to the development of humanity within the parameters of the central path of evolution before it was fully established. Such incidents are described in Hindu mythology and depict the goddess as an all-powerful being; matchlessly beautiful, wholly invincible and utterly relentless in her destruction of the demonic forces arrayed against her.

In Hindu tradition, the consort of Brahma is Saraswati, the goddess of learning and the creative arts. The Swadhisthan chakra is depicted in Sanskrit literature as a lotus emerging from the Nabhi chakra, the seat of evolutionary ascent situated in the solar plexus in the central channel. Shri Mataji described the Swadhisthan as moving in a circle around the Nabhi and creating a void in the Virata known as the *Bhavasagara*, or 'ocean of illusion', within which the material creation took place.

According to her, this 'void' corresponded to a gap in the human parasympathetic nervous system that prevented the attention from rising in the central channel unless it was carried by the ascending kundalini. Before kundalini awakening, she said, the attention could rise only to the highest point of the left or the right channels, and she cited this as one of the reasons why many spiritual or religious activities became so extreme.

It was to guide humanity across this ocean of illusion that another aspect of the divine, the guru principle, came into play, according to Shri Mataji. In Sanskrit, the word *guru* means 'the one who removes illusion' and she described this principle as acting in terms of both individual and collective spiritual ascent. At the collective level she portrayed this as an intervention by the divine in support of the evolutionary process, and spoke of the discerning, prophetic qualities of this archetypal role as having manifested through the teachings of such great historical figures as Moses, Confucius, Socrates and Mohammed. On the individual level, the guru principle was particularly interesting after self-realisation, as Shri Mataji explained that the traditional relationship of teacher and pupil ended, and the soul effectively became both its own guru and its own disciple through the vibratory awareness of the chakras.

It was the heart that had the final say in the completion of the evolutionary process however. Shri Mataji spoke of a direct relationship between the heart and the Sahasrara chakra or 'thousand petalled lotus' in the brain which is difficult to explain in a linear way. She described a special 'nadi' or channel linking them which did not allow the Sahasrara to open fully unless the heart did likewise, at which time the spirit, the 'seat' or core identity of the being, moved from the heart to merge into the integrated awareness of the Sahasrara, and the whole system functioned as one.

All of these things were part of large, complex and interrelated subjects that warrant chapters rather than pages to explain in any real detail, but I have said enough to give an idea of the scale of the canvas that Shri Mataji worked on.

Chapter 17

India

Life went on in Sahaja Yoga as we digested all the information that Shri Mataji gave us, and I had yet another personal drama to go through. I was working as a council gardener, and I had volunteered to spray some weed-killer for a workmate who was reluctant to use it. We were not given instructions or protective equipment, and I cheerfully sprayed away, thinking nothing of the weird taste in my mouth until later in the day when I started feeling unwell. I went to bed and had an endlessly recurring nightmare in which I was trapped in a village where everyone was dying of the Black Death, and I finally awoke feeling horribly ill, with my mouth and throat full of blisters. I had been using Paraquat weed-killer, a chemical that can be quite lethal, and I was in a bad way for the next six weeks.

I spent the first week in hospital having all sorts of tests. The blisters in my throat eventually went down, but my legs swelled up enormously, which was even more horrendous; I could press my fingers into them and the indent would stay in place. I left the hospital after a while and stayed close by, at the house in Euston where we normally met Shri Mataji, returning for various medical tests from time to time in a wheelchair pushed by my sister. Shri Mataji came to see me several times and worked on my chakras, gently massaging my swollen legs and drawing the swelling down towards my feet.

She expressed disgust at the weed-killer, but said it had 'worked out' a lot of the poison in my system from all the drugs and alcohol I had taken. I had no idea what this meant exactly, as I imagined the last thing my body would benefit from would be more toxic chemicals, but I assumed it had something to do with karma and paying for my sins. If so, I had a little more retribution to get through, as the swelling in my legs went down only to be succeeded by kidney stones and the worst pain I have ever experienced in my life. I came through it all, though, and was pleased that Shri Mataji felt some good might come out of it, even if she did say it had been an extremely dangerous way to go about it.

As my health improved, the hospital professed to be as baffled by my recovery as they were by my illness and shunted me about from department to department where I was prodded about by learned persons in white coats with groups of interested students looking on. They asked me a surprising number of questions about my workplace and procedures in place there for storing and using weed-killer, and when I returned to work I found that a minor bank vault had mysteriously been constructed in which to secure it.

I received no acknowledgement that my illness was related to weed-killer poisoning from either the hospital or the local authority I was working for, which seemed quite odd, but those were more innocent days, and I did not pursue it. Eventually the doctors wanted to shoot me full of dye and take lots of x-rays again, something they had done when I was first ill, but by then I had had enough and declined any further treatment, content that Shri Mataji would look after me.

Not long after this, we went to India. Shri Mataji left before Christmas and we followed in early January. We were there for three months or so and had an amazing time, both with Shri Mataji and the Indian Sahaja Yogis and while travelling to take in some of India's rich cultural heritage at Shri Mataji's suggestion.

Our Indian brothers and sisters were somewhat perturbed at the state of our subtle systems and our ignorance of all things spiritual, but concealed this as best they could while showering us with kindness and hospitality. Some of them were at quite a deep level, something that was brought home to me when I saw beautiful golden ripples surrounding one young man I was talking to; and as we got to know the Indian yogis better we began to recognise all kinds of subtleties in their sensitivity to vibratory awareness, and in the way they spoke and behaved with each other. In particular we noticed the protocol they observed in their relationship with Shri Mataji.

We felt an instinctive respect towards Shri Mataji, of course, but we had become used to joking and conversing with her almost as if we were family. We began to realise that we were missing a lot of inner depth and subtlety in this way, and started to consider more carefully what it meant to be in the presence of one in whom all the chakras were fully awakened.

We had been introduced to *puja*, or 'worship', in which the powers or blessings of the different aspects of the divine were invoked at certain auspicious times, and we had experienced some of the effects of this on our chakras. Now we learned more about puja and new depths of vibratory experience that it could bestow; and the more I became aware of the kind of subtleties that Shri Mataji worked with, the more I marvelled at the way she had coped with seekers from so many different backgrounds in London.

Even Shri Mataji's material lifestyle was far removed from the kind of existence we had been leading. At the time her husband was the Secretary General of the United Nations International Maritime Organisation, which was based in London, and one of the things I actually found difficult to accept was that Shri Mataji moved in these kinds of circles. I suppose I imagined that high spiritual beings should lead an ascetic life in a cave somewhere, and it required something of an effort to accept that dynamic spiritual events could take place in a respectable family and social environment.

Shri Mataji told us, in fact, that she had looked for seekers among the diplomats and VIPs she met socially without success and had been forced to search elsewhere. In India, I found it was possible for a high court judge or a senior civil servant to be humble and simple enough to be open to (genuine) spirituality, but I'm not surprised Shri Mataji did not find this in the west.

It was an advantage in the early days that Shri Mataji came from an affluent background as she had no need of money; in fact, she often paid for things that we could not afford. She gave her time freely and comprehensively, as did the Indian Sahaja Yogis. Their generosity was extremely embarrassing, and we spent much of the time in India struggling to pay for things without success. We still managed to run out of money before the end of the trip, though, and ended up borrowing some from Shri Mataji. She never asked for it back, either, as we were out of work for quite a while when we got back to the UK, although we did a small amount of work for her that was supposed to make up for this loan.

The things we were learning in India took a while to sink in, and I fear that we were capable of shocking our hosts right to the end of our stay, but we had a great time. I absolutely loved India. I loved the dusty palm trees and the coarse, discordant cries of the crows flapping lazily over the multicoloured chaos of the streets. I loved the gloriously vibrant sunrises and the dense heat of the day, and the endless, panoramic sunsets and the rich luminosity of the stars in the night sky.

It was a timeless land of slow, ancient rivers and people living in profound simplicity with impossibly complex rituals and beliefs. Hinduism appeared to be a glorious confusion of myths, legends and hopeful superstitions on the surface, but knowledge of the subtle system revealed it in a very different light. Clearly this had once been a very high culture, and even in decline its heritage was impressive, but I was not surprised that the western mind had never been able to understand it.

I really felt deep in my soul that this ancient land had witnessed profound spiritual dramas over long ages of time; its primeval, sun-baked landscapes invoked deep peace and contentment, and it seemed somehow both wonderfully alien and intensely familiar. We travelled much of the time by train, which was a magnificent way to see India. Steam engines seemed hugely romantic, and the train travelled slowly and stopped often, chugging cheerfully past stunning panoramas and winding intimately through the back gardens of simple villages.

Thirty-six-hour journeys were not uncommon, and there were times when I felt this idyllic existence would go on forever. Life seemed one big adventure of spiritual discovery; even lying on the train's pull-down wooden bunk at night, my feet towards the corridor, I would often feel vibratory sensations register in the chakra points in my feet as people walked past.

When we first arrived in India, we met up with the Swiss Sahaja Yogi who had participated in the great drug debate in the house in Euston eighteen months earlier, and attended meditations, public meetings and pujas with Shri Mataji and the Indian Sahaja Yogis in Bombay, now Mumbai, and various other places in Maharashtra.

We then parted company from Shri Mataji for a while, and our Swiss friend returned to Nepal, where he was working. We travelled at a fairly leisurely pace across country, visiting places Shri Mataji had recommended we should see, such as the sculptured caves at Ellora and Ajanta, Akbar's palace at Fatehpur Sikri, and the Taj Mahal, before meeting up with her again in Delhi.

Here we got to know more Indian yogis and enjoyed another round of public meetings and pujas, as well as doing a surprising amount of shopping. We stayed in the background much of the time at the Sahaja events as we did not want to intrude on the Indian yogis' time with Shri Mataji, but she called us over from time to time to see how we were getting on.

From Delhi we set off to Kathmandu, where our Swiss friend was living, travelling by train via Benares to Patna and taking a short plane ride to Nepal. Here we met up again with Shri Mataji, who had come to stay with her enthusiastic Swiss disciple, and we all had a wonderful week together, much as we had been used to in the UK, but with picnicking and sightseeing thrown in. Kathmandu was fascinating, festooned with exquisitely carved wooden buildings; and wandering in its backstreets sometimes felt like going back hundreds of years in time. Shri Mataji would go into a shop first to find out all the local prices and then emerge to wave us all in with a beaming smile, and plunge the proprietor into gloom as she quoted the prices he had given her.

After Shri Mataji left, we said goodbye again to our Swiss friend, who had received us all with great hospitality, and who waved us off with a severely depleted grocery budget, and set off by bus along winding Nepalese mountain roads. We marvelled at spectacular mountain landscapes and held our breath beside precipitous drops, staying in Pokhara and paddling on a mountain lake in dugout canoes. We rode more buses in dusty India, stayed in amazingly cheap hotels and had more glorious train rides, gradually making our way back to Delhi and eventually to Bombay, where we enjoyed many more encounters with Shri Mataji and her Indian Sahaja Yogis.

During our final stay in Bombay, the female partner of my

original 'psychedelic mentors' came out to join us. She had been unable to return to England from France for about a year because of a drugs conviction, and I was very happy to see her, even though she had broken up with her other half. The entire trip was like one long, incredible dream, although I was ill on a couple of occasions, and our subtle systems became 'caught up' at times, whereupon we would be roundly told off by Shri Mataji as she cleared our chakras out.

I brought back many treasured memories from India, especially of Shri Mataji, which varied as usual from the wildly improbable and comic to the poignant and profound. I remember one night we were in a house where a man with a big, bald head was being 'worked on', and Shri Mataji asked one of the Indian ladies to put some of the auspicious red powder, usually applied on the forehead, on the top of his head. At the last moment, the lady stumbled and spilt most of the container's contents, which promptly formed a bright vermillion pyramid on the crown of his head. It is a very light powder, and he could not detect its presence; and all of us including Shri Mataji laughed until we cried as he sat there in perplexed bewilderment.

On another occasion, while staying in Kathmandu, we had gone for a picnic up into the foothills with Shri Mataji when we were told by some local Nepalese that a yogi lived in a hermitage nearby. Shri Mataji agreed we could visit the hermitage, and we walked up to it, sitting down to rest and talk for a while when we found he was not there. We were quite excited by the idea that the yogi would appear and a great cosmic event would take place, and we were thrilled when he actually did arrive, looking very much the part, and smiled a greeting to Shri Mataji.

Next came a lengthy, voluble conversation that we understood nothing of, and we were confounded to see the Nepali boy who was with us circle his finger at the side of his head in a time-honoured indication of madness. In no time at all, Shri Mataji had the man sitting in front of her with her foot on his back, clearing his chakras, and was telling us that the man was actually born realised, but had gone mad in his solitary state in this Kali Yuga. We were quite dismayed, all our cosmic expectations in ruins, but we had not seen the end of this surprising episode.

The yogi seemed quite happy singing to himself, and other

locals had gathered to watch, but when the time came to leave it was discovered that someone had taken Shri Mataji's purse. Various excited but unintelligible conversations followed, and a posse of keen locals set off in pursuit of the suspected offender. We could follow their progress as they ran between the houses dotted about on the hillside, with the posse acquiring additional members at every house, much to Shri Mataji's amusement. Eventually the purse was rescued and returned, and after rewarding the finders she asked if the local children could come and see her. Soon an interested group of children gathered, and Shri Mataji called them to her one at a time, raising their kundalinis and bestowing one rupee on each as they affirmed they could feel the cool breeze. 'Shri Mataji!' one of us exclaimed, 'you cannot pay them to get their self-realisation!' 'I am the Adi Shakti. I can do anything I like,' said Shri Mataji with a smile.

Returning to the west from India was quite a shock to the system. The rigid segregation of every square inch of land into private or public property and the ubiquitous rules and regulations demarcating every aspect of life felt horribly claustrophobic, and the unsmiling faces in the street were dull and depressing.

The worst thing was the reaction of the subtle system to the western world. The mood of light, cheerful detachment I had brought back from India began to flounder amidst the oppressive hustle and bustle of London; and a familiar sense of tension and heaviness crept through my body, it felt a bit like sinking into a muddy pond. Not everything was lost, however. I found I could sit in meditation for forty minutes without driving myself mad, and I felt more grounded in the everyday world, more able to socialise normally and appreciate the struggles and qualities of ordinary people.

A few weeks after we got back, Shri Mataji arrived, and I was plucked back out of muddy shallows into clearer, deeper water; and into another marathon of meditation, working on chakras, questions, answers and discussions. India had given us a greater depth of understanding and humility, and our relationship with Shri Mataji had deepened. I was no longer having 'high' experiences, but I would always experience subtle forces working within me and feel profoundly moved in her company.

We continued to enjoy our unique access to her and basked in it like children at a feast, for although the sacred and the profound formed the foundation of everything she did, she invariably interacted with us in a way that was magical, and full of optimism and fun. All sorts of things happened, including very special times for me personally when I spent time alone with Shri Mataji, accompanying her on house-hunting expeditions or driving her to meet friends or family arriving at the airport.

Three more seekers joined our group during this period. One was an Algerian student who followed up on a leaflet we decided to distribute at the first Mind and Body exhibition at Olympia in London. The leaflet was actually given to him by my brother, who was still busy 'chewing leaves' but had accompanied us to the exhibition. He took some of the leaflets we had been giving out rather diffidently, saying something to the effect of 'you will never get anywhere like this', and enthusiastically gave out lots of them.

I later walked around Shri Mataji's house with our new Algerian friend, pointing out some of the beautiful statues of deities that she had there without realising how shocking this was to him as a Muslim. Fortunately he was a deep seeker and could feel the powerful vibrations these particular statues emitted, and was able to recognise that these different images of the divine were aspects of one primordial being.

Next my old 'psychedelic mentor' reappeared on the scene. I had a dream about him one night, and sure enough he turned up next day at the house in Euston to see Shri Mataji. I mentioned the dream to her in a taxi on the way to the meeting. We were travelling from Victoria, and the journey took a surreal turn when the taxi ended up directly behind a troop of grenadier guards and we followed sedately along behind them for a while as they marched briskly down the middle of the road. It was as if they were providing an honour guard, and Shri Mataji and I laughed about it until, pragmatic as ever, she began to work on the soldiers' vibrations. 'Right side is very bad,' she said.

We arrived at the house to find my Australian friend waiting for us. I had not seen him for over a year, and I was shocked at the state he was in. He had got into all kinds of difficulties and had been badly beaten up in his squat by some unpleasant characters who believed he had a hidden stash of drugs, while the drugs he was taking were now more geared to escaping life than exploring it. Shri Mataji was unhappy at his condition. 'Now what is the situation?' she asked him. 'God save the king?' Our new Algerian friend tried to work on his chakras and staggered back with a crashing headache, agreeing with a rueful grin that he now definitely believed in collective consciousness.

Soon afterwards my old psychedelic companion collapsed in the street with hepatitis, and Shri Mataji scooped him up and took him back to her house, where her startled husband returned from work to find a half-dead hippie wearing one of his suits. She kept him at the house for several weeks while she worked on his chakras and nursed him back to health. I stayed there, too, for much of the time, and when her husband's patience began to wear a bit thin Shri Mataji re-invented us as painters and decorators and announced that we were going to be paid to redecorate the house, which was about to go on the market.

We had a great time doing this, especially when Shri Mataji came and helped us, but painters and decorators we were not. There were a number of long hairline cracks on the walls, and we industriously gouged them into great chasms, then found they were a lot harder to fill than we expected. The house ended up looking a bit like a backdrop for a disaster movie, although neither Shri Mataji nor her long-suffering husband commented on it. The first buyer to look at the house did, though, asking who the decorators were after one incredulous look.

Another new member was a girl from the local squatting community who had been present at one of the early meetings with Shri Mataji. She had had a powerful spontaneous spiritual experience not long before meeting Shri Mataji and had been too absorbed in the personal intensity of it to recognise many of the implications of Sahaja Yoga. She had gone off to spend some time at a circus school in Spain as she was interested in the ancient symbolism of circus tradition, but things had not gone well for her; she had lost her high and become disillusioned and despondent.

A couple of us met her one day, and after we had been talking for a while she started to feel vibratory sensations in her body. In a few surprising seconds she connected what she was feeling with Shri Mataji and recognised its potential, and in no time at all was joining in with everything. A number of people had deep spontaneous spiritual experiences shortly before meeting Shri Mataji. My present wife had a beautiful experience of oneness while sitting by a lake in Poland, where she is from. It sparked her seeking and her various adventures in trying to get to the west, something that was not easy to do at the time.

One day Shri Mataji asked me to accompany her on what turned out to be the inspection of a house for rent in Acton, in west London, to assess it as a possible ashram. She had been saying for a while that it would help us to live collectively in an ashram in a disciplined and meditative environment. The house was owned by an Indian, and Shri Mataji had found out about it through her own contacts; she even paid the deposit as few of us were working at the time. Six weeks or so after we moved in, she found a better place in Finchley Road on the other side of London, and we moved again, with her helping us financially for this, too.

The first day in the new Finchley ashram was pretty surreal even for us, who were fairly used to such things. The landlord was another Indian, who also owned a decorating shop beneath the maisonette that formed the new ashram. As soon as the landlord had left after showing us the place, we set about clearing out the old vibrations we felt there; and my part in this involved carrying around a metal tray of burning charcoal onto which a quantity of ajwain, a seed-like spice, had been thrown. It gave off a sharp, acrid smoke when burned that was extremely potent. This spice has a powerfully antiseptic smell and a mild local-anaesthetic effect; it is brilliant for curing sore throats among other things, and is generally thought to be auspicious and discouraging to negativity.

Ajwain was used sparingly on a few hot coals by some, but things tended to be all or nothing with me, and I got plenty of charcoal going and chucked handfuls of ajwain onto it, thoroughly filling the place with smoke, especially the designated meditation room. I was finishing up in there, inhaling a few additional wafts for the benefit of the ever-present tension in my head and neck, when I noticed a mysterious figure blundering about in the smoke. This turned out to be the landlord, who had returned unexpectedly, and who was unimpressed by our efforts to cleanse the vibrations, despite being Indian. He was eventually persuaded to go away again, but this was not the last we saw of him.

Later that evening, an acquaintance of our Algerian friend's visited us, an unusual individual of vivid imagination and unsteady emotional equilibrium. We put some potatoes in the oven to cook and soon afterwards noticed a strange chemical burning smell, and not having connected it with the cooker we hunted about for a bit trying to figure out where the smell was coming from. Our visitor became convinced that something was burning and was alarmed that it might spread to the paint store in the shop beneath us, and when he announced that he was going off to ring someone for advice we were relieved to get him out of our hair for a while.

Not for long though, because the next thing we knew two fire engines had screeched to a halt outside and the ashram was full of firemen. It was pure Hollywood drama, with fireman all over the ashram, one breaking a window with his axe to get out onto the roof and another shining a searchlight all over the place from the fire engine. Finally, with much embarrassment all around, the burning smell was identified as being caused by the chemical that had been used to clean the oven. Into this mayhem dashed the horrified landlord, who had been rung up by the fire brigade and told his building was on fire, and the look on his face was completely priceless. Surprisingly we remained as his tenants, but I suspect he did not really breathe freely again until we left a year or so later.

Chapter 18
Treading the boards

Finally, in the late summer, Shri Mataji informed us that the time had come to have a public meeting, which was something I regarded with a fair amount of trepidation. She had never made any secret of the fact that she was investing time and effort in us so that we could do the same for others further down the line, and that she wanted to meet as many seekers as possible.

'God has done a lot for you,' she would say. 'You have to do something in return, and the only thing you can do for God is to give realisation to others.'

We had experienced a public meeting of sorts with Shri Mataji some time before, when her efforts to awaken interest in the social circles her husband moved in had yielded an invitation to speak to members of a Christian group in Cambridge. We travelled there in Shri Mataji's husband's car, complete with chauffeur, with my sister sitting on Shri Mataji's lap in front all the way.

On arrival, we were confronted by a troupe of elderly persons who obviously had no idea what they were in for, and Shri Mataji launched into an amazingly powerful speech that took everyone by surprise, including us. When she had finished speaking, Shri Mataji invited her audience to experience their self-realisation, and a white-faced vicar promptly sprang to his feet. He thanked her very much, spluttered incoherently that Christianity was the only true religion, and shepherded his flock out of the room at breakneck speed. Shri Mataji burst into laughter over it several times in the following few weeks.

A meeting open to seekers in central London was a different

prospect, though, and I was apprehensive about it for a number of reasons, among them a strong personal disinclination towards performing in public. I also felt concerned about Shri Mataji confronting the irreverent ranks of the seeking fraternity at a public meeting. I barely understood the gulf between the levels of subtlety that she existed on and the belligerent insensitivity of the western ego, but I cringed at the thought of the cynicism that had developed among so many seekers. Indeed, by this time, the tangled edifice of New Age mythology regarded pretty much anything going as a valid path to enlightenment unless it involved God, religion or morality.

Certainly, in my old identity as a seeker, I would not for a moment have entertained the idea of putting myself forward to promote a spiritual practice as unique or unprecedented. There was also the question of vibratory awareness. As our sensitivity to the subtle system developed, we found that contact with other people could be a bit of an ordeal, especially if they had been experimenting with some of the more dubious practices to be found along the seeking trail. In fact Shri Mataji had found it amusing that I disappeared from a Sahaja Yoga meeting in India when a western hippie couple wandered in, but I had been enjoying a nice but fragile subtle state, and I did not feel like taking on the load of their chakras.

I had learned by experience how sensitive my subtle system could be to the vibrations of people I came into contact with. Annoyingly, although I couldn't feel vibratory indications from their chakras very well, my subtle system could react dramatically to heavy problems they had, and I would sometimes find I had been knocked down quite badly without knowing exactly how it had happened. This situation was intensified if I worked on their chakras and tried to awaken their kundalini, and, although the basic condition of my subtle system had improved, I still got 'caught up' by other people's problems and had not yet built up the strength and detachment to throw them off easily.

This could mean being stuck not just with negative sensations in the chakras, but also with the negative moods and misidentifications that went with them. It was something I was particularly prone to when I worked on people with similar weaknesses to mine, and it could sometimes take a while to get rid of these things. Shri Mataji told us we would have less difficulty with this as our self-realisation deepened and that learning to detach from other people's problems was part of the process. I accepted this fairly philosophically; in fact, I was happy to help people in this way, but I was well aware that interacting with seekers and working on their subtle systems could often mean a subsequent couple of hours of chakra clearing, and I was unsure what a public meeting full of such encounters would be like.

In the autumn of 1977 we hired a large room in Caxton Hall, near the flat Shri Mataji and her husband had bought in Victoria, in central London, and put an advert in 'Time Out' magazine, which advertised entertainment and New Age activities in the capital. I arrived wondering if anyone would turn up and was surprised to see a steady flow of people coming through the door; before long around two hundred people were seated expectantly. To my horror, Shri Mataji asked us all to sit on the stage with her, and I took my place in acute embarrassment, thankful at least that someone other than myself was going to say some words of introduction.

Once again Shri Mataji delivered an extraordinary speech, powerful, dynamic and full of love, and once again it surprised me. Her manner had always been confident and robust, but I had become used to interacting with her in a fairly informal and relaxed manner. Now she spoke with great power and resolution, announcing that self-realisation was an inborn and spontaneous manifestation of the divine that existed in a potential form in everyone.

Her voice resounded throughout the room and, as I felt the vibrations build, my sense of embarrassment was eclipsed by growing discomfort as tremendous forces began to work their way up through my body. It reached the point where it was really excruciating and it was difficult to sit still; and I sat with gritted teeth, trying ludicrously to look evolved, with my attention equally divided between Shri Mataji's amazing speech and what felt like a mixture of serious indigestion, chronic wind and horrendous muscle cramps.

Finally, everything changed; Shri Mataji finished speaking and I felt the vibrations envelop everything in the hall in a great cocoon of compassion and auspiciousness; then she was off the stage and down among the audience, working on people. We followed in her wake without time to think and plunged into a sea of people suddenly awash with energy.

The next hour or two were very intense and quite wonderful; a lot of interesting people were there, and Shri Mataji spent time with almost everyone, talking to them and working on them, and we did our best to do the same. I still seemed to be much more aware of things on an abstract or collective level than I was of my own subtle system, but I could feel a strong current of energy flowing through me, and several people I worked on felt the 'cool breeze', or at least some vibratory sensations in their hands and body.

By the end of the evening, everything was different; it felt as if everyone in the hall was part of one big family, and I had a distinct sense that Sahaja Yoga had changed gear and evolved into something new. It was the end of our exclusive access to Shri Mataji, but we did not begrudge it – we were happy to share what we had with others. We quickly arranged follow-up meetings in the house in Euston and in the ashram in Finchley and embarked on a series of sessions much like those that had taken place when I first met Shri Mataji, except that the numbers were greater and I had a different perspective on it all.

Shri Mataji still dealt with each newcomer personally and in great depth. Long hours passed quickly, with seeker after seeker asking questions of her and recounting the stories of the paths they had travelled, while she probed their subtle system and expressed concern at the problems she found. When she was satisfied she had done all she could for each person, they would join the ranks of grinning onlookers, and the next person would come forward.

It was wonderful to share in the joy and revelation that some seekers experienced on meeting Shri Mataji, but others appeared more interested in advancing their own ideas or those of their gurus and did not seem open to vibratory awareness at all. I could see that all of us had become attached, to some extent, to spiritual practices we had experimented with and books we had read, but some of these people had swallowed doctrines and practices wholesale without any supporting evidence and now defended them to the death.

A great deal of debate went on about various gurus, authors and practitioners of mysterious techniques, to the point where we began to weary of it and feel it was pointless and burdensome for Shri Mataji to have to keep explaining the same things over and over again. As she said repeatedly to some of them, 'If you are so enamoured of this guru, why are you coming to me?' Such misidentifications and 'counter-conditionings' could surpass the problems created in the first place by the ignorance and rootlessness of western society, especially where the black arts of some of the heavyweight 'gurus' were concerned. Some of the things we felt in the chakras of these people were really quite awful and brought home Shri Mataji's warnings that there were negative forces working behind the scenes to destroy the seekers. It was a real battle in some cases to clear this stuff out and establish the vibratory awareness of the subtle system.

The 'battle' part of things was a theme that did not fade as time passed. The experience of being in Shri Mataji's presence did not change; the atmosphere was always full of vibrations, and dynamic processes would work their way through my system, causing aches and pains but steadily transforming me into a more relaxed and subtle state. As more and more people became involved, however, the aches and pains became more pronounced and the depth of experience less blissful.

Shri Mataji explained that when en-mass self-realisation was triggered by the evolutionary process and the Sahasrara chakra at the crown of the head began to open, spirituality ceased to be about individual ascent and became part of a collective event. She said that individual yogis and saints of a high level had done *tapas*, or penance, in the past to consciously work out the collective karma of the human race on their subtle systems. These realised souls enjoyed working for the collective good, she said, because they experienced it as their greater Self, and the more selflessly they worked for the collective being, the higher their own ascent into God realisation became.

She explained that the same thing was happening today, but that it played out slightly differently. Things speeded up when the evolution of consciousness reached its final stage; the seekers got their self-realisation spontaneously without having to perfect their chakras, but repaid the debt by triggering self-realisation in others. She said that many lacked the strength to ascend individually, but could sustain it collectively, and awakening the kundalini of others made our own kundalini flow more strongly, which helped us to deepen and grow in return. Each new realised soul became an instrument through which the collective unconscious could work in a collectively escalating process that generated its own momentum, with the seekers at the beginning of the process bearing a greater part of the burden than those at the end, but with an ultimate reward so great that such distinctions little mattered.

Certainly the field of vibrations was stronger when we were together, and could become incredibly strong when the kundalini awoke in people we worked on. The collective-karma part of things was no joke, however. The influx of new people seemed to create a more powerful field of vibrations in our collective awareness, but it was combined, paradoxically, with more intense negative sensations in the chakras and an increased sense of inertia or drag on our energy.

It was something that accumulated gradually as further public meetings took place and more seekers joined us, and it was not just a question of heat and tingling in the chakras but the weight of conditionings, attitudes, habits, fears and prejudices, not to mention negative entities, that they signalled. I found it was one thing to be loving, peaceful and collective when stoned out of my mind, and something altogether different when only reality existed between the clash of raw egos. They were all special people, though; deep seekers with high ideals, and I had great respect for them all. It was certainly a challenge, but one well worth facing, and we all tried to help each other out as best we could.

The collective vibrational load of people joining us was particularly noticeable when we had a sudden influx of seekers from one of the heavyweight gurus. They were serious seekers, possessed of depth and intelligence, but had astonishingly been tricked into spending thousands of pounds trying to learn how to fly. It was ridiculous of course, but a powerful illustration of the manipulative skills that some of these 'gurus' had, and its credibility was belied by the dreadful condition that their chakras were in.

I did wonder if the fact that they had all been literally hopping about for years, without anyone actually taking off, might have been grounds for the odd doubt, but that was before I really understood what had been done to them. They had been told, when negative entities were introduced into their psyches, that the wild mood swings, manic screaming and jumping, and epileptic-like seizures they experienced were evidence of karma being released from past lives. They had simply been too trusting to suspect what was going on, or even to imagine the motives of a 'guru' of this sort; and their respect, and ignorance, of the ancient spiritual traditions of India had continued to blind them as the deeper souls became weakened, lost and confused and the less sensitive became egotistical automatons.

The state these seekers were in was quite heartbreaking, but some of the situations we got into while trying to help them could be hilariously surreal. When we tried to raise their kundalini, all hell broke loose, they started screaming and jumping and having fits, forcing us to play music at full volume to mask their yelling from the neighbours. I only just grabbed one of them in time as he tried to jump out of a first-floor window. We received a call about the same guy from a hospital casualty ward one night, and ended up having to carry him out to the car in a rigid catatonic state, sitting cross-legged in the yoga 'lotus position'.

There was nothing funny about the effect of their problems on our chakras, though; it was a very heavy time, and everything was dragged down for quite a while. We bore it cheerfully enough out of the concern we felt for them, and because we knew the unconscious was using these situations to work out similar situations for many other seekers on a collective level. We also had frequent meetings with Shri Mataji, of course, who always lifted everything up no matter how heavy it was, and who encouraged, energised and inspired us to go on.

And go on we did. We met hundreds of seekers at Sahaja Yoga meetings and got to know quite a lot about what was happening on the seeking trail, and as time went by we made new friends among Sahaja Yogis from all over the world. Public meetings with Shri Mataji took place in different parts of the UK, to begin with, and then gradually spread to Europe, Australia, the US and many other places. Most people took a while to grasp what it was really all about and to settle down into vibratory awareness in a reasonably stable manner; but a few recognised its potential immediately and rode the initial tide of energy to plunge straight into the real depth of the whole thing. The first awakening of the kundalini was often quite a strong experience, but if the ego thought about it too much or started to doubt, analyse and categorise everything, it could dissipate and reduce in intensity. It was not lost, but withdrew to work out one's spiritual emancipation by a more circuitous route. There were those who recognised that something profound was taking place but shied away from it, feeling it was too much to cope with. I could understand how they felt as Sahaja Yoga was certainly not for the faint hearted, especially at that time, but I could not imagine trying to shut it out like that. My view was that if this was the truth there was ultimately no escaping it, and I wanted to know for certain one way or the other.

I could feel all manner of things happening inside me and was experiencing new depths of pain and frustration as I became more aware of the damage I had done to myself. My kundalini had come up strongly in joy and recognition when I first met Shri Mataji, in a high that had lasted, to some extent, for two or three years, and I had been greatly boosted and supported by spending so much time in her company. Now, with the growing numbers of Sahaja Yogis, the collective weight of the problems on the chakras had grown while individual attention from Shri Mataji had lessened, and at the same time the kundalini seemed to be plumbing new depths in its efforts to root out my problems.

It was becoming increasingly obvious to me that I had taken a hell of a hit in the incident with my friend on the LSD trip, and it had done a great deal of damage to the Vishuddhi chakra in my neck and the Agnya chakra in my forehead. I experienced massive, constant pressure in my head, neck and shoulders. It is difficult to convey how debilitating it was; it felt as if a giant was crushing my head in his hands while twisting the top half of my head one way and the bottom half the other, and resting his ponderous weight on my neck and shoulders for good measure.

The pressure was not actually unbearable, although it could get close to it when the vibrations were at their strongest and the kundalini pushed up with great force, such as at pujas. Sometimes I would tie a scarf around my head as tightly as I could as this was the only way I could get some relief from it, but I could only keep it in place for a short time, as it had to be so tight that the top of my head quickly became numb. More often than not the length of my meditations were determined by how long I could stand the pain because introspection seemed to make it worse, although I always felt better for it afterwards, clearer and more detached.

The fault lines reached deep into my being and generated a lot of tension, making everything I did a strain and doubly difficult, particularly social interaction. Worst of all was public speaking, that is to say presenting Sahaja Yoga at meetings, which I found to be a huge ordeal; in fact, I was amazed I was able to do it at all. It is quite a testimony to the power of the kundalini that I could change from a chronically introspective watcher from the sidelines to someone addressing sixty or seventy people at a time, and later many more. Emotionally, I felt basically numb, experiencing little sense of joy and constantly feeling oppressed and dragged down by emotional stuff from the past, and I could react dramatically to rejection or slights both real and imagined. I often had to witness myself being ludicrously upset, sometimes for days, over ridiculously unimportant matters.

My awareness of the damage I had done to myself was tempered by the knowledge that the kundalini was working constantly to heal and strengthen my system, but a parallel problem was the way it had affected my sensitivity to the vibrations. The heavy damage to the Vishuddhi chakra in my neck meant that I could not enjoy the subtle sensations that many of the Sahaja Yogis experienced; especially the cool breeze and the vibratory indications in the hands. There were times when I felt the struggle was almost too much for me, but there was always an energy and a sense of mission about what we were doing that kept me going.

It was a sobering testimony to the risks that could come with drug experience; and I had to accept the fact that I had done serious damage to deep and subtle parts of my being, and that it was going to take a long time to fix it. The scars are with me still. Weaknesses in my chakras can still react to stressful situations, but the tensions and pressures are gentler, and I can trace them back to their origins and coax them into gradual release. I can also get beyond this and feel fine, and sometimes beyond that, too, and experience wondrous things that I could hardly have dared hope for in those difficult times.

Everyone, especially Shri Mataji, worked very hard for the next few years. We had little personal time, few holidays and limited interest or energy to spend on acquiring material comforts. We meditated, held public programmes and worked at clearing our chakras, and we had marathon sessions with Shri Mataji. We had seminars, pujas and havans. A *havan* is an ancient fire ceremony in which auspicious symbolic ingredients are offered to the flames to cleanse negative problems in specific parts of the subtle system, while invoking the relevant qualities of the divine. Havans these days in Sahaja Yoga tend to be short, sharp and highly enjoyable. These were four-hour affairs and could be quite arduous, with all one thousand names of a deity being chanted in Sanskrit and in English, but had an amazingly powerful effect on the subtle system.

Shri Mataji spoke often and at length, and continued to display an endlessly fascinating ability to unveil unexpected new depths of subtle knowledge. She remained as enthralling and profound as ever, and, although she constantly emphasised that we should work intensively on deepening our self-realisation, she was often very funny, and there was plenty of time for laughter. Things were not easy, but they were always momentous and never boring. I tried to remember her words about the churning process and to be philosophical about the inevitable cycles of tantalising improvement and irritating setbacks.

Chapter 19
A collective odyssey

While all this deep-level vibrational stuff was working out there was a steady improvement on an everyday level, and I began to find new interests in a 20th century world that had little appealed to me in the past. I was intrigued by its mechanisms, social, economic, political, scientific and material; I didn't necessarily like them, but I appreciated their inventiveness and complexities and I wanted to understand them. Old interests such as science fiction and half-forgotten ancient civilisations were still there, but I no longer found current affairs totally irrelevant.

Shri Mataji insisted that we should not reject society, saying that we had a responsibility to contribute towards it materially, socially and spiritually. She told us we had to build strong foundations, choose what was good and avoid what was bad about the community we lived in, and remain free within ourselves to rise beyond its limitations.

It was strange to venture back along the path of social convention. I felt a curious mixture of attraction and repulsion towards it; seeing it would be useful to earn a respectable position in society, but fearing it would impose its own priorities and undermine the desire for the spirit. It was a little alarming how quickly the banal demands of the everyday world reasserted themselves, how convincing its values could appear, and how distant and doubtful the divine could sometimes seem.

However, the divine had not forgotten me. The first ten years were a hard grind that provided little in the way of high spiritual experience. I could feel relatively clear and achieve a certain depth of thoughtless awareness at times, and I was always aware of a strong electromagnetic current flowing through me. The vibratory indications in the chakras and the subtle differences between heat and coolness were less evident though, and I could always feel tension in my body. There had been no escape from the box. One morning, however, I woke up feeling unexpectedly alert and energised and sat down to a meditation so smooth and profound that I failed to notice how extraordinary it was, and set off to work almost as if in a dream. I was sitting on the tube train before I realised how high I was, and that the experience was getting stronger.

I suddenly notice I am 'looking in' at the people in the carriage and the world they live in, as if watching it from a point outside or beyond the physical world. I feel as if I am a large, detached, invisible eye witnessing the scene. There is a subtle quality of vision, a sort of lucidity or transparency about everything together with an elusive shimmering, as if a fleeting, golden dust is vibrating everywhere.

Suddenly the sun is shining in my heart and I am filled with joy and a zest for life I have not felt for years. I feel great, fully alive again, and for long, glorious hours I revel in the rebirth of the immaculate, magical beauty in my soul. I do not know what to do. Should I go to work? Or maybe stay on the Circle line (of the London Underground) and go round and round all day?

I don't really care; I am happy just to exist, so I make my way to work anyway. I become aware of the Spirit of Christ moving like a kind of luminous, phenomenal energy through people and objects. At one point it is reflected back towards me from a wall and takes the form of a great Archangel, shining like the full moon and bowing with great respect and dignity at its own reflection in my heart.

At work I sit for much of the day on the roof or in the loft where I am working, doing little and staring at nothing while seeing myriad things. Again I feel a sense of déjà vu, of awakening once more from an unimaginably ancient cosmic sleep; and a sense of metamorphosis, as though I am a glorious butterfly that has part emerged from its chrysalis into a world of energy and light.

By late afternoon I felt the experience begin to withdraw, and a growing weariness started to weigh on me, a heavy desire for sleep and oblivion. I could not abandon such treasures easily, though, and fought against it with a surge of will that made the joy burn bright again for a while. Again the weariness returned, and again I banished it, but the third time it was too much, and I accepted the inevitable.

Returning to 'human space' was anything but restful, though, and the transition, shockingly abrupt. An iron tension gripped my temples from nowhere and a ton weight bore down on my neck and shoulders, while my mind whirled back into its customary activity. I felt I had been slammed back onto the ground, and I suspected it would be a while before I got off it again, but once I had resigned myself to this I started to look on the bright side again. It had been a wonderful experience, it had lasted more than eight hours and it had happened without drugs. It definitely looked as if I was on the right track.

The opportunities to see Shri Mataji personally continued to diminish as the numbers of Sahaja Yogis grew. Apart from anything else, she was increasingly travelling and giving public programmes in other parts of the world and spending time with the Sahaja Yogis in other countries. I still saw quite a lot of her, though, because of the building projects that began to play an important part in Sahaja Yoga affairs. We needed ashrams and centres, and Shri Mataji invariably chose properties in need of renovation because they were cheaper and it created a chance for Sahaja Yogis to work together. It also gave Shri Mataji a chance to interact with us in many different ways, as she liked to get involved with these projects; discussing plans and overflowing with creative ideas, while taking the time to go round and talk to the people working there. She said that these collective endeavours helped to work out lots of things on our chakras.

The whole building thing really began in the first place when Shri Mataji's husband, who is one of life's natural gentlemen (and used to more honourable behaviour in the circles he moved in) paid some builders in advance for a huge renovation job in a house they had bought in Brompton Square in central London. Shri Mataji was away at the time, and the builders unsurprisingly disappeared well before the end of the work. Shri Mataji asked us if we could help to finish it off, and there was a glut of volunteers, some coming at evenings and weekends or taking days off, and the unemployed amongst us putting in many more hours.

We really had great fun working there together, and we spent a great deal of time with Shri Mataji, with lots of tea breaks that were little different from our usual question, answers and vibrations sessions. Shri Mataji was always amazingly creative and constantly came up with innovations in design and decoration. She suggested, for instance, that I cut out the side of a large biscuit tin that had embossed roses stamped into it, roll it out and fix it to a length of wood together with some wooden beading then make a mould from this and use it to produce plaster-cast lengths of decorative moulding. We fitted these all round her bedroom, dividing the walls up into panels, some of which were filled with mirrors and others, with a patterned silk material stuck on like wallpaper. We picked out the roses in pink and gold, and the result was wonderful. It captured exactly the rich, magical atmosphere of peace and joy that always pervaded her family home.

The work we did went a long way to reconciling Shri Mataji's husband to the growing number of unconventional people who followed his wife around wherever she went. There must be few people in the world capable of putting up with the things he did, especially when in a high-profile job and from a tradition where the man is the most important person in the household. As the years went by, he gradually accepted that his wife was something much more than the housewife she appeared to be, although of course he had always known that she was an exceptional person.

After this, we formed a housing association and took custody of empty properties that we lived in rent-free, ran as centres and looked after until they had to be returned. I became increasingly involved in building work and started training as a plumber, getting lots of additional practice fitting temporary plumbing and heating facilities in the properties we had. Time passed and I was always busy with work, getting plumbing qualifications, meditating, taking part in Sahaja building projects, attending Sahaja Yoga programmes and seminars, meeting seekers and increasingly, as Sahaja Yoga gradually spread, going to collective pujas and get-togethers in other countries in Europe.

Sahaja Yoga was very full-on in the early days, and Shri Mataji encouraged, inspired and insisted that we push ourselves to the limit to break out of the attitudes and compromises of the ego, and to establish the detachment and discipline we needed to strengthen the foundations of the subtle system. It was tough, but the fruits of all this work have become increasingly clear over time and things are very different now, both in the intensity and subtlety of experience and the ease with which Sahaja Yogis can maintain it. It is also mirrored in the initial depth of experience many people are having these days when their kundalini is awakened.

Another important activity that became something of an established Sahaja tradition was the 'India Tour', which normally took place over two or three weeks at Christmas. This was basically an opportunity for Sahaja Yogis from all over the world to meet up in India and spend time together while travelling about to public programmes and pujas with Shri Mataji.

It was always an amazing experience because it created the opportunity to get to know a lot of yogis from different countries in beautiful surroundings and experience a constant exposure to powerful vibrations in a collective group. Without interruptions or distractions from work and the everyday demands of life in the west, we could sometimes get so high and clear that it was possible to feel fine on one or two hours' sleep a night; the vibrations built up to an amazing extent and many problems on the chakras could work out permanently.

It was no package holiday, though; things could be tough if deep-rooted problems came to the surface, and sickness was always a risk when you were off the beaten track as we frequently were; but no one minded because, as with everything in Sahaja Yoga, a serious purpose underlay all the fun.

Even the itinerary of an India tour could be a real challenge, and one particular 48 hours or so is still burned into my memory. We woke one morning after a puja where we had been camping in a fairly remote river valley (the drinking water was distinctly muddy and one guy found a snake in his shoe). 'Quick,' we were told, 'we have to pack up and get to a local school within the hour.' Breakfast was interrupted, and we chucked the luggage on top of the buses we were travelling in, with the usual groans of the men at the weight of the ladies' suitcases, and set off.

Arriving at the school, we were treated to an impressive if prolonged display of gymnastics before being packed back into the buses and driven off to a nearby town. I forget the exact order of the following events, but we watched an Indian movie in a cinema, visited a factory and went swimming in a river before having lunch. I vividly remember the beauty of the lush, exotic vegetation along the riverbank. Shri Mataji had sent word that the mud in the river had cleansing properties, and we larked about for a while, covering ourselves with it and throwing it at each other until we all looked like abominable mud people, before washing it off and having a picnic lunch on the bank.

Next we were in the buses again, bumping and rattling through rural India on hot, dusty roads until early evening, and on arriving at our destination we immediately joined a crowd of Indian yogis who were waiting for Shri Mataji to come for a public programme. She arrived in a bullock cart decked out with flowers and palm leaves, and enthusiastic people with loud, raucous musical instruments appeared, leading a leaping, dancing throng waving flaming torches in procession ahead of her.

The excitement was infectious and it was easy to enter into the spirit of things, so we joined in and danced our way into a nearby village. The simple village buildings had a timeless beauty in the flickering torchlight, and the public meeting in the village square, under the trees and the starlit sky, was equally picturesque. At the end of the programme, a mob of villagers tried to get to Shri Mataji, and we had to form a barrier to let them through a few at a time, struggling back and forth with linked arms before a dense crowd of people.

At about midnight we ate and then boarded the buses again, travelling for two or three hours to a complex of huts near a dam, where we crashed out for a few hours. We were up early next morning eating breakfast when an urgent summons came to jump on the buses again, and off we went, staring back longingly at the huge, steaming urns of tea that had just been prepared. We rattled and banged our way past fascinating but relentless rural scenery all day and well into the night, and arrived at a scattered complex by the sea at about one o'clock in the morning, where we learned that a programme was in progress.

There were a lot of Indian yogis with Shri Mataji under an

extensive, lightly roofed area with open sides known as a *pendal*, and she spoke to us all for a time before recommending that we had a 'foot soak' in the sea before sleeping to clear out our chakras, thus beginning a week-long seminar with a couple of thousand Indian Sahaja Yogis. So it was that I found myself standing in the warm sea under a brilliantly starry sky at three o'clock in the morning, feeling utterly shattered but extremely happy, with my ego thoroughly decoupled from its habitual comfort zone.

To be involved in Sahaja Yoga was to go through a process of change in outward collective activity as well as inward experience. One day Shri Mataji told us that the time had come for us to establish permanent centres and ashrams, and the first of a series of major collective Sahaja Yoga building projects kicked off when we bought a large house in Cambridgeshire.

Shri Mataji put a lot of money into it, with those that could afford it contributing money and those that could not, volunteering labour (and some of course volunteering both). I spent a great deal of time there, and we worked hard and had a lot of fun. It was the first time I had been out in the countryside for quite a while, and I really enjoyed it.

We had not been there long when we discovered that the roof and the top floor were riddled with wood rot, and that the weight of the roof was starting to push out the big wooden beams lining the top of the outside walls on which it rested. We needed to dismantle the entire roof, a large structure with two wings and numerous dormer windows, and rebuild it from scratch. We attacked it without a second thought. We had two or three carpenters, but it was going to take a lot more than that to get the job done, and a couple of experienced builders were discovered among Sahaja Yogis in Australia and flown over to take charge of a large number of keen apprentices.

Standard practice would have been to construct a huge scaffold 'roof' while the work went on, but we could not afford this, and Shri Mataji told us she would hold back the rain as long as we worked as fast as we could. We worked flat out seven days a week for about six weeks, and towards the end even the village postman was asking us to hurry up because the local gardens needed some rain.

It was a brilliant experience; we had large sections of the top of the building off at various points, and standing on the top floor was a bit like being on the deck of an aircraft carrier surrounded by miles of beautiful countryside. I loved to lie back on the roof at night and look at the Milky Way, which was wonderfully clear away from the light pollution of London.

It was about this time that my brother appeared on the scene again. The relationship between him, my youngest sister and me had become strained over time as my sister and I learned more about the damage we had done to ourselves and he had continued along the path we had left behind. Then, some ten years or so after we had first met Shri Mataji, we received a somewhat incoherent phone call from him to the effect that he had chewed a few leaves too many and thought it was too late to salvage himself. It wasn't, of course, but he was in a pretty bad state. Fortunately, the big building project we had going on in fairly isolated countryside gave him somewhere to be away from the life he had been leading and plenty of hard physical work to keep him occupied, and he has gone from strength to strength in Sahaja Yoga ever since.

Not long after my brother's reappearance, I went to India for some months, which I thought quite timely as it gave him a chance to find his feet in Sahaja Yoga on his own (my sister had married and was busy looking after numerous children). Shri Mataji herself had plenty to occupy her, with family matters as well as the work she did for Sahaja Yoga, and she had quite a lot of high-powered socialising to do in support of her husband's work as well. In return for all that she did for us, we tried to help with her family obligations where we could, and I jumped at the chance of going out to India to help with the work on the house she was building near Pune for her husband's retirement.

I went in the hope of leaving western ego problems behind and enjoying a nice, high state, but the unconscious had other ideas and plunged me into the deepest and most difficult cleansing process I had ever encountered. The vibrations were certainly incredibly powerful, but their intensity did not plunge me into bliss - it was quite the opposite, with all kinds of horrendous stuff surfacing from my past, and much of this period turned out to be a real ordeal. I felt as if I was living in paradise and being followed around by my own personal family of scorpions, with my psyche endlessly vomiting up every stupid, adharmic thing I had ever done.

All sorts of strange things happened. One night, I dreamt I was living in a house on a beach and a huge wave swept the house away, dissolving it completely. I woke up abruptly feeling quite terrified because I had lost all sense of identity – I had no idea who I was. A long and frightening moment passed, and then I thought, 'How silly, I'm just me, what does it matter who I am?' It makes little sense of course, but I felt quite content to recognise this basic sense of self - and did not entirely welcome the paraphernalia of my everyday personality as it gradually returned.

It was not pleasant to struggle with all this negative stuff in the company of the Indian Sahaja Yogis, but there was little I could do except witness it happening. It would largely clear out when I was actually with Shri Mataji, but I hated feeling any of this stuff when I was near her. I knew she was using the situation to clear out some really heavy things from my system, but it did not prevent me feeling bad about it. Some of the Indian Sahaja Yogis kept a wide berth around such unfamiliar problems, unable to understand them and incapable of imagining them, but others did help where they could.

Indian Sahaja Yogis have a number of advantages over westerners in that they have traditional knowledge of the subtle system, the kundalini and the deities, and they understand what dharma is. They also have little concept of guilt (and have no idea how lucky they are in this respect). Their biggest problem is a tendency to see Sahaja Yoga through the filter of Hinduism, along with a weakness for ritualism and their traditional family gurus.

Many Indian Sahaja Yogis can be of a very high quality indeed, however. I remember one day being alone in the flat where I was living in Pune and struggling with some particularly nasty stuff inside me when a local Sahaja Yogi called on me. He was a lovely, simple man who had previously invited me to the tiny flat he shared with his three daughters for a meal. The flat basically consisted of a couple of little rooms in which every space and piece of furniture doubled up as something else for day- and night-time use, and it was one of the most delightful places I have ever been to. The subtleties of joy playing out in the family were really quite beautiful.

I felt worse than ever when he arrived as I knew he would feel what was going on in my chakras, and, sure enough, he stiffened slightly as he entered, and I could see him focusing his attention within himself. After a few seconds, he began a normal conversation, behaved in a kind and friendly way and stayed for twenty minutes or so. As soon as he had gone, I realised that I felt totally different; he had cleared me out completely. I felt incredible, as if I had been wearing a set of grimy old clothes that had been exchanged for high-quality linen, and I set off down the road to buy some watermelon to celebrate.

As I walked, my buoyant mood intensified, and I began to feel as if I were climbing out through the top of my head, expanding upwards and outwards until I was one big smile floating above the street. It was a striking example of what vibratory awareness could do; I was just left hoping he had not taken too many of my problems onto his own chakras. It was only a temporary reprieve from the clearing out process, but a very welcome one. Watermelon, incidentally, saved me from an unfortunate fate on one occasion. I overindulged one day when they had just come into season and was obliged to remain in close proximity to the toilet instead of going out to a play, and I was thankful when I learned afterwards that it had consisted of one actor playing three different parts, all in Marathi.

I passed a number of personal milestones during this time in India, one of the more memorable being the occasion I was asked to sing 'Jerusalem' to a large gathering of politely interested Indians.

As well as everything going on inside me, I had much to occupy me in the building work at Shri Mataji's house, and I also enjoyed the everyday experience of life in India. I was staying in the same flat as Shri Mataji in Pune and catching the bus out to site and back each day, and I would get off a good distance from home in the evening in order to wander through the backstreets and take in the everyday lives of the people. I loved to wander past the busy artisans, the little shops and houses and the street markets, delighting in the industrious vitality and cheerful banter of the people under the bright illumination of their haphazardly-slung light bulbs.

On site, Shri Mataji organised everything herself, from designing the building to hiring the labour and buying the bulk materials, and arrived each day to supervise proceedings when she was not travelling abroad for Sahaja Yoga functions. As always with her, everything was on a grand scale, and for little more than the cost of a relatively modest London house she constructed a huge, sprawling building of unique design with three stories of large, high-ceilinged rooms, and balconies and cloistered walkways around the outside. She had the exterior clad with a 'crazy paving' of white marble and the balcony roofs tiled with terracotta, and it looked uniquely lovely when it was completed. I had arrived there ostensibly to do plumbing work but ended up working mostly on the ornamental plasterwork, much as I had done at Brompton Square, but on a larger scale.

Shri Mataji had brought some carved stone architectural elements from a dilapidated palace in Rajasthan, and she had these built into the front facade of the house, where they exactly captured the timeless spirit of India. She continued with this theme in other parts of the building as well, by first asking us to make moulds from them so that we could cast replicas in both concrete and plaster to be used at various locations.

Many of the upstairs rooms had balconies for which Shri Mataji wanted balustrades made with old-style dumbbells, and we produced these by making up a design in wood on a lathe and making fibreglass moulds from it, from which we cast the dumbbells in concrete. I had six moulds, each in two pieces and clamped together with nuts and bolts, but even with an accelerant I could only cast three times in 24 hours, making 18 a day, and it was a long, slow business. Prior to the dumbbell operation I had been catching a bus back and forth to Pune, but one of the mould changeovers was at two o'clock in the morning, and so I began sleeping on site.

There were 50 or more itinerant labourers living there in flimsy huts they had constructed nearby, and the facilities consisted basically of one outside tap, so I had an interesting time. Many of the labourers were women, who carried astonishingly large loads of bricks, or concrete and cement in wok-like containers on their heads. They wore dresses of striking, coloured designs with tiny mirrors and ornaments sewn onto them which they kept remarkably clean, and some had babies with them that they buried up to their waists in sand to stop them straying while they worked. I felt quite humbled by the way they laughed and joked with each other despite the hard life they led, and by how tirelessly they worked in the baking sun.

I had a team of helpers, one of whom was related to a couple living in a pump house close by, and I used to pay a small sum for an evening meal with them. Inside the pump house there was a space of about four square metres with a big old fashioned hand-cranked pump in its centre. There, with her husband, lived an extraordinary young woman with six fingers on each hand who seemed like a nymph or an elemental being out of a fairy tale.

There was a kind of domesticated wildness about her quite alien to anything I was used to, as if her personality sprang directly from nature. There was also no electricity – the only light was from the cooking fire, so I had no idea what I was eating. The view from this spot was a pleasant panorama in daylight, but at night, as the rainy season approached, the lightning in the clouds over the distant hills was hauntingly beautiful. It looked for all the world as if the gods were moving about in the clouds with lanterns of sacred fire.

The rainy season came as a welcome change from months of baking heat, at least at first it did. Its onset was quite dramatic; people actually came out and danced about in the streets, and in no time at all the drains were full and the roads had become rivers deep enough for cars to start losing traction. Another surprise was the way the dry, barren landscape was transformed with greenery in little more than a week. There were a few drawbacks; there was a lot of mud about, especially from the spinning wheels of bogged-down cars, and we had to watch out for bad-tempered snakes flooded out of their holes around the site.

One night an enormous storm developed as I was sleeping up in my 'workshop' on the first floor. Infill walls had yet to be built, and horizontal sheets of water were suddenly being blown right through the building. I jumped up and stood behind a pillar in my sleeping bag, marvelling at the power of the storm as its roaring grew quite thunderous and a waterfall began pouring off the roof.

The whole building began to shake, as if it were being engulfed in a huge, roaring funnel of thunderous power, and for a while it felt as if anything could happen. I began to wonder if a tornado was forming, but the storm gradually abated, and I was left to try to sleep standing up behind my dry bit of pillar without much success. Next morning all was well apart from some new minor river valleys that had carved their way across freshly planted ground around the house.

Towards the end of my time in Pune, I began to emerge from my struggle with the demons of the past, and I returned to England feeling remarkably transformed. 'I have given you a new husband,' joked Shri Mataji when she saw my wife.

One of the nice things about Sahaja Yoga these days is that there is always someone to visit and somewhere to stay when you travel; this often involves helping out with local Sahaja Yoga activities of course, but this is a highly enjoyable way to get to know people and to explore another country. Even when I returned to Hong Kong recently, I was delighted to meet a flourishing group of Sahaja Yogis there.

In the early days we tried to visit and help out in countries where a few Sahaja Yogis were carrying a heavy vibrational load, something that still happens in some places, and of course we had to do these things while earning a living and raising a family. On one occasion my wife and I went to separate destinations at the same time to help out with Sahaja Yoga, she to Poland and I to South Africa, while my youngest son stayed with my sister's family and our second son travelled with me. (My eldest son, from my first marriage, was by now living in Australia.)

Cape Town was beautiful and there was a great group of Sahaja Yogis there. I was in South Africa for a couple of months, and towards the end we drove up to Johannesburg, stopping off along the way to give impromptu Sahaja Yoga programmes to people who had heard about Shri Mataji and invited us stay overnight, calling their friends and neighbours over to meet us. I had more or less overcome my stage fright by this time and could cope with public talks, but it was still not my favourite occupation. In Durban enthusiasts from the Indian community organised a fairly large public meeting in a hall with an extremely temperamental sound system, and I carried away the enduring memory of a sea of faces screwed up in agonised bafflement as I stood on the stage trying to compete with the most horrendous screeching noises imaginable.

Sixteen years passed, during which I was reasonably diligent in meditating and working on the problems in my chakras. I had ups and downs and some very difficult times, but the collective support in Sahaja Yoga on both a vibrational and a personal level was invaluable, and we always retained the ability to laugh at ourselves. There was plenty of fun to be had while the deeper problems in the chakras resolved themselves, and I noticed a gradual improvement in the quality of my experience of the subtle system. I was experiencing a more satisfying depth of meditation, and the flow of vibrations in my body became steadily stronger. I rarely felt the flow was cool, though, and my sensitivity to the various sensations from the chakras, either directly in my body or in my hands (and feet), was not as good as that of many others.

I remember arriving early one morning at Shri Mataji's house in Brompton Square, where many of us had been working (the house was a building site), to find that Shri Mataji had arrived even earlier and was sitting there alone. She greeted me cheerfully and then asked me how my vibrations were.

'Put your hands towards me,' she said.

'Oh dear,' I thought, conscious of a number of my current failings. I put my hands out and felt a strong current of vibrations pouring from her but little of the all-important coolness.

'Do you feel the vibrations all right?' she asked.

'Yes, Shri Mataji, but they are a bit, um, warm,' I admitted, a little uncomfortably.

'That's all right,' she replied with a smile, 'you need some warmth in this country.'

Perseverance, I felt she was saying, was acceptable in lieu of perfection, and love was as important as commitment and discipline.

Chapter 20

Knocking on heaven's door

There were advantages and disadvantages to the various adventures I had gone through before encountering Sahaja Yoga. I had done a considerable amount of damage to myself and went through a lot of pain and frustration because of it. Nevertheless, it helped that I had some knowledge of higher dimensions of consciousness, and the struggle I went through in putting myself back together taught me a lot about the kundalini and the chakras. Many who encountered Sahaja Yoga with their subtle systems relatively intact could enjoy a spontaneous experience of thoughtlessness and vibratory awareness without recognising its real significance or potential. They could easily lose the subtle connection if they tried to evaluate the experience through the ego's mental perceptions and conditionings instead of nurturing its growth and development.

I had accepted Shri Mataji's assertion that we had to work towards a collective spiritual ascent in terms of both Sahaja Yoga and the destiny of humanity. She said that what she called the 'second stage' of self-realisation - the flowering of overt divine experience - would be a broadly collective happening that would start to manifest when we were ready for it. This was certainly more satisfactory from an evolutionary perspective than the self-interest of the individual ascent - as Christ said, 'The first will be last and the last will be first' - but I longed to return to the fabulous dimensions of existence I had known on LSD.

In fact I was close to becoming re-acquainted with such heavenly realms, but up until now, apart from a few brief episodes, my consciousness had been pretty much grounded in the everyday world.

It had been far from boring, though; the years had passed quickly and I had had an amazing if challenging time. I had gained a lot of experience and insight into the workings of the subtle system, and my life had been enriched in many different ways.

At first, when the kundalini rose with any force, it tended to become stuck in the Nabhi chakra in my solar plexus or the Anahat chakra in the heart, and when this happened the whole system seemed to work against itself in chaos and confusion. The kundalini would pulsate erratically in my stomach or in my chest, caught up in an intense, urgent excitement, and I was unable to establish the calm or stable basis for its further ascent. The left and right sympathetic systems appeared to be fighting with the central power of ascent and with each other, as if they were each struggling separately to resolve the problem, with the result that I never got off the ground.

It was incredibly frustrating and infuriatingly difficult to resolve, reminding me of the story of the monkey with its hand stuck in a narrow-necked jar. The creature reached in to grasp some food but could not pull its hand out again without letting go of the prize and, unable to give this up, remained trapped. I had to learn to extricate my ego and superego from their obsessive agendas, work on the subtle system with the clearing techniques Shri Mataji had taught us and allow the kundalini to heal and strengthen the chakras. It was a cyclic process of change and transformation that required patience, but it was stable and balanced and worked itself out on multiple levels. It allowed me to confront the root causes of the problems on the chakras without becoming overwhelmed by them, and to steadily build my knowledge of the strengths and weaknesses of my subtle system as I penetrated deeper into the psyche.

The kundalini was both ever present and elusive at the same time. I could usually feel vibrations flowing in my body, no matter how faintly, but it could manifest more forcefully and withdraw back into itself for no apparent reason. There was always a reason of course; it was a matter of developing the subtlety of attention to recognise it. Many things could affect the kundalini positively or negatively once it was awakened, but the ego required a great deal of re-education in this respect.

The ego feared and resisted the divine, in fact. I noticed, for instance, when I was in a higher state, that the involuntary shiver of excitement I sometimes experienced racing up my spine was not what it seemed. At a higher 'frequency' of consciousness, this took place almost in slow motion, and I could see it was a violent reaction by the ego and superego to a spontaneous surge by the kundalini. Powerful tensions clamped down instantly to suppress the rising energy, and the 'shivering' appeared symptomatic of a considerable struggle taking place at lightning speed before the ego regained control.

I had quite a bit of difficulty establishing the clarity and simplicity of the Mooladhara chakra at the base of the spine. Much time had to pass before I experienced positive vibratory manifestations in this chakra, and it was strange and delightful when it happened - as if an air conditioner had been switched on in my nether regions! Physically, a 'catch' on this chakra manifested as a deep, painful aching, as if in the bone at the base of the spine, that could sometimes extend into the pelvis and the thigh-bones. An unpleasant, hot tingling could also often be felt at the base of the spine and in the heel of the palms of the hands. Personally, I also registered problems from this chakra quite strongly in the heels of my feet. Vibratory sensations related to each of the chakras could be experienced in specific parts of the feet and body, in fact, but often less distinctly than this.

Life when the Mooladhara was 'caught up' was uneasy, with a susceptibility to boredom and self-consciousness, not to mention a tendency to read sexual nuance and innuendo into everything and everyone around me. Simple joy – as opposed to ego gratification – was impossible, confidence and spontaneity were somewhat contrived, and the kundalini would keep falling down or would not rise at all. There were many subtle qualities to this chakra, most of which went right over our heads to begin with. One evening, on our first trip to India, Shri Mataji spoke to us in great depth about the problems in the Mooladhara chakra in the west, and that night I had a horrific dream in which I saw that the heel of the palm of my left hand, which registers the vibratory sensations from this chakra, was completely eaten away. A gaping hole remained, exposing the bone and layers of disintegrating flesh like ragged strata in a cliff face. It was a disturbing image that stayed in my mind for a long time.

Vibratory information from the Nabhi chakra in the solar plexus registered in the middle fingers. I could also feel all manner of aches, pains and dramatic physical reactions in the stomach area caused by difficulties with this chakra, including stomach upsets, wind, diarrhoea and even vomiting. This was responsible for an interesting, if embarrassing, episode when I accompanied Shri Mataji on a plane ride to Italy, having been invited to help choose bathroom appliances and tiles for the ongoing works in the house in Cambridgeshire. As I sat next to her on the plane, I felt some fairly spectacular activity start up in the Nabhi area, various aches and pressures pushing and heaving about that started to produce some remarkable gurgling noises. This activity escalated steadily throughout the flight, although the sound was somewhat muted by the background noises of the plane. Certainly Shri Mataji made no mention of it, and we talked normally about various things that were going on in Sahaja Yoga.

When we arrived in Milan, we were met by lots of Sahaja Yogis who quickly departed with Shri Mataji, leaving me to follow in another car a little later. Arriving at the flat where Shri Mataji was staying, I found she was in deep meditation with a room full of Sahaja Yogis sitting in silent meditation around her. I sat down with some foreboding and, sure enough, the grand symphony in my stomach achieved new heights of volume and virtuosity, greatly magnified in the profound silence, and treated me to the most self-conscious meditation of my life.

The agitated, erratic pulsation that could occur when the kundalini was blocked at this chakra was a very physical sensation too and was sometimes quite visible in the body, both in the stomach area at the front and close to the spine in the corresponding area at the back. It felt a bit like trying to stand in quicksand and seemed to epitomise the restlessness and discontent that defects in this chakra gave rise to. When properly established, though, the Nabhi had the opposite effect, generating a broad sense of stability, balance and satisfaction and a temperament inclined to competence and consistency in life.

The Swadhisthan chakra was associated with the Nabhi chakra and, according to Shri Mataji, could act all around the perimeter of the void that encircled the Nabhi. It was difficult to pinpoint in the body, but vibratory sensations could manifest painfully enough in the pelvic and stomach area when problems were highlighted. In the hands it registered in the thumbs, and stabs of pain, heat, aches and heavy tingling sensations could extend right down into the ball of the thumb if the catch was deep enough. This chakra was doubly problematic for me because I had both done physical damage to my liver and kidneys and become entangled with the illusions and delusions of negative psychic entities, all of which came under its remit.

The creative mental and physical faculties of my right side were shattered and drained, my quality of attention dull and restless and the pure knowledge of the left Swadhisthan overlaid by a hotchpotch of indiscriminate experience, things I had read, speculation and hearsay. I had acquired a lot of information via copious amounts of the printed word and found I had absorbed a lot more than just facts, suppositions and convictions from them.

Everything I put my attention on reacted with the subtle system, and it seemed that immersing myself in a book was a particularly intense way of doing this. It appeared to grant an inside track into the psyche, and I discovered that my chakras could differ considerably from my ego in their opinions on the quality of literature, especially where spiritual subjects were concerned. I could put my hands towards a book - or even simply place my attention on it - and feel anything from a strong flow of cool vibrations to some extremely unpleasant 'catches', and I learned that these things could affect me in all sorts of subtle ways. It applied to music as well and, perhaps to a lesser extent, to television and movies.

Left Swadhisthan catches made the psyche prone to illusion and fantasy and were difficult to get rid of. I found it hard to extricate myself from ideas I had mentally identified with, even when I could feel negative reactions to them in the chakras. The ego's capacity for mental projection seemed to encompass a distinct reluctance to let go of beliefs it had held to be real, and a stubborn persistence in clinging to belief systems that could be inversely proportional to their credibility. An unreal spookiness often lurked in off-centre spiritual pursuits, that was very different from the rich, auspicious nature of vibratory awareness, but some people could be quite insensitive to the difference between the two.

Vibrational information from what Shri Mataji called the 'void', the gap in the parasympathetic nervous system corresponding to the 'ocean of illusion' in the Virata, registered in the area encircling the centre of the palms of the hands. It could also be directly experienced in the area surrounding the solar plexus and, in my case, could give me cramps right across the body, although they might be anchored more on the left or the right side. I became mainly familiar with the negative reactions from this aspect of the subtle system to begin with, both through facing repercussions from my own past and through encounters with some of the more obscure and extreme practices being experimented with by some of the seekers I met.

The void was home to the guru principle and related to the self-discipline and balance required to manage the spiritual ascent, but it also manifested the confidence and certainty about spiritual reality that the vibratory awareness of the subtle system bestowed. Its positive qualities generated an enthusiasm for the spiritual ascent, a simple enjoyment of austerity and discipline and a clean-cut sense of meaning and purpose in life.

My heart chakra was as badly damaged as the Vishuddhi chakra in my throat, if not more so. The arrhythmic pounding I had felt in my heart for years proved to be symptomatic of a great deal of hurt - physical, emotional and spiritual - that had been compounded by the trauma of my nemesis trip. Part of my trouble seems to have been a predisposition to open up too much to people and make myself vulnerable in an age when many hearts were closed, or masked by heavy conditioning. At a certain level, human emotion gave way to the love of the divine, and unconsciously confusing the two could have dramatic repercussions. It was always all or nothing with me, and I reacted violently to rejection, deliberate or otherwise. The deepest aspect of the heart chakra was the reflection of the spirit on the left side, the essential spark of divinity that sustained existence itself, and I had acted against this principle in a big way by flinging myself into self-destructive extremes in life.

The damage to my heart chakra was so deep, Shri Mataji told me, that my ego perceived the ability to feel as a matter of life and death. I learned to calm the heavy agitation and tension in my heartbeat in meditation over many years but small, anxious and apparently random palpitations could still occur. If I went deep enough, I could see that these little flutters of uncertainty took place as the ego began to surrender its grip and I stood poised to open up to life and love at the deepest level - to re-establish oneness with the primordial being. Sometimes the tenuous connection would be made and sometimes it wouldn't, but everything would clam up again all too easily. The heart chakra registered in the little fingers, and its activities, emotional, spiritual and physical, were plainly obvious. Pains in the heart area could sometimes be so dramatic they raised fears of a heart attack and surges of joy so intense they invoked tears of wonder.

Vibratory information from the Vishuddhi chakra registered in the index fingers, and the condition of this chakra affected the sensitivity to vibratory sensations in the hands from all the chakras, which was something I had problems with from the start. I was conscious of the tension in the Vishuddhi chakra in my throat before I met Shri Mataji, and afterwards the pressure in my neck and shoulders became massive. Even then, I would often realise I was holding myself taut in postures I was locked into as a result of tension in my neck and shoulders, especially when driving, in confrontational social situations or at work. Sometimes the tension was so pronounced it seemed to extend right down into my legs.

The most extraordinary thing was the way that this chakra would sometimes open out and cause the pressure to vanish. When this happened, the relief was amazing, and the way the pressure could reappear was pretty extraordinary too. At the beginning its reassertion could be sudden and dramatic, but as time went by the chakra closed down in a subtler way. I would feel a light pressure begin to constrict the smooth flow of energy in my neck, pushing in from each side. At first it would not seem significant, just one discordant note in a song, and it would seem surprising somehow when the constriction increased, as if its absence was normal and its reappearance alien and wrong. But reappear it would, the pressure growing until it formed a solid block from shoulders to jaw and clamped tightly around the sides of the temple. My throat often ached too, with that strange intensity that occurs in highly charged emotional situations, as if powerful feelings were dammed up there. I often had to resist the urge to cough or swallow away the discomfort if the kundalini moved with any force through the Vishuddhi. It was a strange experience, not painful in the ordinary sense, but unbearable just the same, bringing tears to my eyes and an almost irresistible urge to escape it.

An interesting experience was the unexpected reappearance of the fluctuating sense of expansion and contraction I had felt as a child. It occurred while I was meditating one day and was exactly the same oscillation between being very tiny and absolutely huge that I remembered, except that I was now precisely aware that it originated in the Vishuddhi chakra in my throat.

Vibratory information from the Agnya chakra in the forehead registered in the ring fingers. Problems with this chakra were pretty much all-pervading in the western lifestyle, very apparent in all the excessive mental activity and the constant clash of egos. The endless, meaningless chatter of the mind and the restless shifting of the attention were a kind of modern insanity, a constant evasion of reality and an obsessive preoccupation with the past and the future. Tension in this area could be experienced before self-realisation, but afterwards a 'blocked Agnya' was an obvious affliction, with the pressure of the kundalini pushing up tightly behind the eyes and forehead and making the inside of the head feel as if it was tied up in knots.

Many conventional forms of mediation directed the mind to imagine restful and positive scenarios to calm the psyche, but this barely scratched the surface where the Agnya was concerned since it was responsible for generating the mental activity in the first place. I found that the only successful way of transcending the Agnya was to bring the attention into the present in thoughtless awareness and allow the activities of the ego and superego to recede while the kundalini pushed up through the centre. Of course this was not possible until the first strands of the kundalini had risen through the innermost channel of the subtle system and achieved the connection with the all-pervading power. It could be difficult for even this minute shoot to penetrate the Agnya, but once it had done so a natural state of meditation could occur spontaneously, if only temporarily. It took much longer to work through the complications of the ego and superego and establish thoughtless awareness as a natural state of being.

As the kundalini widened and my meditation deepened, higher

energy levels began to manifest and the tensions in the Agnya started to resolve themselves. The involuntary twitching of my eyes slowed as they ceased to rigidly avoid the here and now, and the pupils began to alight tremulously on the elusive intensity of the present moment. My eyes started to sting, a kind of 'peeling onions' effect taking place as subtle nerves delicately unfolded, and the tears of love began to flow. The relief as such deep-rooted tensions started to release was wonderful, but the ego still shied away from it, trying to glance aside and blink the tears away at the slightest pretext.

Vibratory sensations from the Sahasrara chakra in the crown of the head registered in the centre of the palms, and 'catches' on this chakra usually indicated an egotistical or heavily conditioned view of life, especially where spiritual truth was concerned. The Sahasrara was probably the area where I experienced most vibrational activity to begin with, and sometimes in the early stages it was the only part of the subtle system that showed any signs of life at all. Typically a subtle flow of cool energy was experienced rising from the top of the head when the kundalini was raised; a 'cool breeze' that could be felt literally blowing cool high above the head by placing a hand there. Some people felt a sense of pressure building up at the top of the head before this happened, or heat being released before the flow cooled down.

Each of the chakras related to a different part of the Sahasrara and as time went on I could feel various vibratory sensations all over my head. It was surprising how sensual the release of deep-rooted tensions in the Sahasrara chakra could be. Pleasure and pain mingled in a deeply satisfying way as numbed and bruised nerves came back to life. Specific points of pressure appeared and disappeared with slow deliberation, and long, delicate tendrils of sensation unwound themselves to flow in liquid-cool dissolution and relief. At other times excitable whorls and patterns of exhilaration raced around the scalp, gushing with energetic rushes of cool vibrations.

Many of these sensations were symptoms of the ego and superego dissolving, and I had to wait a long time before the Sahasrara started to fully come to life. When this happened, everything could come together in the most amazing way. I felt completely free, whole and complete, with all tension gone from my body in a silky-smooth sense of ease. The jumble of glitches in my subtle system was miraculously resurrected into a single, fully integrated instrument, precisely tuned into the matrix of energies I perceived all around me. The chakras functioned as one, and a single all-seeing, all-knowing focus of perception opened in the centre of my being. The possibilities were boundless, but I also felt wide open and vulnerable – a rush of awe and exhilaration battling with a precarious sense of balance and control. Part of me still anticipated pain or oppression when such experiences took place. I would sometimes feel a bit like a kind of amateur silver surfer, and I knew it would take time before real stability could be established.

I had to go through a lot before this started to happen, but much of what I experienced along the way was just as magical and intriguing; the collective being of the Virata was made up of countless dimensions of beauty and wonder, and the kundalini began to take me through many of them, presumably in an effort to repair the harm I had done to my subtle being. I had kept myself occupied with the day-to-day experience of Sahaja Yoga for many years and had almost forgotten the higher dimensions of consciousness I had once known. Then, quite unexpectedly, the day came when I began to awake into these fabulous realms again and the wondrous delights of the divine returned like a long-lost friend.

It happened on Shri Mataji's birthday. A puja was being held to celebrate the event, but I had not gone to it because I had an exam the following day, and I was studying at home. Taking a break from my work, I passed a newly framed photograph of Shri Mataji we had recently been given, and for no particular reason I paused for a few seconds to look at it. Suddenly, without warning, the picture seemed to come to life, and I felt I had awoken abruptly out of a dream:

My eyes feel incredibly relaxed and fused with a blissful energy that permeates everything in existence; light flows through them in a tangible stream. My vision merges with a subtle new field of perception that lifts the veil of the everyday world with a feather-light touch, penetrating its illusory nature. For a long moment I glimpse a stunning divine reality, a luminous existence of wondrous bliss that forms the foundation of this physical existence, yet flows eternally far beyond everything we know.

A profound recognition rocks me to the core of my being. I know I have touched the divine, and I want desperately to grasp this bliss, to seize this vision revealed so unexpectedly before me. I cannot cling to it, however, and fall away from it.

Immediately afterwards, looking again at Shri Mataji's photograph, I realise that something remains open or awakened in me. I find myself looking at the Agnya chakra in the centre of Shri Mataji's forehead. It has become beautiful and golden, and my attention seems somehow to roll or be drawn effortlessly upwards in a blissful sensation of surrender and release.

Awe fills me as Shri Mataji's face becomes that of a divine patriarch; timeless and golden, the essence of authority, nobility, dignity, beauty and love itself. Is this the reflection of Shiva? - Of the divinity within my own soul? I do not know. I know only that I have entered the kingdom of God.

These few moments triggered a continuous flow of experience that built steadily to a peak over the next few days and lasted, in only gradually declining intensity, for several weeks after that. I was quite unaware at first of the ongoing spiritual 'happening' that began to unfold within me. Over the next few hours, I did notice a subtle sort of 'spiritual essence' that seemed to permeate my surroundings, together with a lingering undercurrent of magical joy that evoked memories of Christmas as a child. I assumed at first that this was a kind of 'after-effect' of my experience with the photograph, but by the next day the experience had enveloped me completely. This is some of what I wrote about it at the time:

I am walking along the road, and I feel as if a light bulb has been switched on inside me. I have a distinct impression of Shri Mataji's presence existing within and around me, bestowing a subtle yet profound sense of lightness and holiness on my being.

I begin to feel Shri Mataji's presence very intensely along the whole length of my spine. She takes the form of a friendly, self-illuminated column of consciousness that also shines inside my head. The top of my head feels 'open' and very light. I feel that the top of my head has become like Shri Mataji's head. Instead of my own hair, I feel it is Shri Mataji's hair that is growing there. I feel alive in a completely new way. I am part lost in wonder and part anxious that it will all go away again.

As hours and days pass, I feel myself increasingly to be an elusive, detached personality passing through everyone and everything around me. The image of the timeless archetypal figure, indescribably beautiful, is now reflected back at me from the eyes of everyone I look at. I begin to feel I am everywhere and nowhere at once.

I do not feel any barriers between myself and others. I have nothing to fear in this world because I am enveloped by a profound sense of oneness that binds everything into an ocean of love. Looking at other people in the street, I see only one playful, divine personality smiling back at me from everyone.

My heart is open and overflowing with joy. I want to be an artist, a poet, a musician to express this joy. I begin to take an ecstatic delight in everything I do. I feel quite detached from my body and yet the simplest physical act, walking, sitting, eating, cleaning my teeth - even just breathing - is supremely satisfying.

I feel time itself is slowing down, or maybe I am speeding up. I am aware of a series of images of myself following and anticipating my actions. I am not sure which one is really me, but I am enjoying myself so much that I don't really care. My every movement leaves golden traces in the air.

The material world is fading, dissolving, appearing more and more unreal like a myth or a dream. I feel I am awakening out of a dream. Only the dimension of spirit that I exist in is real, more intensely real than anything I have known.

I am aware of my dream-like body, which seems somehow small and below me. I feel that to die and leave my body would be a matter of no particular concern; it would mean only changing one dimension of existence for another. It would mean no more to me than moving from one room to another within my own home. I feel that a lifetime in a human body is a very short time indeed.

I see that the spirit permeates and transcends the material universe and all matter is reduced abruptly to an illusory, uniform 'stuff' that I look down upon as I would the cloud layer from an aeroplane. The transition is stunning; I have escaped from a dull and oppressive material existence, and the luminous beauty of the divine shines through the dissipating fog of space-time. With a delightful sense of freedom, I realise I have left all of my past, my past lives, the whole history of evolution behind me.

With growing wonder I realise that my sense of identity has grown rather than diminished in this new, subtle existence. I become aware that I have a subtle body. I feel blissfully relaxed, almost as if I am clothed in soft, silk-like garments. I feel a profound sense of dignity; I am wearing a beautiful crown that has a kind of fan radiating out from the back of my head, and I realise it is an expression of a chakra that is open.

I recognise my state of consciousness as that of a deva, a celestial being out of Hindu mythology. With sudden insight I realise this is a higher or more subtle expression of the divinity of the soul, and I marvel at the accuracy with which it has been depicted in the ancient Hindu scriptures.

I feel pure and serene. The material world becomes real again, but now I appear to be seeing it from another dimension. Everything looks divinely beautiful and deeply profound. A golden eye floats in the air before me, and I feel I am witnessing not so much a human drama as a divine fairy-tale. I look at Sahaja Yogis around me and they all look like divine beings, like devas. It is like taking part in a scene out of an ancient Hindu epic. The girls look like celestial princesses, with beautiful ornaments decorating their foreheads.

As I wander through this enchanted fairyland, I feel that my awareness is being carried further into unknown realms. I become aware of a sort of current or stream of particles flowing from my back, leaving a trail behind me as I move. It begins to feel as if long, delicate wings are growing from my shoulder blades.

I go through more changes. I feel more and more blissful. I am becoming conscious of a vast, unimaginably ancient divine realm, a kind of 'divine super civilisation' existing in the depths of eternity. It seems to be inhabited by fabulous, immortal beings whose origin and purpose form part of a much greater story than that of our physical universe, but it is far beyond my comprehension. It is overwhelming, awesome, and yet it is so familiar. It is where I belong. It is the home of my soul.

Gradually I realise that I am a fabulous being myself. I have a divinely beautiful form and a timeless knowledge and understanding. I have huge, stunningly beautiful wings. I am an angel! I look at other Sahaja Yogis and see the same being reflected back from each of them. I see no difference between the sexes at this level, or perhaps they complement one another so completely I cannot tell them apart. In the spirit it seems we are all angels, sleeping in the kingdom of God and dreaming of this transitory existence. It is all too much - and yet it does not end here.

Day after day I move through ever-changing dimensions of consciousness. I go to sleep in bliss and wake up in bliss. The cool breeze flows strongly. The everyday world seems to have no real substance; everywhere I look I see only manifestations of my inner nature reflected back as from a mirror. I feel I am being taken on a journey through the mind of God. Each day, each hour, the bliss is different, each form it takes expressing its own unique beauty. Each state is completely satisfying, and yet every time a new dimension of bliss and revelation follows that is, if anything, even better.

- *I am a Buddha-like golden being emerging from a lotus. I am rising from a great primordial egg, while all around me awesome cosmic energies dance in myriad dazzling patterns in celebration of my awakening.*

- *I am dissolving in an ocean, swimming in and out of my eyes like a fish. Everything looks divine. An electric lamp looks exquisitely beautiful. The simple design on a carpet sends a thrill of joy through me and makes the whole room ripple with life and colour. Every object seems to bear the hallmark of its divine creator.*

- *I feel the presence of Christ shining within me like a dazzling sun of divine glory more beautiful and precious than all the jewels of the earth. I feel profoundly relaxed yet full of light and power, and possessed of a tremendous strength and confidence. A beautiful, soft, luminous lightning flows through me, flows from my finger-tips. I feel I could touch anyone and cure them of any disease; I feel the kundalini, the primordial divine power, rising within me like the tip of a mountain of ecstatic bliss that could make the whole universe burst into song.*

201

- *Delicate petals unfold within me. I peep out at the world from a secret, inner self of subtle beauty and joy. A timeless innocence and purity fills my consciousness, and I recognise the 'personality' of a divine archetype manifesting within my being. It is Ganesha. I am filled with an overwhelming sense of auspiciousness and my nose has become an elephant's trunk. I look at my small son. I see how simple-hearted he is. I feel the purity of Ganesha rise in me, in him. He looks at me. We are lost in each other's eyes, absolutely one in the same, innocent being.*

- *My consciousness soars high above me like a great eagle, looking down in complete detachment and pervading everything with a presence that is light and subtle yet vibrating with power and dignity. I feel the kundalini within me like a subtle golden rope with many strands.*

- *I feel Shri Mataji's presence in the form of a golden goddess in my spine. Symbols and patterns of breathtaking beauty and simplicity float in the air, expressing ever-greater depths of divine love and bliss. Wondrous designs, ravishing beyond imagination, frame magical doorways into fairytale worlds.*

- *I awaken into majesty and splendour. I see chakras opening out their petals like beautiful flowers. My spine feels strong and substantial like a kind of massive, richly decorated totem-pole. A dynamic authority crackles like lightning in me. It seems to flash directly between my spine and those of people around me, communicating forcefully with them on a profoundly spiritual level.*

Numerous states of consciousness come and go for which no description is possible. I do not have to make any effort to experience things – on those occasions when I try, they go away. I am often vividly aware of Shri Mataji's presence. Sometimes I feel as if her personality is surrounding me and at other times I am aware of a shining image of her within me, as though she is sharing these experiences with me.

Music is a whole new experience. It has a magical intensity that strikes powerful responses from deep within my being. Almost any music is a joy to listen to, seems divinely beautiful - a mysterious, primordial language with a life all of its own that conjures up the essence of the higher worlds in a way that words could never do. As the material world dissolves into a mythical dream, only music resonates in the spiritual realms beyond.

I see no negativity in anyone or anything; beauty shines everywhere. Only modern architecture is dull and lifeless. I see that each human being reflects different dimensions of the divine in his or her personality, with some who are especially blessed making good use of their talents and others exploiting them for personal gain. People in the streets and actors or politicians on TV are all profound spiritual beings who have forgotten their real nature. Everywhere in nature, in all human relationships, I see the timeless poetry between the masculine and feminine principles of the divine, between glorious majesty and infinite love, as they work to bring enlightenment to their child, Creation.

The pomp and grandeur of a royal state occasion reflects the power and majesty of the collective being, its riches, the beauty of the divine and the royal crown, the open Sahasrara chakra of a realised soul. Many ideas seem to originate from the collective unconscious. Traditional marriage celebrates the primordial symbolism of the union, and the auspicious founding of a new family. Even the humble Christmas tree represents the tree of life, its lights shining with the magical beauty of the chakras and its gifts symbolising the blessings of the divine.

I cannot understand how I feel so pure, where all of my problems have gone. It is as if all the old dirt was only encrusted on the outer skin of the chrysalis and I have emerged as a beautiful butterfly, immaculate and untouched. I realise all the energy, innocence and joy of my childhood had been gradually blotted out by layers of ego. At last I can really like myself again.

As I have a coffee while waiting to meet a friend at Heathrow Airport, a stranger comes to my table. I look up as he sits down and a flood of recognition washes through me. It is extraordinary. I have never met this man before, yet I know him, he is absolutely familiar to me. It is like meeting an old friend unexpectedly in a foreign land, the feeling so strong I almost speak out at once. I pause, telling myself I should evaluate the situation more carefully. The vibrations seem fine; the chakras register nothing negative about the situation. I can see into his inner self and almost laugh out loud as a beautiful, shining, joyous being beams, smiles and waves back at me. (I don't know how else to describe it.) But the man himself is not reacting at all.

I decide to probe a little and strike up a casual conversation. He seems nice enough, an American, but amazingly he seems completely unaware of what is going on. I see that his human consciousness is assiduously identified with his ego despite his higher self being so awake and aware of what is going on; it is quite extraordinary. I realise that something similar happened during my meeting with my 'dream psychedelic partner' in Cornwall, but now I am at a higher place and he is quite unaware on a human level. There is also nothing sexual about it to confuse things. What is it all about? I have no idea. I see that the ego can be completely unaware of the subtle spiritual being within, even when one is quite evolved. Much depends on the circumstances and society one grows up in, I suppose. All I know is that this kind of relationship is timeless, and as I return a silent salute of farewell there is nothing sad about it. I feel that to meet again in ten years or a thousand makes little difference.

I feel I have gone inside a great, hollow building. I am aware of all the chakras in my being. Some have weaknesses, but all are opened out. Only the Sahasrara chakra at the crown of the head is not open wide. I can see the petals of the chakras and the reflections of the divine archetypes that control them.

I watch the Hindu epic The Mahabharata on TV and feel the presence of Krishna, watching this drama about his life from within me. I put my attention on Ganesha and his manifestation fills my awareness. His divinity and holiness is an intoxicating nectar that overwhelms me. I feel utterly pure, and the purity turns into a flood of bliss.

I put my attention on Shri Mataji and I see a great light shining in the distance. I see that my heart has opened out just a little bit, and it sends out a pulse of love. I feel an answering pulse from a great divine heart that waits, open wide, to pour its love into me. I peep into the Sahasrara chakra. It is full of light and an almost overpowering sense of Shri Mataji's presence.

I look at Shri Mataji's photograph. It has become a magic mirror and is reflecting the spirit within my own heart. I am amazed at the beauty I see within myself. My heart is as pure and spotlessly white as snow. I feel more and more blissful. I am golden, blazing with light and impossibly beautiful colours.

I watch a video of Shri Mataji speaking at a public programme. I am astonished at the crystal clarity with which she is speaking, at how plainly obvious the truth is she is proclaiming, and on how many levels her words can be understood. I feel that the people of the future, when they see these videos, will be completely at a loss to understand how so few people have recognised her at the present time.

I am aware of changes and transformations in the Sahasrara chakra on the crown of my head. I feel the vibrations and the chakras more clearly than ever before. Rays shoot out of my body in every direction and a pure essence of spirit keenly penetrates everything around me.

I feel the petals of the Sahasrara chakra opening one by one all over the top of my head in a series of delightful, feather-light eruptions until the whole thing begins to open out and send a torrent of cool breeze pouring down into my body. My head sometimes feels so light and clear it is as if the top half is completely missing, while a bright, golden purity shines within me. I feel cheerful and serene. Sometimes it is Shri Mataji herself, in the form of a deva, who watches smilingly from within.

I am a being whose innate nature is that of deep inner peace, a serene witness of the cosmic drama. Thoughtless awareness is my natural state of being. There is complete relaxation, total comfort, as though I am luxuriantly cushioned by a soft velvet bed of vibrations. I am like a fish in an ocean, completely at ease with the profound depth of silence that envelops me.

The flow of experiences ceased quite abruptly about a month after it had begun, on the day of another puja, that of the Sahasrara chakra at the crown of the head. I just felt as if something had closed in my head, and it was gone. Suddenly I was back down to earth again, and the heavy pressure in my head, neck and shoulders returned, though less violently than before. For some days I felt quite clear and peaceful then gradually returned to a more familiar cycle of struggling with thoughts and working with vibrations on an everyday level. I was left with the impression that I had gone through, or had been put through, a deliberate process of some kind that was as yet incomplete. Certainly it was quite spontaneous and outside my control.

I wrote the experiences down at the suggestion of a friend, and showed them to Shri Mataji to see if she had anything to say. 'I would like to have time to enjoy these things,' was her comment. 'Your attention is moving a little on the left and right, but it is sufficiently anchored in the centre. Now, where are the plans I want to talk to you about ...?' and we were back into the building work. Her message was clear; yes, such things awaited us, but we had to keep our attention on the work at hand.

Chapter 21
A castle in the mountains

Life went on, and Sahaja Yoga grew slowly and steadily. Money was always a problem because Shri Mataji insisted that money could not be charged for awakening the kundalini or for helping people to establish their self-realisation, and we had no way of raising funds for Sahaja Yoga projects other than among ourselves. This we did mostly by contributing money at international pujas (as opposed to local pujas; international pujas were those at which Shri Mataji was present and were attended by people from many different countries) – over the years the money raised has gone into all kinds of Sahaja Yoga projects in different parts of the world.

The house in Cambridgeshire had served us well in England for collective gatherings, but we soon outgrew it, and in 1990 Shri Mataji purchased a huge old mansion in Italy that overlooked a small village in the hills about an hour's drive from Genoa. We then acquired a 'big top' ex-circus tent that was erected on some land down by the river that ran through the valley, and for quite some time international pujas were held there. Instead of staying in hotels, we camped in the big tent or in our own tents around it and brought, cooked and served our food ourselves.

As I have said earlier, the purpose of puja was to awaken the power of the divine within us, something the western ego could find difficult to relate to, as it was used to achieving things through its own efforts. Instead of mental, physical and emotional activity being externalised, the attention was focused inwards and the ego surrendered to allow the divine to manifest. This 'worship' is a somewhat alien concept to many western people, but is an instinct that has long existed in humanity and was perfected in ancient times in India to invoke the blessings of the divine. In its purest sense, worship is a means of focusing the attention intensely on the divine, of invoking the powers of the deities in the chakras and surrendering to the manifestation of the vibrations they release. The required humility brings down the ego and superego and opens up the psyche to the divine, incidentally denying access to divine power by egotistic personalities.

The puja weekends were actually a lot of fun and helped us to face all sorts of things in ourselves, shaking up habits of personal comfort and private space and teaching us to enjoy the company of people from all over the world. They were also very powerful, and the greater the number of people attending, the greater the number of channels for the vibrations and the more powerful they became. They usually took place on a weekend close to the traditional or most auspicious date associated with a particular archetype or aspect of the divine such as Shiva, Krishna or Christ. The energy would build up over two or three days until, at the climax of the puja, every molecule in the body shimmered with vibrations and a thousand subtle processes whirred away in the chakras.

The puja itself consisted of mantras and songs, many of them in Sanskrit, and the offering of symbolic, auspicious substances such as honey, ghee and fruit to Shri Mataji to invoke the blessings of a specific **as**pect of the divine. The effects on the subtle system were intense and ranged from extreme discomfort to profound peace and joy, depending on the condition of the individual's chakras. Whatever we felt, many things worked out in the course of a puja, and by the end of it there was always a deep sense of contentment and collective accord, and the atmosphere would be thick with vibrations. It was often not until we returned to our everyday lives after the weekend that we realised how high we were, and we often continued to be so for days afterwards.

The local Italian community was understandably a little bemused by the whole thing, but, apart perhaps from the priest and a few of his cronies, they soon appeared largely reconciled to having hundreds of people from dozens of different countries wandering around their village. The shopkeepers were delighted at the extra custom, of course, and the majority of locals were cheerful and friendly in a way I cannot really imagine happening in England. They were surprised at how such numbers of people, sometimes two thousand or more, could coexist in such a good-natured way, and indeed these events were really quite wonderful. The vibrations were strong and meditation was effortless, and there were kindred spirits to meet from all over the world.

There was a lot of work needed at the 'castle', as we called Shri Mataji's house, and I spent some months there with dozens of other volunteers from many different countries. It was a big, old building with four floors and walls a metre-and-a-half thick at the base. I spent weeks with a jack-hammer cutting channels down the inside walls for waste and soil pipes; and we constructed a new drainage system around the building and ran it down the hill in a 250mm pipe complete with deceleration chambers, to prevent the locals from being blown off their toilets when it hit the village sewage system.

My sojourn in Italy started in typical Sahaja fashion. Shri Mataji's car had to be transported from London to Italy, and I took it in turns with another Sahaja Yogi to drive it there. All went well until we hit the Italian border at the end of the Mont Blanc tunnel; where the fact that the car was crammed with goodies for the puja didn't go down well with Italian customs, especially as we were carrying numerous presents that Shri Mataji had brought for Sahaja Yogis coming to the puja from afar.

The customs officials were not impressed with our explanation that it was all for a camping weekend, and we were sent back into France to obtain impossibly complicated paperwork. Plan B was to drive a hundred miles or so along the border and try to sneak across on a remote road over the mountains. We planned to position ourselves near the border post during the night and join the first of the traffic going through early in the morning, when we hoped vigilance would be low.

The roads over the mountains were extremely steep, unbelievably bendy and went on for miles, and we unexpectedly shot past the border post, cunningly hidden around a bend, at three o'clock in the morning. We screeched to a halt with clouds of smoke billowing from the overheated brakes on the wheels and could not have looked more conspicuous if we tried. Nor did it help when I opened one of the doors and a big drum of mustard oil fell out and rolled down the hill, but surprisingly we were let through and drove thankfully into Italy, parked up and crashed out for a few hours.

We arrived at the castle in the early afternoon and went to see Shri Mataji, who after some incidental conversation said that she had something she wanted me to do. She showed me her bathroom and pointed out the toilet, which was up in a kind of raised alcove, and said that she wanted to move it down to floor level at another location. The soil pipes from Italian toilets exit straight down into the floor beneath them, and are invariably buried in walls and floors, which meant I had to find where the pipe was running and dig it out of the solid floor on the lower bathroom level in order to connect the toilet in its new position.

'I don't know where the pipe is, Shri Mataji,' I said.

'Try there,' she replied, pointing to a particular spot.

'When would you like me to start?' I asked.

'Straight away,' she said, and promptly went to take a siesta on a bed on the other side of the door, about three or four metres away.

I stood for a while with a hammer and chisel in my hand, thinking about the noise it would make and smiling at the impossibility of the situation. Shri Mataji went straight to sleep, something she could do whenever she chose. Sometimes, when she was working on people with deep problems, she would go off to sleep, saying that she could work things out better in the unconscious. She would ask them to put their hands on their chakras, or towards the ground or out to the open air and fall sleep, awakening briefly every so often to ask them to change what they were doing in various ways.

I felt quite daunted by the idea of trying to break up cement a few metres from where she was sleeping, especially when lots of ladies were tiptoeing about whispering to each other. I gave a small experimental tap on the chisel and then another, and any hopes that I could work quietly steadily evaporated until, after ten minutes or so, I was pounding away as hard as I could. Shri Mataji awoke a couple of hours later, just after I had found the pipe exactly where she had told me to look for it.

It was the start of yet another special episode in Sahaja Yoga in which lots of hilariously improbable things happened, far too many to record here, as well as much profound personal and collective experience. Eventually the circus tent near the village was replaced with a more permanent structure to gather in, and for a number of years many international pujas took place there, probably averaging around five or six a year.

Sahaja Yogis arrived from every part of the globe and it was always great to meet them. Different countries would be given responsibility for specific pujas, looking after the puja ceremony itself as well as logistical arrangements, musical and dramatic entertainment, cooking and serving the food, etc. The entertainment took place over several evenings and included performances by world-class Indian musicians, as well as music, songs, dancing and plays created and performed by the 'host' countries.

These shows ranged from the courageously amateur to the talented and professional and were often unusually original and creative. I remember a dynamic dance sequence choreographed between western classical ballet and traditional Indian dancers that was absolutely stunning. It was an intense and exciting time; there was always a lot happening with the work in the castle, and soon after the last people had departed from one puja, advance parties would begin arriving to start setting up everything for the next.

In the early weeks, the power supply was rather limited, and all the power tools in use often overloaded it. Some of us would be talking to Shri Mataji in her sitting room in the evening when everything would suddenly turn black and the cacophony of banging, grinding, cutting and drilling noises would abruptly cease. She would continue to talk quite normally in the darkness, and eventually someone would find the circuit breaker and the lights would come on again, followed a moment or two later by an all-pervading chorus of machine tools.

Shri Mataji would often call us in to see her and share news about Sahaja Yoga in other parts of the world, or to give us unexpected presents she had picked up on her travels. Occasionally she would invite us to watch videos late at night, usually Indian films. These were always interesting or amusing, but sometimes I would really just want to sleep and had to struggle to keep my eyes open as endless laughing bad guys with big moustaches filled the screen.

It was a pretty extraordinary time, and one from which many

images of Shri Mataji remain vividly imprinted on my mind. In perhaps the most powerful of these, she is sitting utterly still and in complete silence in her bedroom one afternoon as a dense cloud of white dust from an angle grinder pours in under a doorway on the other side of the room. The dust rises steadily towards the high ceiling, lit a pure brilliant white by the light from the windows, and drifts slowly across the room to descend onto her silent form. I had just walked in, and the sight was so stunning and its beauty struck so deep I could not react at first, despite the threat posed by the dust to her beautiful sari and the lovely furnishings in the room – or perhaps it was her complete indifference that held me. It was an astonishing sight.

Around the beginning of the time I spent in Italy, I had another high experience that started during a music programme on the evening before a puja:

I am listening to the Indian musicians performing on the evening before the puja and begin to notice new levels of delight and appreciation of the music. I recognise that a new subtle experience is starting to take place and I feel a thrill of excitement and anticipation.

The sound becomes more and more delightful until the individual notes seem to hover in the air like shimmering jewels of magical joy. I see them collecting in beautiful patterns high in the air near the top of the big circus tent, weaving a divine enchantment that lifts everyone higher and higher into the spiritual realm.

What happens when Shri Mataji arrives a little later is absolutely astonishing. It is like the sun coming out in the middle of the night. The sudden manifestation of a divine presence in our midst is overwhelming and unmistakable; countless glories spill and pour from her being with every step that she takes.

The Sahasrara chakra at the top of my head opens out and a dazzling vision of divinity manifests itself. I behold a great golden being that seems to oscillate through many levels of consciousness and whose magnitude and brilliance surpass them all. I feel I have stepped beyond the reflection of the divine in my own soul and entered into a universal arena.

A large, cool flame burns silently in my heart, its living essence at one with infinity, and a vast, majestic lotus fills my vision like a great celestial city in the sky. Everything about it, its beautiful colours, its royal simplicity, its very essence, seems a subtle expression of Shri Mataji's personality.

The remainder of the evening passes in deep delight. The music scintillates in sparkling tones of joy, the notes twinkling like bright Christmas lights against the magical backdrop of eternity. I want the music to go on forever, and the later it becomes the more wide-awake I feel. Its magic returns next day at the puja, although less intensely, and I feel weaknesses highlighted in my chakras. Still it lingers for a day or two before disappearing.

The elements played a prominent part in my time in Italy. The summer was baking hot, but it began to rain in autumn and at times it seemed as if it would never stop. The village was at a fairly high altitude, with the result that for long periods we were literally living inside a cloud, and this sometimes seemed to complement the surreal atmosphere in the castle. Shri Mataji spent a great deal of time there, and the vibrations built up steadily until the whole place hummed with energy.

It was not all bliss, though; people often felt amazing for the first week or two, but then weaknesses in the subtle system could start to reveal themselves and confrontations begin to take place with deep-rooted problems. It was something I had been through before in India and become used to, and in any case it was much lighter this time around. Some people found it too much and left, but most managed to face the music. Despite this serious side to the purpose of our stay and the hard physical work we did, life there was always extraordinary and I wouldn't have missed it for the world.

We had limited washing facilities for a lot of the time and many of us went down to wash in the river in the evenings, after which we would have a cappuccino and a game of table tennis at the 'young persons' bar' in the village (so named because it was frequented by elderly Italians with time on their hands). Among the regulars was a local policeman who used to leave his machine gun hanging over a chair while he moved around the other tables chatting to people.

The river water was extremely cold, and I began shampooing my hair first so that I would be forced to go into the water to wash it off.

The cold increased dramatically as winter approached, but we were still swimming in December when there was frost sparkling on the ground and steam rising from the water into the freezing air. My shampoo trick still worked, but even the quickest ablutions left my head completely numb.

We had some really great storms, including one at the end of the last puja of the year that was positively Armageddon-like. The wind built up so much that scores of us had to jump up and hold down the support poles of the big circus tent, and the rain came down in a great deluge. An armada of shoes, customarily left outside, sailed majestically in through the main entrance at the head of a river that had formed in minutes, and mothers plucked sleeping children from its path moments before it reached them.

We received an SOS from the castle; work on the roof had left parts of it open and tarpaulins had collapsed under the deluge, and those of us that had been working there scrambled to get back in any way we could. It was pitch black outside, with huge flashes of lightning illuminating a solid wall of falling water. I saw that someone had got a car going and ran out through impenetrable darkness that alternated violently with blinding white light, the rain hammering all over me like needles, and dived head first through an open window as the car roared off, with my legs sticking out in the rain.

In the castle a waterfall was running down the main staircase, and lots of fun and games ensued on the roof, with much mopping up to be done. By morning the river had become a roaring brown torrent a hundred times its original volume that raged across the whole floor of the valley, and huge rocks crashed and pounded into each other amidst its tumultuous violence with a sound like a sullen giant grinding his teeth.

Various parts of the castle were prepared as a venue for Sahaja Yoga activities and as accommodation for Shri Mataji and her family. Rented accommodation was also made available for yogis and their families who wanted to live there, which helped to pay for the building's upkeep. Shri Mataji paid everyone who was working there full time; although this was something I disliked as I preferred to work voluntarily for Sahaja Yoga, and on several projects she summoned me personally and insisted I take the money.

She also invited several of the key workers to join the India tour at the end of the year without cost, and on this occasion we travelled around southern India in relative luxury in a hired train and things were fairly laid back. It was as if we were being given a treat after all the hard work we had been doing; we were even put up for the night in a five-star hotel in Bombay when our plane missed a connecting flight to Madras, where we had a good laugh over all the unaccustomed opulence and ate everything in sight. After India I went home to London for a couple of months before returning to Italy to work and, around the time of a puja dedicated to Shiva in February, I started to have high experiences again.

This time I notice subtle sensations and changes in perception occurring over a period of two or three days, but once again the experience begins in earnest on the day of a puja, in this case that of Mahashivaratri, or Shiva.

During the puja the divine patriarchal image of my earlier experiences reappears, though subtly, as though at the edge of my awareness. Now grown in stature, it shines in a diamond-bright cascade of fabulous beauty that seems to flood from the gates of paradise itself.

Slowly I notice that my perception of this divine image is beginning to alter. It starts to become infused with a sense of Shri Mataji's presence, and by the end of the puja I am aware of a beautiful form of feminine divinity expressing the familiar essence of Shri Mataji's personality.

The next day, despite some pressure in my head, I feel quite light and relaxed. A gentle coolness flows around my body and a hole seems to float at the top of my head. It opens into a realm of brilliant colour, beauty and joy that shines down to illuminate my whole being.

Shri Mataji's subtle new form has grown more dazzlingly beautiful and now looks down from this paradise directly into my heart. I feel her presence there and thrill at the recognition I feel of her divine nature – marvelling also at the friendly reassurance I feel emanating from her being – and touch for a moment the boundless love I have always looked for.

This glorious, subtle reality shines down on me for the remainder of the day. My body feels empty of everything other than a feather-light awareness of the divine qualities shining in my chakras, while beauty reveals itself in everything around me. I am enthralled even by the beauty I see in the white paint on my paintbrush! An absolute simplicity has come into my being, and I feel the beginning of a perfect joy.

Shri Mataji's bright, divine image hovers in my awareness over the following days, growing all the time in depth and substance. Finally, as I am singing a traditional invocation in praise of the divine mother with other Sahaja Yogis, she emerges suddenly from the depths of my being like the sun bursting out from behind a cloud, and I am dazzled by a flood of divine beauty that leaves me totally stunned.

All of the chakras are seamlessly united in a vision of such blinding, divine splendour it can scarcely be endured – a treasure trove beyond the wildest dreams of humanity. I literally feel as if my brain has become physically numb as it struggles to comprehend the magnitude of it all.

During the next few days I drift effortlessly, my attention drawn deeper and deeper into silence. I feel I am becoming like Buddha, the door to eternity drawing nearer with the growing awareness of the oneness of all things.

I am a wondrous child emerging from a cosmic egg, an ego-less being gazing upon a primordial landscape where the masculine and feminine aspects of God are merged into one, simultaneously emptied of content and fulfilled in completeness.

I see that human beings are truly created in the image of God, each with the potential to rise from this tomb of matter to become something greater than the whole universe. Multiple images of divinity radiate from the Godhead in a seemingly endless stream. I know a profound peace and contentment and linger joyfully in the fathomless honeycomb of the thousand-petal lotus, drinking the precious nectar of God's love.

Again the experiences waxed and waned for weeks before finally ceasing. The churning process went on, but subtle states of existence that once seemed unobtainable now seemed closer at hand. Each time

I awoke from the maya, however briefly or incompletely, my faith in humanity's collective awakening into the divine grew stronger.

Many other things pointed to this as well, for the collective vibrations had changed enormously over the years, and it no longer felt as if we were constantly struggling through an all-pervading soup of inertia. As this weight began to lift, it became easier for Sahaja Yogis to maintain the condition of their subtle systems and to raise the kundalini of others, while newcomers had stronger initial experiences and made faster progress than had been possible in the past.

Chapter 22
Fledgling flight

Yet it has been a long and difficult struggle, and one that Shri Mataji has borne the brunt of, and I have watched her sacrifice everything to work out our problems, taking more and more of our karma on in her being. She has said many times that the only use she has for her body is to work out the problems of humanity, and she has proved that in ways that have been heartbreaking to witness.

I suspect she hoped we would be more capable and that our ascent would be faster. It must be hard for her to understand why we cannot grasp something that is so simple and obvious from the other side of the mirror. Nevertheless, I remain confident that she will achieve her goal and we will awaken to the reality of her vision at last.

One of the trickiest things about Sahaja Yoga is the power of the vision it reveals, and this can be difficult for the ego to cope with, particularly where leadership and organisational responsibility are involved. As our numbers grew, Shri Mataji appointed people to leadership or coordinating roles to organise Sahaja activities in their countries and to communicate between her and the local Sahaja Yogis. These were difficult and demanding roles that could sometimes lead our friend the ego to develop an exaggerated sense of its own importance and of the current depths of its spiritual understanding.

On occasion a certain amount of posturing could creep in, of politicising Sahaja Yoga activities with an eye to one's place in history, and it could create additional friction in the struggle for our collective ascent. However, Shri Mataji always showed great faith and respect towards those she asked to take on a position of responsibility; she largely left them free to do as they thought fit, and would not lightly ask them to stand down. Instead, she reminded us to keep our attention on our inner being and to witness the ego, both our own and that of other people, and the ways in which they reacted to each other. 'There is no greater entertainment,' she would say, and I must admit there have been times when everyone was sharing the joke except the person up at the front doing the talking.

At every stage in Sahaja Yoga, my impression was that Shri Mataji wanted us to learn to stand on our own feet, and learning to cope with organisation, delegation and coordination was all part of the process. Where Sahaja Yogis had weaknesses or ego, she did not encourage us to confront the situation but to witness it as part of a collective play of maya, allowing the actors to recognise and grow out of their problems or eventually become exposed by their folly.

Her approach to self-realisation was much the same; she awakened our kundalini in all faith that we would live up to it, and was patient and forgiving of our mistakes. She did often lambast many of the more idiotic and destructive forms of human behaviour, but always in a general, collective sense. She was invariably gentle and respectful with those she spoke to personally.

It took me a while to appreciate how free I was in Sahaja Yoga because, once it realised how many things it had been doing wrong, my ego leapt from vociferous self-justification to guilty self-condemnation in the twinkling of an eye. This was a notorious hurdle in Sahaja Yoga known as 'left Vishuddhi' that related to the left side of the chakra at the base of the throat. Shri Mataji taught us that, among other things, this chakra represented the relationship between the macrocosm and the microcosm and engendered a sense of greatness and self-respect in the human personality.

She explained that the more the ego crossed the bounds of dharma, the larger it had to grow to bury its dwindling sense of self-worth; and this all came home to roost when the time came for the ego to face itself. This has proved an endemic problem in the west, with its severity exacerbated by the gargantuan stature of the western ego and the huge gulf between western 'culture' and that of the divine. It is certainly much less evident in more traditional cultures, although these can have other problems, such as a deep identification with time-honoured conventions that may be quite rigid or nonsensical.

Shri Mataji was sometimes strict with people, and could ask a lot of them on occasion. My own experience was that she did this rarely and always for a reason, and to those she was particularly concerned about. Her imperative was always to liberate the divine within, and this could sometimes be diametrically opposed to the designs of the ego. As I have said before, Sahaja Yoga is not for the faint hearted, and this was particularly true early on when some people faced tests they could or would not deal with and dropped out.

A few became resentful and critical of Shri Mataji and Sahaja Yoga when this happened, and I was sad about this, but maya is a wonderful thing; one does not have to stray far to lose sight of the path, however, its shifting perceptions of reality can lead full circle to rejoin the trail with new strength and understanding. Some people have left Sahaja Yoga for long periods, worked through all manner of things and returned with new vigour. Some have left for trivial reasons and remained petty in their criticisms and complaints. Others have had a tough time, people I cared about and still do, and I hope to see them again one day.

Several more years passed before the cycles of change and transformation brought me up out of the maya again. This was a really powerful experience and one that made me quite certain that events were gaining momentum. The scale of the vision was awesome, revealing the entire history of humanity to be but a precursor to a glorious, transcendent future, and confirming that the real story of our existence has yet to begin.

The feeling grows over several days, a sense that something is rising from deep within me. It comes to a head suddenly, without warning. There is a great wrench in my heart and I am instantly separated from 'myself' in an extraordinary way. To my astonishment, I am looking at a kind of caricature of myself, a sort of robot running a ridiculous program of fixed attitudes and repetitive routines. I experience a real feeling of shock. This horrendous bundle of madness cannot be me! No, it is not me; but then who, or what, am I?

The next moment I realise I am floating free, a limitless, formless being of pure joy. It is my ego I am looking at, or rather the ego of the limited being I had thought myself to be. Almost immediately, in a way impossible to explain, I recognise that I am looking at the inner surface of a kind of shell that surrounds me. A piece of the shell has broken away, allowing me to become aware of limitless space beyond. It is like a piece of the outer pod of a beautiful divine seed or of a wondrous cosmic egg. I have broken out of my old existence into something new and wonderful.

For hours I remain in an ego-less state. [I do not have a very clear recollection of where I was or what I was doing during this period, only of some of the things I was feeling. Yet I seem to have done the things I needed to do, such as driving a car or speaking to people.] *At some point I experience myself flowing throughout a building, apparently as electricity moving through the electrical wiring system. I also have the exhilarating experience of existing as a small, individual point of consciousness that is free to move anywhere and everywhere. It is like becoming a single pixel in a living 3D kaleidoscope of dancing images that make up the appearance of reality, moving joyously around the room in a sort of carefree conga dance to become randomly a part of everyone and everything. I see Ganesha existing everywhere, formless yet imbued with form, a multi-dimensional being manifesting in three-dimensional space in a way that looks right and yet defies any attempt I make to grasp it. Life is absolutely simple, pure and intense, and everyone has a huge, joyous heart dancing deep within.*

The initial intensity of the experience gradually dies down a little, but continues to flow in the days that follow. I feel powerful emotions. My feelings have come back to life in a way that I have not felt since my youth. They are so intense that at times I find it hard to believe that friends I have not seen for twenty or thirty years are not about to walk in the door.

I feel that this is the real manifestation of Sahaja Yoga, the full potential that Shri Mataji has always talked about. The kundalini and the chakras have gone into action like a dynamic, well-lubricated machine, and vibratory awareness has suddenly become amazing. I can feel everything in my own and other people's chakras with what seems like digital precision. At work I find it hard to concentrate on what people are saying to me because I am so fascinated by the things I am feeling from them.

Mantras work like magic, the primordial cadence of the Sanskrit language at one with the energy of the subtle system. I can hear the power resonating in my voice as I speak; the sound echoing back from the walls of the room as the words rip through time and space and penetrate deeper realities beyond. I need only utter a single mantra to release a flood of vibrations that propel me deep into mediation for hours. It is as if I have been trying to drive a car through slippery mud for years and have suddenly struck firm, dry tarmac. I have only to put my foot down to accelerate with all the power I could wish for.

Deeply profound experiences occur without warning. I sit in front of Shri Mataji's photograph and the bottom half of my body becomes instantly cool. A moment later the top half is completely cool. Then I realise this is just a prelude to the main body of the kundalini rising, and it ascends like a broad, majestic, royal golden cobra. As it touches the top of my head, I touch eternity, and a wall of thoughtless awareness descends. The state of meditation is rock-solid, the detachment absolute, as if the whole world is suspended in glass. I feel I could rap on it and it would ring like steel. I can step back out of my body and stand in the land of the father, of Allah, of Sada Shiva. It is absolutely awesome.

I walk around a DIY store, and it is as if a portal into a higher world has materialised in the air above me. It is a dimension of blissful existence straight out of the Saundarya Lahari *('the flood of beauty', an ancient Sanskrit work describing the qualities of the Goddess). I feel an immaculate, soft, golden-white purity within me, the presence of Ganesha. It is he that is connecting me with this higher existence. I perceive my subtle system as a ladder I need to climb up to this paradise, my body a temporary necessity to be left behind when I reach it. I feel a sort of luminous, blissful umbrella open over the top of my head, golden and lustrous with vibrant colour, as though infused with living gems.*

A slow, broad river of vibrations is flowing up my spine, and the Sahasrara chakra at the top of my head suddenly opens out so wide it seems to turn itself inside out in the most unbelievable way. Immediately I become part of a vast ocean of the Holy Spirit that floods out of me in a great tide. It is almost like a scene from a comedy movie in which someone opens a door in a house filled with water, except that it is an absolutely profound and glorious experience. I am one with the essence of Shri Mataji's personality and ride with her in an outpouring of spirit that flows deep into the eyes of those around me and passes on into eternity.

I smile a greeting as a visitor comes into the room. I am feeling rather like a half-hatched bird of paradise, an enjoyable confusion of vibrations, feathers and petals. To my surprise, a golden ray travels out from my heart and into the person I am greeting. I somehow expect a reciprocal ray to return but instead back comes a whole bundle of information about this person's chakras, complete with attached physical, mental and emotional sensations. I feel like a cartoon character that has inadvertently swallowed something too big for its body. I gulp and my smile becomes a little fixed for a moment, but then I feel my chakras start to work on the problems and I feel happy about that. Within an hour or two everything has worked out and I feel back to normal.

I am walking along the pavement near my house and I feel an intoxicating joy begin to permeate my being. It is as if the whole world is saturated with bliss and it is seeping into me through all of the pores of my skin. I feel totally ecstatic just to exist, and the everyday scene of the street where I live is transformed into the most beautiful place on earth. As I place the key in the lock of my front door, I feel I am a character in a magical fairy tale, living a perfect, utterly fulfilled existence.

Deep in sleep, I dream of a great mountain of bliss. It is a great, eternal flame, luminous, blissful; incandescent with cool, white fire. It is the absolute promise of immortality. I cry out and run to place my hands at the foot of the mountain. The light is pure, divine love, and my hands become fused to its surface. A miraculous power flows into my arms, transforming the molecules of my being into a blissful, divine substance. I am instantly wide awake and sit bolt upright in bed, yelling in excitement.

As before, music has become absolutely magical, but this time I am much more sensitive to its quality. There are not many pop songs I really enjoy listening to, and some seem much on a level with television, which mostly seems incredibly stupid or horribly violent. Western classical music is pleasant, but Indian classical music is in a class of its own. It is so obviously in tune with the divine. The base rhythm of the tabla resonates with the oneness of the primordial being, and the crystal-clear notes of the sitar create specific tones of joy directly within my being. Rather than me listening to the instruments, it is as if the instruments are playing me, creating a beautiful melody of feelings in my subtle system.

I watch Shri Mataji walk onto the stage at the Albert Hall [one of a series of programmes we held there] *and she seems to become a gigantic being that has to crouch down somehow in order to fit into the suddenly tiny space of the great auditorium. Her body is a limitless storehouse of spiritual treasure, and I know if I can only open myself up to her she will fill me with all the divine riches I can hold. Only a tiny part of myself is open to her, though, and it eagerly tries to absorb some of the staggering abundance of spiritual blessings. I feel awed, yet saddened. It is like seeing a beautiful fountain pouring out precious, sparkling water that is being lost in a desert.*

Thoughtless awareness is a constant and comforting companion, a profound sense of oneness that envelops and binds me to my surroundings in a great cushion of love. I see that ordinary people sense this oneness and are drawn to it, its presence awakening the innate goodness and simplicity in them. They forget their everyday distractions and begin spontaneously to talk of deeper things. I feel myself entering further and further into the ocean of consciousness that surrounds me, and the less concrete the objects of the everyday world become, the more solid the foundation of reality seems to be.

The constant play of maya halts abruptly, as if I have put my feet down through shifting waters onto solid rock. Here, at the centre of everything, exists the almighty sacred mother, the foundation of reality itself, and in the hub of her being is a golden peace where all is utterly pure and blissful. Here the miraculous seems commonplace, and I see that atomic structures can be manipulated with the attention. It makes modern technology and medical science look sadly primitive, but I note it with only passing interest, because I am awakening into an eternal divine reality of such fabulous wonder and beauty that words for it simply do not exist.

It is utterly stunning, unimaginably glorious, an eternal, divine existence that sheds the material universe like the dead chrysalis of the butterfly. Absolutely one with the primordial being, fabulously beautiful and awesomely powerful, I see that the immortal children of the primordial mother will rise from their cosmic eggs to turn the spreading of enlightenment on this earth into mere child's play. The vibrations from the wind of their wings alone, as they take flight into eternity, will create an age of wonder on this earth for thousands of years.

I had always viewed my spiritual ascent as rather like climbing a mountain, a process requiring considerable effort on my part, and proceeding in increments (with frequent slips downward) as I struggled to rise higher and higher. In a way I felt it was something my ego had to accomplish. Now, as I bathe in the limitless beauty that oneness with the divine brings, I remember Shri Mataji's joke about people carrying their luggage on their heads in the plane. All I have to do is allow the kundalini to flow and feel great joy and gratitude for all that it is giving me, for, when I am one with everything, everything is divine.

It is hard to believe that something so wonderful can be true, even though Shri Mataji has always said it is our birthright. The ego does not seem to have played any part in the proceedings at all. Meditation, discipline and attention help the process along and a desire for the spirit is essential, but the end result now seems almost inevitable, like a child being expelled from the body when it has reached full term.

There seems to be a natural sense of balance. I do sometimes veer into the left or the right, into lethargy or restlessness, but on the whole it feels normal to feel centred, energised, thoughtless, alert and positive. It is quite effortless, sustained by the kundalini. Even when I am not plunging deeply into amazing experiences, I am aware of a unified field of the all-pervading power humming within and all about me.

I realise I have experienced this before sometimes, usually at pujas, but was never fully aware of what was happening, or how to sustain it. Now maintaining it is easy; all I have to do is desire it. I see I can begin to emerge into this state despite unresolved problems in my chakras, just as I did when experiencing the initial stage of self-realisation. But now, although sensing that some of my karma is too deep-rooted to shed, I feel my 'catches' are parts of the cosmic egg that have not yet fallen away, they are not really part of me.

The spirit is the very bedrock of reality; it remains where space-time ends at the foot of the towering cliff-face of eternity. It is the material world that is illusive and transitory, the ego that is mythical, and the human body that is the least part of what I am.

Shri Mataji looks like a living miracle. She shines with a perfect, luminous beauty. There is an infinite depth of majesty within her, with tantalising glimpses of divine brilliance flashing briefly in her words and movements. The very timbre of her voice resonates with a power and love that it is almost unbearable, yet I know my attention is penetrating very little into the real nature of her being. She is utterly enchanting and endlessly fascinating.

Shri Mataji manifests in me as well; my hair, my face, my hands feel as if they have become hers, while her presence within me reveals ever-new dimensions of bliss and beauty as the power of the kundalini grows. As I watch Shri Mataji's videos, every expression she makes, every movement of her body, every word that she says enraptures me completely. My favourite pastime is trying to catch the swift, loving glances she bestows on the yogis around her. I can see how much she loves her children, and it is extraordinary to see such power expressing itself in such a gentle way.

Another revelation is the yogis themselves. I feel tremendously proud of them all. I am filled with love for them as I watch them with Shri Mataji on the videos. I see their courage, their dedication and their sacrifices, and I see how we will work together as one as our divine nature manifests. I smile with amusement and some trepidation, wondering if we really understand the vast powers we are invoking with our pujas. I remember many of the beautiful people I knew during my seeking days, brave, lost souls on their seemingly hopeless quest for love, and my eyes fill with tears as I see that our dreams really can come true, and this fractured world be made one again.

Yet I remain aware that my subtle system is not yet able to complete the transformation. I feel 'stuck' half in and half out of the cosmic egg I am trying to emerge from. Intense emotions course through me, often reducing me to tears. I cry tears of frustration at *not being able to break free and tears of joy and wonder at the beauty that awaits me. I cry like a baby as I feel the miraculous love of the divine mother. She is an immaculate, ecstatic sea of utter bliss, the elixir of the gods, the treasure of all treasures. Her touch intoxicates with love, and her gift is infinite power and immortality.*

I know I need to surrender completely to be cleansed and transformed by her love, but I cannot. I cannot bear to be apart from her, yet I cannot reach her. I cannot stay with her; I cannot immerse myself in her love. At one point I completely break down in desolation. Yet I know I am not yet ready to know my divine creator fully. Despite being thrown into such amazing dimensions of consciousness, I can still feel problems in my chakras. I long to be able to surrender them and to dissolve into bliss, but I know the time has not yet come.

Slowly, as the days go by, I feel the opening to the divine closing over again. I can feel the auras shutting down one by one. It is like putting on layer upon layer of old clothes. Still, I enjoy the fading splendour, right up to the last moment. It is like watching a beautiful sunset. There is one last revelation, a sudden surge of love for the mother earth as I drive through the beautiful autumn countryside, and it is gone.

The vision and purpose of Sahaja Yoga is not small, and neither has been the motivation and dedication of those who have worked to establish it; and as time has gone by more Sahaja Yogis have started to have higher experiences in a process that began slowly but is starting to accelerate with each passing year. Nevertheless, self-realisation is the birthright of every human being, and it is not necessary to stand on a soapbox, pay any money or 'join' Sahaja Yoga in order to participate in the process.

Most of the work has already been done by the divine and by saints, sages and yogis over the thousands and millions of years that have passed in preparation for the final collective awakening. It is necessary only to experience self-realisation, keep the subtle system clear and balanced and allow the inner process of transformation to take place. Of course it is easier to maintain this in the company of other realised souls, especially to begin with, and often it is when awakening the kundalini of others that its real potential becomes clear.

The collective vibrations have changed tremendously over the last thirty years or so, and people are increasingly experiencing spontaneous manifestations of the kundalini, often without fully understanding its nature. Only a little knowledge and support is required for it to blossom. Many can experience the kundalini awakening just by putting their hands out towards Shri Mataji's photograph, and information can be shared over the internet; certainly there are kindred spirits all over the world who are happy to share their knowledge and experience.

Chapter 23
Love's labour's lost

However, we are not out of the briar patch yet. It is easy to laugh about maya when one is out of it, but to struggle within its shifting folds can be no joke at all. For the most part we do not even know we are lost, and it often amazes me how courageously many people struggle in the cruel and nonsensical world in which they find themselves. It was Shri Mataji's view, however, that most of the cruelty and stupidity we faced sprang from seeds we had sown ourselves. There was no doubt that we were emerging from long ages of ignorance into a world full of technological wonders. But it was a world in which the most scientific of minds could have deep and mysterious flaws lurking below its orderly sense of self or display ferocious cunning in the pursuit of personal ambition, and dismiss these failings as irrelevant to its understanding of reality.

It was not difficult to see that advances in technology had far outstripped our emotional and social maturity. The role the rational mind had played in dragging our consciousness out of the conditioning of the superego had been a positive one, of course, or it would have been had it not gone on to assume command of creation. Even then, Shri Mataji said, we had not emerged completely from the ignorance and darkness of the past; we took refuge in rationalising all that we saw but were still swayed and driven by forces we did not understand.

She stressed that the rational mind was just one of our faculties. It could bring balance into the system, manipulate the material world and make choices about the future; but, until the system itself surrendered to the flowering of the evolutionary process, we remained a hybrid;

neither wholly physical nor wholly spiritual beings, but something in between. From her perspective we had undoubtedly become extremely clever and successful caterpillars, but were missing the point somewhat if we didn't achieve our metamorphosis, especially when we had eaten most of the leaves in the neighbourhood.

It is hard to know which thread to try and pull first to untangle the complex web of human affairs that Shri Mataji portrayed, or, perhaps more accurately, the limitless vagaries of the human ego that she identified. I suppose there were basically two points she was making. One was that we had been selling ourselves short as seekers and our destiny was far greater and more glorious than we imagined. This was something I could concur with, to some extent at least, from my own experience. The other was that life was not the bowl of cherries we liked to think it was, and this was not at all easy for me to come to terms with.

Shri Mataji spoke of major pitfalls in the western lifestyle beyond its unsustainable growth and global irresponsibility, of powerfully destructive forces at work behind the scenes and a deep and widespread ignorance of genuine spirituality. She depicted some surprising correlations and contradictions between what seemed quite innocuous, everyday behaviour to us, and vitally important qualities of the subtle system. According to her, some of our most casual and deeply ingrained habits and beliefs conflicted with the fundamental principles of the chakras, and denied us the subtle depths of consciousness that they sustained. Moreover, she told us, the interrelated nature of the subtle system meant that deficiencies in one area undermined other aspects of its operation and the overall viability of the instrument was impossible unless all of its parts were configured correctly.

At times it felt as if I belonged to a lost colony of a great civilisation; in which a traveller had arrived from afar to point out that the box I was sitting on was a computer, the cables the washing was hanging on were power leads and the frame with a drawing of the village headman on it was a video screen - never mind learning to surf the internet and deal with computer viruses. I was initially surprised, for instance, at the importance Shri Mataji placed on the quality and stability of personal and social relationships, not just where our personal happiness was concerned but in relation to our individual and collective spiritual ascent as well. She placed a high priority on the foundations we built in life and constantly impressed on us that emotional dramas and distractions could undermine our efforts to progress on subtler levels.

I faced a number of challenges in trying to live up to these priorities too, and one of them was accepting her suggestion that I marry a young lady from Poland who had become involved in Sahaja Yoga. Shri Mataji felt it was important for me to have a partner and set up a home with my son, who was still living with my parents; and my proposed partner was in difficulties, living illegally in the UK because the Polish government would not renew her passport.

My perception of relationships had changed quite a lot since meeting Shri Mataji, but even so I did not find this an easy thing to contemplate. I could see that the arrangement would be mutually beneficial, and I very much wanted to create a home for my son. I also knew that I hadn't made the greatest choices of partners in the past, but I was still discomforted by the idea of marrying someone I was not emotionally involved with. It was hard to let go of the romantic ideal, although I was beginning to understand Shri Mataji's rather pragmatic attitude towards human relationships, so I sat down and tried to contemplate the situation in meditation.

I felt my ego sulking a bit because it would not be embarking on a romantic adventure, but after a while I entered a deeper, more subtle state. I felt a powerful sense of auspiciousness in my left side that soothed my confused emotions, and a cool, blissful, melting sensation flowed in the right side of my heart chakra. I immediately understood that my unconscious mind approved of the marriage, and although I still felt a certain amount of trepidation I decided, as I had with everything else in Sahaja Yoga, to give it a go and see what happened.

Poland was still behind 'the iron curtain' at this time, and we had a bit of an adventure tying the knot, as in addition to an expired passport my prospective bride had a husband who had disappeared in Kathmandu; a friend of a friend from West Germany who had gone to Poland to marry her so she could obtain documentation to travel to the west. She managed to get divorced without anyone discovering she was an illegal alien, and we experienced an equally hair-raising episode getting married without the registrar noticing it either. My new wife celebrated her achievement by jumping up and down on a chair waving the marriage certificate above her head, while I tried to shepherd her and my bewildered parents out of the room as quickly as possible. We received a cross letter from the Home Office afterwards, but we have lived happily together ever since.

Essentially, I suppose, dharma was all part of living life for a higher purpose than the gratification of the ego. Shri Mataji was adamant that ultimately only oneness with God would satisfy the desire for completion that drove us, and that everything else was fine but should be balanced and dharmic. She supported marriage because it represented a collective recognition of the union and symbolised the profound nature of the relationship between the masculine and feminine aspects of the divine. She also said it was important that we create dharmic families where self-realised souls could take birth and prosper.

I went through quite a lot of soul-searching about love. First, I suppose, was the recognition that the divine forms of the archetypes and the subtle qualities of the chakras were the templates that fashioned the aesthetic ideals of proportion and beauty in the unconscious mind, and that we constantly looked for these expressions of beauty in the physical forms and personalities of others. With each chakra reflecting many radiant aspects of the divine, infinite visions of loveliness could shine through every human being, and we could glimpse magical depths of beauty and magnificence in the soul of another.

I knew that these unique qualities were not always as they appeared, however, for each soul had its own motives and desires and its ego did not necessarily reflect its inner nature, while the shifting mirage of maya could create all kinds of false perceptions. If we really wanted to enjoy the beauty in others, Shri Mataji told us, we must first find the beauty in ourselves; and we would achieve this not by trying to possess other flowers but by tapping into the sap that sustained the life process itself. She explained that the quality of life depended on the quality of the attention, which should be immersed in the spirit to sustain the tree of life reflected within us.

Gradually I saw that, if my attention was clean and centred, the energy of the subtle system could be conserved and focused within, reducing the exterior distractions of the ego and deepening and widening the central channel, which in turn opened out the chakras and enriched the quality of consciousness. Conversely, energy was lost when the attention was identified with the ego as it was constantly dissipated in projecting desires and ambitions onto the outside world. Once the attention began to separate from the desires of the ego, it became increasingly obvious that inner qualities such as self-respect and the quality of experience were being sought through acquired social status and material trophies, and collective identity, by identifying with religion, country, class, tribe or caste, and even street gangs. The greatest quality of all, the love and beauty of the divine, was being sought through its manifold reflections in the forms of others.

Shri Mataji was not at all impressed with the serial romantic infatuations we indulged in, saying they were unreal and destructive; creating successive shocks of love failed or betrayed that damaged and desensitised important aspects of the subtle system. From her perspective, we were projecting our primal desire for the divine onto the outside world, searching for perfection and fulfilment in all who crossed our path and investing our faith in souls as flawed and frail as our own. The fascination and enchantment of successive objects of desire was inspired by the divine archetypes they reflected rather than the individuals themselves.

She explained that the overwhelming intensity of falling in love might be triggered by the vision represented in another person, but it was the deep yearning for oneness with the divine that it invoked; and she described the myth of 'salvation through romance' in western society as a ruinous sacrifice on the altar of the spirit, and one that market forces exploited to the full. She did not say that people could not fall profoundly in love with each other in a dharmic way, just that it was rare and not something we should pursue at all costs, especially if we were seeking the divine.

According to Shri Mataji, if a couple's subtle systems had evolved to a high degree of subtlety and were pure and balanced, it could happen that they spontaneously complemented one other and experienced an intense state of oneness together. Nevertheless, she said, even the most ideal experience could only be a temporary idyll, tempered by eventual loss and sadness unless lived as part of a greater awakening. Of course relationships could work relatively well in less-than-perfect situations; what concerned Shri Mataji was the constant hopping about from one partner to another in pursuit of a fantasy. She encouraged us to look for qualities other than irresistible attraction in prospective partners, and to trust in vibratory awareness to give more reliable information about the true potential of a relationship.

Shri Mataji encouraged marriage as a stable foundation for family life, but it was the attitude and depth of commitment to the relationship that was important, rather than the institution of marriage itself. One did not need to be in a relationship or have a family to progress in one's self-realisation, of course, but much could be learned and worked out by the curious combination of enrichment and self-sacrifice that family life created, and re-experiencing the pangs of childhood from a parent's perspective was an education in itself. It certainly seemed to be an important factor in achieving real maturity in life. The freedom of the single state had its advantages, too, although self-discipline could be both more difficult and more necessary and it was easier to go to extremes. The most important thing was to recognise the dharmic boundaries in individual and social behaviour and to dedicate one's life to the pursuit of inner spiritual growth and the collective emancipation of humanity.

There were various attitudes towards arranged marriages among Sahaja Yogis. Some chose, or were already involved with, partners outside Sahaja Yoga, but most of us felt it was important to have a partner who shared our values and aspirations. Shri Mataji discouraged us from constantly distracting our attention by searching for boyfriends and girlfriends amongst ourselves, however. It was something we felt comfortable with, generally speaking, particularly the ladies, because it made for easy social and spiritual interaction without being constantly hit on by members of the opposite sex. Instead, she would suggest marriages on a vibrational basis between couples, who had not necessarily met before, on occasions when Sahaja Yogis got together from different parts of the world in India or at international pujas.

She was in favour of marriages between different nationalities because she said it helped to dissolve the barriers between different countries and religions. Those who wanted to marry would put their names forward, and often a large number of couples would marry together in a Sahaja ceremony. However, it was quite possible to decline the proposed partner or to cancel the arrangement, if necessary, before a civil marriage took place, or at any point for that matter. Otherwise some yogis did chose to marry each other of their own accord.

Shri Mataji's concerns were not just about a downward spiral of frustration and disappointment in individual relationships but also with the effects of all these broken relationships on the stability, quality and prospects of society as a whole. I could see that plenty of people learned to cope with the rough-and-tumble of diverse relationships even if deeper, more subtle feelings were numbed and diminished; but Shri Mataji was worried about the escalating casualties this inflicted on increasingly weakened and confused personalities in western society, and the creeping negative effects on the quality of consciousness at every level. She spent a lot of time talking about the processes of degeneration that could take place in an adharmic society, and the way that the collective attention was gradually subverted as more and more individuals lost cohesion with the whole, and began to act in a radical manner.

Probably the closest thing to the divine in everyday human experience is love and, at its core, the passion and mystery of sex and procreation. Its power and fascination is unrivalled, its powerful drive to reproduce, an important evolutionary mechanism; but it is unique in the range of contradictory experience that it can encompass, from the loving and magical to the depraved and the sadistic. It seems that sex can retain a degree of sensual intensity no matter how divorced from love it becomes and, although its quality can be sadly diminished, for some it appears to be the only way they can feel much at all.

Shri Mataji's views on sex in western society were quite simple and pragmatic. It all went on in our heads, she said, and in its performance we were sadly lacking; and, as my subtle system started to clear, I realised that we had never understood the rules of the game where love and sex were concerned. It was quite unnecessary to hang oneself in a hotel room trying to circumvent the ego's stranglehold on the intensity of feeling. I rediscovered something I had known in my early LSD days; that sexual love merely hints at the true intensity of the bliss of the divine. Sex on LSD may have reached amazing heights of pleasure for some, but we had missed the pot of gold at the foot of the rainbow.

According to Shri Mataji, sexual reproduction was regulated by the Mooladhara chakra at the base of the spine. She described it as the only chakra placed outside the spinal cord, and the one chakra from which the release of *prana*, or divine energy, could be experienced in the central nervous system before self-realisation. Even then, only a tiny fraction of divine power was released during orgasm (but quite sufficient to encourage us to procreate!). According to her, the missing magic ingredient in the quality, intensity and unity of love and sex, and more importantly in the spiritual ascent itself, was purity or, more precisely, innocence.

This was no Walt Disney idealism she was speaking about but the innate purity of the high-energy dimension of spirit. Shri Mataji described innocence as egoless awareness and a powerful quality of the divine in its own right, and one manifested and maintained by the Mooladhara chakra on both microcosmic and macrocosmic levels, where it formed the foundation of both the subtle system and the whole of creation. She said that innocence underpinned everything we really cared about, and taking it for granted risked a deterioration of every aspect of our lives. She maintained, in fact, that the quality of our lives had already been greatly undermined. There was nothing healthy about masturbation, according to her, and, I would add, nothing healthy about trying to violently suppress such things either. The problem was the gross and stunted nature of our awareness in these dark and unenlightened times, and I began to see that in a balanced, dharmic society of the highest level the spiritual integrity of the being – its depth and quality of joy and fulfilment - would be such that the need for sex outside a mature, adult relationship would simply not arise, something the western mind was all but incapable of imagining.

This was not about a 'fall' from the Garden of Eden in the Biblical sense - something Shri Mataji said was an allegory about the ego phase of evolution and the inevitable lot of the journey to self-realisation. It was more to do with the subtlety (or otherwise) of the culture and the times we lived in, and the knowledge and will to keep the attention tuned to the divine qualities of the chakras. Nor was dharma the be-all and end-all of everything; seeking was also important because the ego had a marked tendency to become self-satisfied and fixed in its perceptions and goals in life.

Shri Mataji told us there had been advanced cultures in the ancient past that had lived life on a much higher level than we did in many ways, albeit at an earlier evolutionary stage where further chakras were yet to unfold in the psyche. It became a problem, in fact, according to her, because they had developed extraordinary supraconscious powers that made them exemplary in character and invincible in battle, but obstructed and diverted the attention from the evolutionary process. She described much of Krishna's incarnation as being engaged in ending the dominance of the glorious but proud and inflexible warrior class in India, and in establishing an awareness of the oneness of God and the play of the collective being in life.

Ironically, according to Shri Mataji, the highest breakthrough of enlightenment occurred at the grossest stage of ego (by which time it had presumably outlived its sell-by date and become too full of itself for its own good!) She would laugh and say that the lotus had to grow out of the mud; and that sages had foretold in ancient times that the flowering of collective self realisation would take place at the darkest point of the Kali Yuga.

'You have to have confusion to seek for the truth,' she said, 'and to be tested.'

In her eyes we were like children, unaware of our real nature and purpose and straying into dangers we did not understand. I had known that the quality and spontaneity of sex was an indication of a healthy and relaxed personality, and that obsessive and destructive sexual behaviour was symptomatic of insanity and pain, but I still listened to her words in some perplexity. At one time I had seen sexual repression as the root of all evil, but the increasingly seedy nature of burgeoning sexual 'freedoms' in the west were showing little sign of heading towards any kind of enlightenment. Now I struggled to reconcile the differences between equilibrium and inhibition, spontaneity and abandonment, and, worse, found myself having to consider a conflict of a more sinister kind.

Chapter 24
Dangerous liaisons

Shri Mataji spoke of a relentless assault on innocence that formed part of a much greater and more ancient struggle between the evolutionary power of the divine and accumulated negative mutations throughout the millennia. It was something she had talked about in general terms before but, when going into the subject more deeply, she said that its most dangerous manifestation had its origins thousands of years in the past, in the east. Of course, the qualities and functions of sexuality and the weaknesses of the ego would always have been a potential Achilles heel in human development, but this was of a different order entirely.

She had already told us that there had been a sustained, collective movement of the attention towards the future-orientated, mental/physical 'sun channel' among the people of those times, in which extreme asceticism was practiced in pursuit of supraconscious powers. She had also said many times that any extreme human behaviour generated a momentum within the left and right channels that led, sooner or later, to a swing in the opposite direction. According to her, it was something that could manifest individually from life to life and collectively in societies down through the generations. In the case of the extreme right-sided behaviour of ancient India, she said, a reactive drive was ultimately created towards extreme sexual indulgence, giving birth to the Tantric movement that adorned its temples with endless copulating couples.

Unfortunately, Tantric practices did not stop at human experience; they went on to try and sexualise the relationship between human consciousness and the divine. The destructive potential of this kind of transgression was not necessarily obvious to the western mind, but, according to Shri Mataji, an attempt to awaken the kundalini through sexual practices was the complete opposite to the egoless innocence that the soul needed to approach the divine, where the relationship was that between a child and its mother. I suppose it might be described as an attempt to force a gross low-energy function from one level onto an extremely pure, high-energy function on another, but this does not capture the heinous nature of the association. The utter disparity between the immaculate purity of the kundalini and the vulgar nature of the flotsam and jetsam of evolution has to be experienced to be understood - think oily sewage in the swimming pool and raise it to a significant power. It came to be about something much more than the redundancy of sex at high-energy levels of existence.

However ignorant or naive the original instigators of Tantric practices may have been, acting against the purity of the kundalini in this way seems to have given rise to some particularly nasty mutations of consciousness. According to Shri Mataji, these practices had gone on to become the principal focus of resistance and hostility to the divine, a hoary, malicious hatred that haunted the collective psyche of humanity.

They formed the fundamental tenet in the practice of black magic, she said, where the destruction and degradation of innocence insulted the divine principles in the chakras, causing the attention of the deities to withdraw and creating a vacuum in the psyche through which negative spirits could manifest. It was something I had detected in my early LSD days and interpreted as the collective pain and frustration of repressed sexuality. I had failed to recognise the brooding malcontent lurking within its universal profanities, or the insidious nature of its pornographic anthem to the death of love.

This was the origin of stories about the 'danger' of kundalini awakening, Shri Mataji told us, for if people tried to awaken the kundalini through Tantric practices a violent reaction could take place, created not by the kundalini but by Ganesha, the principle of innocence in the Mooladhara chakra. She explained that this powerful archetype controlled access to the immaculate purity of the primordial power and this behaviour was one thing he would not tolerate. He could create nausea and shaking in the body, and waves of intense heat, cold and pain, she said, which manifested in the emotional and physical being through the left and right sympathetic nervous systems. This could even happen if Ganesha detected such gross vibrations at second or third hand, according to her, through those naively attempting to follow the teachings of others they believed enlightened and sincere.

Shri Mataji described the accumulation of negative right side, or supraconscious karma, as having played an equally destructive role in human history, but on a less subtle level. She portrayed the gross levels of the collective supraconscious mind as containing countless ambitious, fanatical and violent souls that thrived on chaos and hatred and delighted in shattering the peace and stability of dharma. They formed the horn of ego, just as the sexual degradation of the *Tantricas* formed that of the superego, and between them they cast a dark and sinister shadow over the fortunes of humanity.

She spoke of this heavy collective burden as encompassing multitudes of negative entities that hated love and innocence and constantly strove to debase and destroy it; and she talked about the way we were manipulated and exploited in a materialistic society, with dharmic boundaries constantly being broken to create shock, novelty and sensation. It was certainly not difficult to see that innocence and auspiciousness were being steadily leached from our lives, even if it took a while to accept the more sinister side of the picture that Shri Mataji painted. However, as the quality of my awareness improved, I began to see that many things that appeared relatively harmless in themselves did seem to be contributing to a general subversion and suppression of the spirit.

I noticed this even in fairly unremarkable forms of general entertainment, such as when some friends put on a fairly 'middle-of-the-road' film with a lot of dramatic action and special effects while I happened to be experiencing a high subtle state. Normally, I would have been quite happy to watch it with them, but suddenly I could not believe its violence and barbarity, how brutal and relentless the action was and how deafening the noise seemed to be. I could not actually look at the screen as I felt the images would shatter the beautiful state I was in. It was not that I was incapable of watching it - I could still have appreciated the film on a certain level, but I knew that the subtle experience I was enjoying would have shut down if I did so, and it was far more interesting than the film was. So I left the room, having learnt one more lesson in how insensitive the ego could make us.

Science had not helped matters by gleefully informing us that life was a random and meaningless process, nor psychiatry by following the machinations of Freud rather than the subtlety and depth of Jung. It was typical that the ego could propose the existence of an infinite number of random, meaningless universes to be sensible and realistic and belief in an intelligent purpose behind creation foolish and absurd. It left us with little chance of making sense of anything at all, and open to pretty much any influence that came our way.

Shri Mataji talked about collective trends in society, of recognising how small changes in individual behaviour were part of a pattern affecting the direction and momentum of the whole and how dharmic values sustained collective energy and cohesion while negative forces broke it down. The picture that formed during long conversations and debates with her was that there was always an attraction between the masculine and feminine aspects of the divine, but that a finely tuned interplay was maintained on many different levels for the dance of duality to sustain itself. In human society it operated a bit like the positive and neutral potential of the power supply to a complex electrical circuit. The potential between the sexes energised social behaviour in many different ways, but it needed to flow through a finely tuned matrix of checks and balances to maintain stability and harmony in human life and to enrich and evolve the quality of consciousness. Constantly seeking to short circuit this potential for dramatic effect was pointless and destructive.

This, Shri Mataji said, was why a sense of relationship that respected the spirit was important in a dharmic society, for it allowed social interaction to remain free of the designs of the ego, particularly in situations where entanglements of a romantic or sexual nature were inappropriate. She felt it was extremely destructive to pursue impulsive desires in any and every situation, especially at the expense of established relationships and responsibilities. She maintained that the dharmic family unit was important not only because it reflected the archetypal forces at the roots of creation but because it created the ideal protective cocoon in which children's spiritual subtleties could unfold, and that this became increasingly important as the evolutionary process neared its completion.

Relationships were not just about pursuing self-orientated needs and wants, she told us, for the things we reached out for could harm us as well as the family and society we lived in. Self-centred, egotistical behaviour could debase the subtle web of social and family relationships and undermine the collective depth and quality of experience. She likened the family to the atom in material structure, in which the breakdown of dharma and cohesion in one family could release radicalised egos to destabilise the members of another, in a destructive chain reaction that could escalate in momentum.

It was certainly tough looking for happiness amidst the relentless pressures of the materialistic society we lived in. Where spirituality was a myth or a delusion and the passions of the ego ran free, notions of dharma and innocence were laughable and compromise ruled – no one looked too deeply into the lifestyle of another for fear they would have to look more closely at their own. The ego soaked up its surroundings like a sponge, accumulating layer after layer of artificial identity as it was buffeted and subverted into conforming to the prevailing level of awareness. The body, mind and emotions disintegrated into separate, warring factions, and the soul wandered in confusion, seeking consolation where it could.

Of course, few people would jump straight into the worst excesses of self-destructive behaviour, but I could see how a paucity of real emotion and the festive gloss of western society could lure us into ignoring caution and crossing more and more boundaries. There was little room for genuine love in a society without innocence and dharma, and many frustrated souls seemed doomed to pursue empty dreams of emotional fulfilment. If emotional wounds were deep, sex could become compulsive and emotion hijacked by risqué excitement, and love and lust could intertwine in a siren song of unrequited longing.

While sex looms large in the lens of human consciousness, Shri Mataji described it as the least important aspect of the human personality from the standpoint of the divine, and a mechanism that became basically redundant at the end of the ego phase of evolution.

Diverting the attention from the ego in this respect could be a real problem, though, and demonstrated an important part of the raison d'être of a dharmic lifestyle in the first place; it kept the attention in the centre, the ego and superego balanced and the consciousness clean, and allowed life to be lived in a way that was both joyful and fulfilling, and in tune with the evolutionary process.

The fabulous divine being that ultimately unfolded its wings in a flood of immaculate beauty was neither masculine nor feminine, but this supreme desire of the heart could be realised only when it came from the innermost part of our being; the pure desire of the kundalini. Shri Mataji warned us that to try and seize this elusive intensity of self through the fragmented reflections of its parts in restless humanity was to wander deeper into the tragic comedy of human affairs, and further away from the reality of the divine. Our struggles with love and infatuation, with lust and desire, looked very different from the other side of the looking glass. From the perspective of the divine, we were lost, foolish souls, emotional junkies caught in a web of illusion spun by the ego and chasing temporary fixes of conquest or acquisition, or indulging in exquisitely tragic dramas of emotional agony.

The ego often seemed to respond more powerfully to its unreal projections onto other people than to the real thing, I suppose because the myths of the ego were often charged with underlying pain or unfulfilled primal needs. I imagine we remained largely unaware of it because we saw our new western freedoms as modern and enlightened, and did not consider that the fleeting bubble of contemporary life has a lot more to do with fashion, the weaknesses of ego, and artificial inner city environments than the evolutionary story of the human race.

Each generation's conviction that it was savvier than the last seemed to be a fairly routine function of the ego's 'herd instinct', a syndrome with a chronically short attention span and an unquestioning identification with the attitudes and aspirations of the day. Every culture incorporated a fundamental collective inertia that resisted profound change and transformation; a shared convention of ego that encompassed all of its incarnations, from the learned, ambitious or dogmatic to the romantic, self-indulgent and anarchic. Scientists strove for eminence among their peers, religious scholars nit-picked over details of translation in antique scriptures, politicians pursued cheap popularity and consumers scrambled to seize their share of the loot. The passionate dramas of humanity, it seemed, were fought out within tacitly accepted boundaries that obscured the discerning eye of pure intelligence, and a selective blindness maintained that underlay the ancient and modern mind alike.

"Men in general judge more from appearance than from reality." said Machiavelli, writing hundreds of years ago, "All men have eyes, but few have the gift of penetration." Little seemed to have changed since he wrote so cynically about the foibles of human nature, self-knowledge remained superficial, our quality of consciousness poor and our perceptions dimmed by the patina of ages, like old buildings darkened with embedded grime.

It was difficult to separate consciousness from ego, and there could be scant difference between the ego's agenda and that of extraneous psychic guests. All kinds of dissatisfied souls could lurk behind the scenes in the western social jamboree, according to Shri Mataji, and the dimmer the light of the spirit the more they came out to play. It took a while to get used to the idea that we might sometimes fall in love with ghosts, or ghosts fall in love with us, despite the popularity of the film of that name. Funnily enough, Shri Mataji said that the events depicted in *Ghost* were quite accurate in many respects. It was not uncommon for dissatisfied souls to orchestrate our desires and emotions, according to her, and even to interact through different human hosts.

My first real insight into this kind of thing occurred unexpectedly one day when I was startled to perceive a feminine psychic entity regarding me through the gaze of a gay colleague at work. He was a nice guy and someone I was friendly with, not obviously gay; in fact, I did not discover his sexual orientation until after this incident. I just saw how this feminine entity manifested through his personality and how identified he was with it. It was an unusual experience, in fact, a collective subconscious manifestation; because, although in time I became quite aware that such incorporeal entities could act through people's psyches, as I became more centred I would feel vibratory reactions in the chakras and sense the presence of spirits rather than see them. They could also, sometimes, be associated with a strange or unpleasant smell.

The problem was that the dissatisfied souls who desired to interact with the living were not Hollywood heroes and heroines according to Shri Mataji, they were fundamentally weak and flawed spiritual beings, and she repeatedly warned us that nothing good could come out of entertaining their dreams and aspirations.

I began to see how breaking the dharmic mould exposed the psyche to all kinds of seductive influences that could undermine the qualities of the spirit, with stronger personalities struggling as the foundations crumbled and weaker ones succumbing more quickly to the appetites of a wide variety of quirky psychic entities. This seemed to be especially true where the more promiscuous aspects of western society were concerned, for wild excesses, unrestricted sex and emotional excitement were just what the doctor ordered as far as negative spirits were concerned, especially when free of consequences or responsibilities.

It became apparent that any feeling could become sexualised in an adharmic and materialistic society, and that sexualising feelings could make them more susceptible to the games the ego liked to play. Once the sexually charged romantic quest for intensity and completeness became the driving impulsion on a primal level, it could be hard to escape, despite its frequently inconclusive and compulsively repetitive nature. It seemed we were no different from so many other, failed societies in the past. Degeneration appeared to constantly reinvent itself, often under the guise of freedom, while the self-determination and radicalisation of the western lifestyle had elevated the whims of the individual above family, social responsibility and the interests of the evolutionary process alike.

LSD had shown me that the western dream was exactly that; a living dream from which we were destined to awake into a higher reality. Instead, I could see that our ultra-science-fiction vision of the future was a mirage the ego had created in the belief that it had to invent its own destiny. The smug, biologically enhanced antihero that we imagined would be scooting about the Galaxy was a classic supraconscious projection, a daydream extending the fiction that our clever, self-indulgent material lifestyle could go on forever.

We were certainly beginning to stir from the long sleep of ego, and there was a growing sense of self-awareness, but there was also an identity crisis because the material illusion was home to the ego and not to the nascent divine being within. We were trying to liberate ourselves from ignorance and prejudice with a rational mind that was itself part of the problem; the ego awarding itself rights and freedoms without responsibilities - the bird of paradise trying to take flight while still confined within the cosmic egg.

Ultimately, it seemed, we all faced the same dilemma no matter what our place in the scheme of things; to divert ourselves in the playground of the ego or to seek to transcend it. For this, Shri Mataji was adamant that the human personality had to reflect the archetypal balance of feminine and masculine energies in the subtle system and maintain the dharmic qualities of the chakras. There could be no compromise with this, she said, because the subtle system had to mirror the image of the Virata for the evolutionary 'program' to fully engage and the process of integration and transformation to take place.

This could mean difficult choices for an ego heavily identified with a lifestyle at odds with dharma. The restless pursuit of emotional and sexual desire could cause problems in heterosexuals and homosexuals alike, although each lifestyle had different kinds of conditioning and misidentification to contend with. Ultimately, the myths of the ego were superficial relative to the kundalini and, unless the personality was particularly extreme, self-realisation could be experienced and evaluated step by step before committing to it fully, with an equally long rope available to everyone. We had to be free to choose, though, because the pure desire that awakened the kundalini had to be heartfelt and genuine, and the absolute realm of the spirit sought with the whole of our being.

Chapter 25
War in heaven

The suggestion that we could be possessed by troubled or obsessive spirits was hardly fashionable, and an anathema to the modern mind, although there were actually plenty of western people who believed that spirits existed. Generally speaking, there appeared to be a strange mixture of belief and disbelief at work. One view held that spirits did not exist and that belief in them was harmful or at least foolish, and the other, that they did exist and that belief in them was beneficial; and it could be a thankless task trying to get past ingrained attitudes in this regard either way. The ego's self-perception seemed pretty much set in stone whatever world-view it adopted, and sometimes the only common thread seemed to be an equal ignorance of humanity's inner divine nature.

The champion of spiritualism appeared quite oblivious to the effect of psychic possession on the subtle system, in the short term at least. An exaggerated awe of the dead seemed to have developed in the west in recent times, with almost any perceived spirit, real or imaginary, bestowed with mysterious wisdom and kindly intentions. It sometimes seemed that every other New Age acolyte had some kind of psychic entity tagging along as a spirit guide. Perhaps it was the overblown fear of the death of the materialistic ego that created this veneration. It is hard for the modern mind to imagine conscious existence independent of the physical body, and I suppose spirits are seen as reassuring proof of life after death, even if one strangely preoccupied with the minutiae of human affairs.

Surprisingly, the mediums involved in the symbiotic psychic relationships that existed in spiritualism seemed to be able to continue for some time without any negative mental, emotional or physical symptoms showing themselves, despite constantly interacting with the subtle systems of so many disturbed and devious entities. At the same time, their chakras registered some quite horrendous things on the vibratory awareness of a realised soul; intense heat, numbness, violent tingling and aching pain. Presumably it was in the interest of the entities that made use of them to keep them functioning as a channel, although it would be interesting to see some statistics on the long-term effects on their well-being. It may be that such mediums had strong personalities or were insensitive in a true spiritual sense and thus resisted the negative vibrations for longer, for I often noticed that seekers with subtlety and depth seemed to suffer more from the effects of drugs and dodgy spiritual practices than their more egocentric associates.

There seemed to be a broad spectrum of interaction between the living and the dead, with large numbers of these beings haunting the fringes of human consciousness and looking for opportunities to propagate their interests. Their intentions could range from the relatively benign to the outright destructive, but even the most harmless functioned as a parasite on the subtle system and a diversion from reality. This continues to be the case today, but is not something that impinges much on everyday consciousness because our awareness is not particularly subtle and our attention is focused on the demands of a tough material existence. We are also used to living with the consequences of adharma and psychic meddling; the mundane, the inauspicious and the eccentric are not unusual, and we are unaware that we are missing out on a much higher quality of life.

The explosion of energy in the sixties brought vibrant new life and colour into the shell-shocked post-war world, and for a time it seemed that we stood on the brink of a whole new era of consciousness, but it spiralled down through frustration and despair into a nihilistic cynicism and a materialistic free-for-all that now appears well on the way to creating a complete spiritual wasteland. There seems to be a creeping negative encroachment of the psychic environment at all levels, the overall quality of awareness slowly degenerating into a bankrupt moral lassitude and an empty narcissism.

Superficially, the influence of these negative entities can be seen in such things as the romanticisation of the vampire myth - its parallels with the activities of parasitic psychic entities only too obvious - and the idiotic introduction of Halloween festivities in many western countries (the modern mind too smart to fear such primitive superstitions). At the upper end of the scale, the excitement of the ego at savouring daring new experience blurs with the thrill of the negative spirit in subverting a fresh new system, and the more extreme adharmic behaviour becomes, the more prominent a role the despoiling of innocence seems to play. Presumably, this is what lies at the root of paedophilia.

Looking back at the psychedelic era, my feeling is that it kicked off in a tide of idealistic optimism that seemed unstoppable, with high-energy experience commonplace and the dawning of a new age of enlightenment seemingly obvious and inevitable. Then suddenly it was over. The dream was dead, but it took a while to realise it; its most ardent apostles struggled to keep the flame alight, and thousands still flocked to its banner, while it slowly and inexorably fell apart.

During my time in the drug scene, we tried to regain simplicity and spontaneity by opening ourselves to each other as completely and honestly as we could. We shared experiences richer and deeper than anything we had known before, but unlocked mysteries beyond our understanding and lost our way. I suspect we had a store of spiritual currency from previous lives to thank for much of our high experience and we failed to understand how quickly this spiritual legacy could be depleted. I also have little doubt that we opened the floodgates to the collective subconscious and allowed the restless souls dwelling there to pour into our systems like an army of viruses. Right sided supraconscious entities could also have come into play, but extreme personalities of this type had already wreaked havoc on the subtle systems of millions through the brutality and destruction of war, and the desire for peace and love was a swing away from this.

It is a simplistic view in some ways, although accurate enough; many factors would appear to have combined to cut 'flower power' off at the roots, and a large part of the negative impact seems to have been absorbed by the Nabhi chakra in the solar plexus. Many drugs, including alcohol, seem to have had a destructive effect on this chakra over and above their toxic effects on the physical organs it sustains.

Shri Mataji described the Nabhi as a complex chakra that sat at the hub of human affairs and not only maintained the balance and stability of the personality, but the quality of awareness, peace and satisfaction in life as well. It formed the centre of gravity in a human being, according to her, with its ten petals, or sub-plexuses, manifesting the ten basic principles of dharma that underlay the essential strength and weight of a person's character. She also described the Nabhi as the fundamental driving force of the evolutionary process; generating the primal desire for sustenance in nature and progressively refining this in human beings into the aspiration for shelter, family, social cohesion and culture, and ultimately, into the desire for the spirit.

In Hinduism, the evolutionary principle of the Nabhi chakra is represented by Vishnu, whose power or consort is worshipped as Lakshmi, the goddess of wealth and prosperity. In typical human fashion, this quality of the divine has been translated into a supposed cash machine that dispenses material riches to its supplicants. Good fortune did indeed form part of the Nabhi's blessings, we were told by Shri Mataji, but its most important rewards were the depth and quality of stability and satisfaction it bestowed in life, and the rich tapestry of peace and harmony it created within a dharmic family and, on a collective level, within the culture of a society.

An ideal life led in tune with the divine would be played out on a gracious and dignified level impossible for the western ego to conceive of. Instead of a competitive world populated by friends, enemies, and objects of desire, the spirit would perceive a divine drama in which the primordial being was acting out many different roles and the purpose of the collective play was to deepen the experience of the mystery. Everyday life would become the magical enactment of a living poem, vibrant, deeply profound and full of transcendent beauty.

The Lakshmi power manifested where the role of wife and mother was held in high esteem, according to Shri Mataji, and was the source of nurture and sustenance in the family on every level. It was a role she said was little valued in our materialistic society because it did not generate ready money. Short-sighted ambition seemed to have ripped the guts out of many things where the Nabhi was concerned, and drug-taking or heavy drinking degraded it even more, with all of these things combining to undermine the quality of life.

I came to see that the rich, auspicious nature of the divine had no place in the bleak life I had been leading as a squatter. This was nothing to do with impoverishment, for I had seen the poorest of families in India invite us into tiny huts where the atmosphere was thick with vibrations and overflowing with hospitality. I realised that my imagined detachment from materialism had (basically) led to a rudimentary existence that merely provided the crude essentials required to get high. It was an environment that leached all that was stable and sublime from life and was the antithesis of the Nabhi's succour and support.

Drug experiences could blow holes in one's aura and create openings for negative entities to invade the psyche, according to Shri Mataji, who said that these interlopers delighted in dragging down those who were seeking the divine. She said the attack was even more specific than this and unveiled a further chapter in the ancient chronicles of spirit possession, known traditionally in India as *bhootavidiya*, or 'the non-knowledge of the dead'.

This, she said, was a well-developed black art that employed methods of overpowering and taking control of dead spirits to manifest psychic phenomena and control the psyches of others. She said it was used by all sorts of people, who manipulated spirits both knowingly and unknowingly, but that some of the gurus who had come to the west from India were masters of the craft. They spun a web of psychic tricks, she told us, and overawed the trusting seekers with reams of grandiose quotes from ancient Sanskrit scriptures.

These wily operators seemed able to project compelling illusions about themselves, and to trigger overwhelming emotional responses in their followers, similar to those experienced in unreal romantic infatuations. They couldn't awaken the vibratory awareness of the chakras however, and this remained the only independent way of establishing their spiritual credentials. Nor did they appear able to conceal their tantric nature, and some form of promiscuity often formed part of their creed, or else rumours of sexual misconduct would surface from time to time.

All of these things contributed to the disintegration of the psychedelic scene, I suppose, with the gradual contamination of our subtle systems inexorably excluding us from high-energy experience and the one vision scattering into a myriad spiritual pursuits. Heaven remained unimpressed by our efforts and witnessed our naive assault and bitter retreat with equal indifference, much as I imagine the primeval shores watched the first creatures try to struggle from the sea onto the land. Somehow, though, I did not associate my failure to achieve the divine or the deterioration of my quality of life with my own actions or my own ignorance. It seemed impossible that the drug experiences which had opened me up to such amazing things could have been destroying me. It was a baffling and frustrating situation, and I could understand those who blamed God and turned away in bitterness and despair.

I was certainly quite naive in my perception of maya, which proved far more subtle than I had imagined. I suppose that on some level I believed it was enough to be aware that this material existence was an illusion, and I was certainly too dazzled by glimpses of higher dimensions of consciousness to question the nature of my efforts to experience them. Before my nemesis trip, I had not believed that attempting to explore my inner being could harm me, and afterwards I became desperate enough to try anything. Looking back, it was the overwhelming nature of high-energy experience itself that was perilous because it was impossible to resist, and we hurled ourselves at its immaculate beauty like moths at a flame until we were burnt and broken.

Of course the wisest or more fortunate psychedelic explorers stopped at one, or a few, profound experiences and felt their lives enriched by the insights gained. Much may have remained undiscovered but the stability and experience achieved was compensation enough; although this did not prevent the perceptions or understanding of such experiences being overlaid by more subtle conditionings and misidentifications.

I suppose the final coup de grâce to the ethical justification of drug experience was the arrival of the designer drug, which completed the downward slide from the exploration of consciousness into hedonistic excess. The encroaching criminal element in the drug scene developed entrepreneurial tendencies and began to create a new and more diverse range of products. Drugs were tailored to trigger 'party highs', enhancing physical energy and emotional intensity so that people could feel great and dance for hours. These drugs could enhance a sense of collective identity, but in a relatively superficial way, and boosted the ego in an experience that was available to anyone regardless of the depth and quality of their personality.

The rich and famous seemed interested only in enhancing the ego's prowess, while the extreme concoctions at the lower end of the market delivered a euphoric intensity that destroyed the personality in an orgy of insatiable craving. My feeling now is that the direction the drug scene took could hardly have been more opposed to the original spirit of the sixties had it been deliberately engineered.

With the royal oneness and ecstatic bliss of the divine comes the realisation that a deep, unconscious longing for this state has always existed in humanity, and that the use of all kinds of drugs and fermented brews has been a crude attempt to reach out for its comfort and fulfilment. These days, I suppose, we sense the need for a higher, more vibrant life, and the bright lights and technological wonders of the modern world seem to promise this. But the excitement and optimism of youth is inevitably ground down by the remorseless financial machine, the lottery of broken relationships and the gradual deterioration of the quality of awareness.

We console ourselves with alcohol or try to rekindle the fire with drugs and little realise we are further eroding our strength, or what greater heights we could aspire to. The counterfeit animation of the designer drug tricks us, and we are lured by its easy comfort, like snakes into the snake catcher's sack.

The power of high-energy experience in the sixties certainly had an effect. It reverberated around the globe, shaking up social conventions and alarming the material establishment; but the empire struck back to create Aquarian-age consumers with must-have style accessories tailored to the designer ego. I sometimes think we have created a world that is even more superficial than the stolid imperialism that preceded it.

It can be difficult to communicate with anyone on a profound level. In conventional society, only money-making and political correctness are taken seriously, talking about religion is taboo and everything else is a joke. In the 'counter culture' it is the liberty to follow any and every path in life that is imperative, questioning the credibility of any lifestyle or spiritual pursuit that is taboo, and everything else is a conspiracy.

The seekers appear to have abandoned the heights they once reached for, admittedly with justification where the heavyweight gurus are concerned, and retreated into a wistful, fairytale world of crystals, herb lore, colourful yoga practices and mysterious energies. Not that these things are necessarily without value, but they are peripheral activities compared with the real potential of the spirit. Some New Age activities are perilous, in fact, as they involve the blind channelling of energies through the left and right sympathetic systems and can play right into the hands of our busybody friends the spirits. There is little awareness that seekers could be vulnerable to the unknown.

The perspective that Shri Mataji cast on human experience was always quite sobering. She portrayed the history of evolution as a vast panorama in which we lived extremely short lives within very limited horizons, and in which it was not easy to recognise the long-term consequences of our actions. According to her (and despite appearances to the contrary in the case of the unfortunate John Lennon), karma was not instant, but it was inescapable, for we stored the consequences of our actions within our chakras.

We were free to act as we chose, she said, but there could only ever be a temporary escape from karma, as the play of maya was acted out against the immutable backdrop of eternity and we were judged on the scales of our own subtle systems. It could seem a tough position to be in, but it appeared to be the price we paid for the freedom to choose our destiny. Nor was it really a penitential process, according to Shri Mataji, for she spoke of dharma not in terms of good or bad but as the parameters required to maintain and fly the plane, and of karma not as retribution but as the natural consequence of ignorance and neglect. We learned from consequences, she said, with our actions swinging us from the left to the right in subsequent lifetimes, gradually approaching the centre in an upward spiral movement if we were evolving, or swinging downward into increasing extremes if we were not.

The subtle system appears capable of absorbing a lot of punishment with little apparent effect on the surface; the repercussions only become obvious when we try to turn the situation around, and we seem to be able get away with a great deal over a long period before some kind of tipping point is reached and things start to go wrong. All too often we seem to get stuck, calcified into a fixed personality at a certain age with insufficient energy to change, and can only wait for death to release us for another chance to pursue our destiny.

All this obviously does not figure much in the world-view of the average ego, which is mostly too caught up in the struggles of everyday life to consider profound truths about its existence. Most of us know we are not really bad people and assume that being a bit naughty is all right, especially if everyone else is doing it. Daring lightning to strike if we cross the line is about as far as it goes, and we remain in a kind of limbo in which the accumulated effects of our actions on the subtle system go unrecognised. However, while not everyone wants to fly off into fabulous cosmic realms, living in tune with the spirit is deeply fulfilling at any level and could prevent a huge number of the problems that the human race is struggling with. A value system based on the subtle principles of the chakras would both enhance the quality of life and phase out the destructive traits of the ego that are squandering and polluting the wealth and beauty of our planet.

I suppose the slow-motion consequences of karma reflect the vastly different time scales of higher levels of consciousness, especially in relation to the mayfly-like existence of the ego. Certainly, I have noticed on occasion that, when something knocked me down from a high state, I would feel 'catches' in the chakras without experiencing any immediate change to my state of being, then would watch the whole thing slowly tumble down over hours or days before the state of consciousness disappeared completely. Conversely, awakening for a moment into a higher world could keep me up there for hours, days or weeks, and I would descend only gradually back 'down to earth'. Likewise, the measured pace of spiritual process required perseverance to deepen self-realisation, as a substantial amount of meditation and attention to the chakras was needed before these activities bore fruit.

Gradual though the effects may have been, they have been accumulative, and there has been a growing sense of momentum that has gathered pace with every passing year. The childlike abandon with which we enjoyed Shri Mataji's company in the early days developed into a more focused recognition of our responsibilities towards our own ascent. Ultimately, Shri Mataji said, each soul would be judged by the condition of its subtle system, but her emphasis was always on the positive potential of self-realisation on both an individual and a collective level.

Mostly she spoke radiantly about the joy and fulfilment that spiritual maturity would bring. She did speak of the unhappiness and disease that imbalance and adharma could create, but was less forthcoming with regard to the dire warnings contained in many spiritual traditions about the consequences of failing to live up to our spiritual potential. My impression was that it was a subject she did not much like to talk about. Shri Mataji put me in mind of an anxious mother at times, concerned that her young ones would have to face the unforgiving laws of reality. She did say that those who did not desire to evolve would ultimately forfeit their chance of doing so, and on occasion gave more ominous warnings. 'Nothing can stop the manifestation of truth,' she said once, 'and if we are not prepared it may break many things.'

The main problem seemed to come down to the fact that the primeval struggle between negative psychic mutations and the forces of evolution had become subtler and more internalised over time, with these ancient foes now warring in the human mind. It was easy for the divine to destroy negative people or psychic entities, Shri Mataji said, but 'free will' really did mean complete freedom. According to her, human identification with the desires and ambitions of negative spirits meant that the children of the divine had effectively become hostages in a cosmic drama in which the divine could not directly intervene.

'Now the battle of Kurukshetra [the epic battle described in the Mahabharata in which Krishna orchestrated the destruction of the ruling warrior class dominating the Indus culture] is being fought in the human brain,' she said. At the present time, the principle of free will seems to require that the final battle be fought by the emerging divine beings themselves.

The struggle takes place on many levels, in many guises. Even the spiritual instinct has been harnessed to work against itself. Each soul has an innate desire for the divine, but the mind has worked to create its own visions, interpreting the teachings of the truly enlightened according to its particular understanding, and claiming ownership and control over them. Nor are the obsessions of the past restricted to carnal appetites; the fanatically religious seem prolific too, and haunt the hearts and minds of their spiritual heirs, further entrenching dogma and bigotry. Combined with the ego's tribal mentality and its propensity to entwine religious zeal with material and political ambition, this has spelled disaster for universal spiritual accord and led to unspeakable intolerance and cruelty, not to mention a considerable glitch in the evolution of consciousness.

The main difference between the vast majority of pundits and preachers in this world and those that follow them is that the former have adopted a fixed set of practices and beliefs and the latter believe what they are told. No one is awake in the divine realm. Often, ironically, the pupils have better vibrations than the masters and are quite unaware that their spiritual aspirations are being hijacked. Dissention and passions are stirred, and we are pitted one against the other, belief against belief, religion against religion, fanatic against fanatic.

It is, unfortunately, a battle into which we seem to be sleepwalking jaded and drained; there is little firm ground on which to make a stand, and the seeds of egotism are manifesting a catalogue of woes on every side. We are certainly racing to destroy the ecosystem that gave us life in an orgy of greed, the millions of years the earth has laboured dismissed by a game-show mentality that takes our miraculous existence for granted in the stupidest way imaginable.

The problem is not just the difficulties we are creating for ourselves; it is also the limits of tolerance and patience on the part of the collective being. Life is aware and purposeful on every level and has its own rhythms and harmonies, and, if it is sullied and ignored for long enough, unexpected reactions can build up in nature that spread calamities in their wake. The earth is no abstract, organic Gaia, Shri Mataji explained, but an embodied archetypical entity. She is an aspect of the primordial mother that has managed the creation and evolution of life and her innate and routine processes can interact spontaneously with the higher functions of the collective unconscious mind.

The primordial being stirs as the power of the kundalini grows, and the demarcation between the inner and outer worlds becomes less distinct as our unconscious self interacts with the living environment. Universal communications and the trans-cultural aspirations of the young reflect the emergent collective awareness, positive developments, but entwined with the wreckage of the ego phase of evolution. It seems that the closer we draw to collective consciousness, the more our karma is reflected in the world around us, with our ancient earthly home reacting with slowly increasing wrath at our destructive irresponsibility – or perhaps forcefully hinting that the time has come to break through the outer shell of ego. Nor is it just the living earth that we need to worry about. The primordial being is present everywhere in existence, both within and without, from the subatomic realms to the mightiest galaxies and beyond. There are an infinite number of ways it can play around with the delicate balance of forces that sustain us, if it chooses. It is present even within our innermost thoughts, and constantly plays tricks with the complicated intrigues, vanities and ambitions that we think so clever.

We remain stubbornly oblivious that we exist on the sufferance of a vast collective being with an agenda far removed from the everyday preoccupations of the human ego. Although it operates on an immense timescale, its patience is determined by its purpose – Shri Mataji was clearly concerned that there would be consequences if we did not awake from our foolish obsessions. The earth bears the ego's transgressions, though with decreasing tolerance, for the sake of the divine souls in its care, Shri Mataji told us, while the potential power of the emerging collective being is enormous, with forces building that place an unconscious but massive pressure on the ego. It is resistance to the divine that is the problem; the processes of nature change and flow spontaneously with the collective unconscious, and so could we if we could only yield to it.

I have a little experience of how even a partial manifestation of the power and majesty of the divine can affect the ill-equipped psyche. The tsunami comes from within and the personality disintegrates in panic and confusion; everything it has known is overturned and there is nowhere to run. The 'last judgement', I feel, could be as gentle and compassionate as a mother's caress or as relentless and implacable as a storm surge; ultimately only surrender will save the sanity of the soul, but the capacity to surrender is a blessing not easily won.

The western dream seems to have pretty much shot its bolt and begun to enter a period of collapse and decay, although the fiction is maintained that everything can be fixed and limitless growth can continue. In reality, I suspect, it has already stretched itself too far, with such finely balanced and interdependent financial, communication and transportation systems that unexpected glitches in key areas could have catastrophic consequences for everyone. Little seems to have been learned from the banking fiasco, and the collective head remains firmly buried in the sand, presumably because it cannot think the unthinkable, that the Titanic might actually go down. The downfall of materialism does not have to be a catastrophe, however. A certain amount of material development is no bad thing, and much of the problem seems to stem simply from the ego's identification with material wealth as the primal source of security and self-fulfilment. It is, ironically, a situation that turns humanity into a slave of matter rather than its master. Also, I suspect, matter's subtlest secrets will not reveal themselves until we come of age.

Nor does the discovery that we are not the highest form of life, or that there may be responsibilities and expectations implied by our existence, have to be an alarming or oppressive one. The knowledge that we are not alone and that the primordial being underpins everything we do can transform the psyche, while the disintegration of materialism can be a positive transformation, if we recognise that eager shoots of spiritual reality are pushing through the cracks. If the value system is transferred to the enrichment of consciousness, we can stand on the solid foundation of eternity, there is nothing to fear and we become heirs to an awesome legacy that transcends this material existence completely.

Chapter 26
Stranger than fiction

Sahaja Yoga remains something of an enigma because it has yet to reach full maturity and its true nature continues to unfold. Self-realisation is a universal phenomenon, but each soul remains unique and the pace of individual development, diverse. Sahaja Yogis can be found at various stages in the process of growth and transformation that self-realisation initiates; it has little to do with the length of time spent in Sahaja Yoga, or the prominence of the role one may have played.

Ultimately, the tree of life has to bear its fruit - the spiritual transformation has to take place, and this is the only thing that matters. The doors of Sahaja Yoga are open to anyone, and some have entered with motives and weaknesses that are at odds with the values of the collective unconscious; but this is true of every one of us to some degree, and all such things can be dissolved in the collective ocean of vibratory awareness. The spirit forgives many faults, however those who prove unable or unwilling to let go of negative misidentifications may eventually be asked to work out their problems on their own for a while, or else try their luck elsewhere.

It has been amusing to see Sahaja Yoga branded as a cult when it encompasses such a disparate band of freewheeling intellectuals and irrepressible spiritual rebels, albeit our personalities are bound together by the depth of vision and vibratory awareness of the collective unconscious. I suppose any new spiritual upwelling in the world will be a cult to the established order and a religion to its descendents. The western mind has no real tradition of the guru/ disciple relationship and can only judge by its own material values;

its observations can be accurate enough in some cases, but it cannot easily envisage what it would mean to find a real flower amongst the mythical representations of its image scattered throughout the spiritual folklore of this world.

Nor has the work of establishing Sahaja Yoga been without difficulty. There have been excesses, particularly in the early days, not to mention the occasional touch of megalomania - hardly surprising, given the potent mix of such a fired-up bunch of seekers and such potentially explosive ideas. Do I hear the faint sounds of laughter from the future? Yes, I know these are early days still. I fear that our progeny may regard us more as a bunch of hopeful amateurs than as the exalted pioneers we sometimes imagine ourselves to be, but they will never know the appalling realities of the burden the seekers have had to bear.

There have been problems with some who took on organisational or representational responsibilities in Sahaja Yoga; both people of high calibre and the more bureaucratically minded, for the ego takes time to reduce after self-realisation and can sometimes become subtler and trickier before its reign is over. Acting as an intermediary between Shri Mataji and the rest of the Sahaja Yogis has been a difficult and demanding role, and one's weaknesses and vanities are subjected to additional pressures which could sometimes lead to problems.

Fortunately it is a position that becomes increasingly unnecessary as the inner experience of the yogis deepens. The real backbone of Sahaja Yoga has always been represented by the ordinary yogis, who maintain an ironic sense of humour and strive for high standards in vibratory awareness, while sharing what they have with others. It has been a long, hard struggle against the things that hate joy, spontaneity and innocence in life, and at times the churning process has been more akin to being rattled around in a concrete mixer.

It is difficult to understand Sahaja Yoga when looking in from the outside, as its values are learned from the subtle system and its activities are designed to increase the intensity of vibratory experience and the quality of consciousness. There have been criticisms levelled at Shri Mataji and her work, and it is tempting to refute them in detail, but suffice it to say that the money raised in Sahaja Yoga is really very little relatively speaking and has been spent on Sahaja projects all over the world. It is amusing that the western ego should find fault with this, in fact, since it is quite content to worship ruthless businessmen and money-guzzling celebrities. Indeed, it is perfectly possible to learn about Sahaja Yoga without any outlay whatsoever, and even the DVDs, literature, etc can all be borrowed if necessary.

Likewise with the international schools that Sahaja Yoga has set up. The intention was to try to give our children a chance, at least for a while, to grow and develop away from the destructive nonsense they are bombarded with in western society. It is something that perhaps can only be understood after seeing the depth of magical wonder and innocence in the eyes of the children in the villages of India. It is easy to forget that the whole western teenage ego syndrome, the source of a whole host of troubles on an individual and collective level, is largely an artifice of market forces. Each Sahaja Yogi has free choice in this matter, however. I sent my two sons from my second marriage to the Sahaja school in India for two or three years, while my sister sent none of her children, and my brother sent one of his for only a year.

All of my sons have grown up to be excellent young men, certainly far more balanced and mature than I ever was. The youngest is currently still at university after taking a couple of years out to see a bit of life, and his brother has completed his degree and is currently backpacking around Australia, New Zealand and Asia. My first-born, too, is a deep and perceptive soul, who has done his own share of travelling and is much more of a writer than I will ever be. He feels the vibrations well when he wants to and engages with Sahaja Yoga accordingly. The younger two are also very sensitive to vibratory awareness, but they are still at an age where they can take many things for granted. I would like to see them settle down and deepen their experience of Sahaja Yoga, but that is for them to decide.

In 2007, I sat listening to Shri Mataji speaking at a puja in Italy when a strange feeling came over me. She was talking about love, saying that love was the most important thing, that it was the key to everything, that love was really what it was all about. Something about the way she was speaking put me in mind of a beautiful sun setting at the end of the day, and I realised I felt quite sad. 'Oh no,' I thought suddenly, 'it's as if she is saying goodbye to all of us.' The puja was powerful and my mood gradually dissolved in the sea of vibrations; I didn't forget about it but it was hard to feel bad about anything with the chakras of so many realised souls buzzing with energy around me. I did not really know if it had been a significant perception either, and over time I let it drift to the back of my mind.

There had been intermittent reports for some time that Shri Mataji had been suffering from bouts of unspecified health problems, but the following year I began to hear that something more serious was going on and that she was 'not speaking' now. It was a while before I saw her in person, and when I did it was obvious that 'not speaking' was something of a euphemism. To all intents and purposes she was no longer there; she seemed largely unaware of her surroundings, with her eyes constantly shifting focus in an apparently random fashion, while her body appeared to be racked with pain and discomfort.

It was a real shock and extremely distressing, and a very difficult thing to make sense of. I had been aware for a number of years that Shri Mataji had been putting her body through a great deal of *tapasya*, or penance, of a sort, in trying to work out the problems in our subtle systems on her own chakras. I was aware, in fact, that she had had higher expectations of us in the early years, and had gradually appeared to re-evaluate her approach to our ascent, reducing the gradient and extending the timescale of our projected emancipation.

Now what was happening, I wondered sadly? Had she given up and taken herself off to some other realm, or was she sacrificing everything to accelerate the process? The vibrations in her presence were certainly very powerful, but they lacked the abounding joy and exquisite fragrance of her normal personality. I knew perfectly well that a spiritual personality of Shri Mataji's stature existed on a level far beyond that of the physical body, and she had said on a number of occasions that the only use she had for her body was to work out the problems of humanity. However, this was of a different order from anything I had ever conceived of, and very difficult to deal with on a human level. I could imagine how Christ's disciples must have felt when he was crucified; how confounded they must have been.

Yet on reflection, many great spiritual personalities ended their lives in ways that seem strange and unfortunate from a human perspective; Rama, Krishna, Christ, Buddha, Socrates and Mohammed all had a traumatic end to their days on earth. Nor, initially, was their spiritual stature universally obvious. It was only with the passing of time that their teachings really began to resonate in the collective psyche, sustained by the fundamental truths they represented within the collective unconscious mind.

My best guess is that Shri Mataji is working out the problems in the Agnya chakra (in the forehead) where the attention of humanity is well and truly stuck - where the detritus of the ego and superego, all the madness of the human mind, exists, and where the soul clings most desperately to its identification with this material existence. A fellow yogi spoke to me of being confronted by the unfocused confusion of an awesome primordial child in Shri Mataji's gaze as he passed close to her; and as I watched her movements and expressions I grew increasingly certain that he was right. It was like witnessing the pain and bewilderment of blind humanity as it struggled to awaken to its divine nature; as if she had fully immersed herself in the birth pangs of the collective being.

There have always been profoundly elusive depths to Shri Mataji's personality, and doubtless many other things are going on as well; certainly Sahaja Yogis have been forced to face a scenario in which all of their understanding, weaknesses and misidentifications are being tested to the limit. The maya surrounding her remains as powerful as ever, more powerful, in fact, and we remain in a kind of limbo in which clarity has yet to establish itself. One thing for sure is that the collective field of vibratory experience has never been stronger, and the sense that the destiny of humanity is rushing towards some climactic conclusion is increasing all the time.

In her present physical condition, Shri Mataji is being cared for by her family, who are trying to help preserve and continue her work out of their love for her. They are good and dharmic people, but they have never fully understood Sahaja Yoga (although one of Shri Mataji's grandchildren is certainly very special in this respect). They have lived too close to the mountain, I suppose, and have basked in the richly vibrated environment that Shri Mataji has created without ever recognising the true depth and magnitude of her personality.

For the time being, the Sahaja Yogis feel the need to meet with Shri

Mataji and enjoy the intensity and fulfilment of collective vibratory experience, and Shri Mataji's family are keen for her to attend pujas, so outwardly things remain much the same. To what degree and on what level Shri Mataji acquiesces to this I am uncertain; I suppose the drama continues until enlightenment is achieved. Thankfully, the majority of Sahaja Yogis are of a deep and subtle character and keep their own counsel, maintaining the development of their subtle system and evaluating events as they unfold.

Not all Sahaja Yogis have achieved this depth of understanding it is true; some who are more identified with the right side tend to see it as a linear, physical process and are concerned with putting organisational and material structures in place for the future, while others on the left can be reluctant to accept that anything has changed. A certain amount of confusion seems to be generated by the entirely human habit of identifying with Shri Mataji's physical form. Many Sahaja Yogis are comforted by her physical presence and are content to enjoy the collective vibrations at pujas and wait for her 'to talk again'. A few have perhaps become a little over-comfortable with this scenario, with Shri Mataji's family trying their best to fill the void with social niceties.

Nor is Shri Mataji's family alone in being susceptible to the maya that surrounds her. There are some in Sahaja Yoga with a cultural tendency or a personal inclination to transfer the mystique of divinity onto her family as well, thus completing the circle of illusion in a rather amusing way. Discrimination is the name of the game, applying due diligence with all of the faculties at the disposal of a realised soul. The powerful spiritual environment that is generated through collective consciousness when realised souls meet is invaluable in the early stages of self-realisation, but the development of an inner depth of experience is an equally important part of the equation, and an overdependence on collective events can sometimes distract from, or dilute, the necessary introspection.

Shri Mataji does come out of her current state on occasion, sometimes speaking and sometimes sitting and watching without interaction, but for the most part she has remained withdrawn from engagement with the outside world, and there is a risk that carrying on with things in the same old way could delay the progress of spiritual maturity. I have always felt it important to remember that Sahaja Yoga is a means to an end, not an end in itself, and particularly so at present. I suppose I am fortunate in having already seen big changes in the past in the way that Shri Mataji conducted events, when everything I was used to went up in the air and things moved on to something new.

Some do treat Sahaja Yoga as a religion in a traditional sense; they are following their gut instincts to search for truth and light, and the mind has been conditioned throughout history to put God on high and out of reach. They are not really aware of the stupendous spiritual riches that will be bestowed on them; but ultimately the clouds will part and the sun will shine through. Others do not quite appear to have grasped the notion of the spiritual ascent and dally a little with convenience and compromise, happy to attend pujas and enjoy the vibrations, but reluctant to face and work out their deeper problems.

Shri Mataji's insistence on complete personal freedom has always created a certain amount of anarchy in Sahaja Yoga, and there are a few loose cannons around who avoid facing themselves for less innocent reasons, supraconscious personalities stuck at the level of the Agnya Chakra who pursue the status of leadership and seek to impose their own view of Sahaja Yoga. Others are nervous of real freedom and try to impose various degrees of organisation and control. Eventually these people run out of rope or transcend their limitations, but inexperienced Yogis can be led astray. The struggle against the negative legacies of the past goes on in Sahaja Yoga as much as anywhere, but becomes subtler and subtler.

Even the collection and preservation of the physical mementos of Shri Mataji's life, her recorded talks and writings, things she has used, presents she has given, are only of relative importance in some respects. They are unique and have fantastic vibrations, but everything that Shri Mataji is; was and always will be - infinitely more than we have known in this physical incarnation - will ultimately be experienced directly within.

At one recent puja, much to everyone's surprise, Shri Mataji did actually give a powerful talk, in which she spoke forcefully about what it would mean to become a guru, and the changes that would be involved for those who achieved it. It was a remarkable exception, however. It is difficult to convey the phenomenal nature of Shri Mataji's personality and the lasting resonance of her impact on the psyche. It is not easy to let go of the way that things have been for so long. She has displayed so much power and knowledge, such a depth of love and compassion, that it seems impossible a light of such brilliance could withdraw into itself, and it is only natural to desire for it to return in its familiar form. It is not a strong and commanding personality that is missed, but the extraordinary sense that sometimes, when she spoke, the whole of creation spoke with her.

Nevertheless, Shri Mataji has always had as much faith in us as we have in her, and everything she has done was for a reason, often one that only gradually became apparent. She may well throw off the burden she has chosen to bear at some point, but in the meantime she has given us all the tools that we need, and we have many video recordings of her speaking in great depth about Sahaja Yoga. For the time being, at least, it is up to us.

Shri Mataji has always been an extraordinary person, a force of nature, and when I knew her best she was as elusive and unpredictable as she was dynamic and profound, although consistently practical and diligent about the condition and improvement of the chakras. At the same time, she was always fun to be with, endlessly creative and taking joy in the tiniest detail of the world around her. Her words could act powerfully on every aspect of the being, particularly when she spoke in public, although the yawning gulf between the perceptions of the spirit and those of the ego could make it difficult for the western mind to grasp her vision.

Much of the information she dispensed was actually understated, expressed in simple terms that left much to the recognition and discrimination of her audience. Even seemingly light-hearted or incidental comments carried a subtle undercurrent of meaning for those with ears to hear. Certainly her words could be understood on many levels. I would not have recognised some of the things she alluded to without having had some experience of higher levels of consciousness, and doubtless such meanings resonated with higher dimensions still.

She rarely followed the predictable linear course that the mind plots through life. For instance, an architect discussing a Sahaja building project might become impatient or bewildered by an apparently irrelevant deviation Shri Mataji made during discussions about conflicting elements of a design proposal, only to find forty minutes and many twists and turns later that the ideal solution turned out to be the very thing she had first spoken of.

These disparities between everyday reality and the perceptions of the collective unconscious could surface in surprising ways at times. I remember meeting an excellent young Sahaja Yogini (as the female of the species is known) in Cape Town many years ago, who was quite perturbed by a vivid dream she had had in which a specific sequence of events had taken place. What concerned her was that each of these events was now happening one after another in everyday life, a week or so apart. I told her I thought it was nothing to worry about, that she had probably just entered a high state of consciousness in her sleep and had a glimpse of life from a different level of perception. It may have been a supraconscious manifestation as it was future orientated, but at a certain level the collective unconscious encompasses the subconscious and supraconscious realms within itself, and I did not see this as a problem. It is only when such things happen frequently or one seeks to experience them deliberately that there might be cause for concern; however, it does show that there can be very different perspectives on everyday life from higher levels of consciousness.

A more striking example occurred when Shri Mataji spoke after a puja on the day following the 1985 Bradford City fire disaster in England. She said that the football stadium disaster had been terrible, and that one part of the crowd had attacked another part and many people had been killed. I could not understand this because I knew the deaths had been caused by an accidental fire, but a couple of weeks later the Belgian football stadium disaster took place where the attack described by Shri Mataji actually happened, and it gave me goose pimples to realise that to the collective unconscious the two events were connected outside time, with the violence on the terraces at the Heysel stadium reflected in the raging fire at Bradford.

While Shri Mataji unfailingly generated a powerful field of vibrations at pujas which set the chakras buzzing for days, she rarely gave any obvious demonstration of the power she wielded. I knew from my own experience that the potential power of the divine is enormous, and there were many ways she could have impressed if she had chosen to. Perhaps the only exception was the way in which she awakened the kundalini on a collective scale; for, whether they were few or many, the 'cool breeze' of vibratory awareness would always manifest in the majority of the people who asked for it in her presence, and in India I have seen these number thousands. This is described in ancient Sanskrit literature as one of the powers of the Divine Mother, for the primordial kundalini of the Virata is one of her aspects, and it is the reason that Sahaja Yogis have given her that title.

Many aspects of the Primordial Mother are described in the *Shri Lalita Sahasranama,* the '1000 names of the Goddess,' and one of the greatest and most enigmatic of these is that of *Shri Mahamaya,* 'the creator of illusion and confusion to the greatest of Gods.' This addresses the Divine Mother in her greatest and purest form; the original primordial power that generates the Virata, the great archetypes of the collective unconscious and the whole of Creation. She is represented as the essential nature of everything that exists, remaining unknowable except on her own terms, and the ultimate source and arbiter of the illusions of duality. She is equally the ultimate refuge and the champion of the seekers and the evolutionary process.

My experience was that Shri Mataji often acted as a mirror to my fears, doubts and weaknesses; they would look right back at me and I would sometimes squirm uneasily under her gaze. It was a mirror with an ocean of vibrations swimming behind it however, and I felt simultaneously cleansed and soothed by myriad subtle energies working through my system. There was certainly an aura of 'illusion and confusion' surrounding Shri Mataji on many levels. Her manner could be deceptively unassuming, and it helped to bear in mind the mind-blowing heights of majesty and power I had glimpsed within her on occasion. She maintained an essential simplicity that drew the attention from the circuitous and particular to the abstract and profound, and this could frustrate the convoluted mind and test the humility and sincerity of the seeker. Ultimately her purpose was to deepen spiritual experience and understanding, and the ego could flounder hopelessly as it tried to impose reason and order onto light hearted spontaneity and playful misdirection. Events around Shri Mataji played out in all sorts of unlikely ways and the trick was to witness the drama and learn from it, and increasingly, as experience grew, to enjoy the subtle humour of the divine.

So is Shri Mataji the incarnation of an archetype, of the Divine Mother? That is something every individual has to discover for themselves. Sahaja Yoga is all about inner experience, after all, and the experience is available to everyone. The only price is a little humility. It is not something the modern ego can easily contemplate as it has no template for the unlimited depths that can be plumbed by human consciousness and it is always on the lookout for its own failings in other people. There are templates for the manifestation of universal archetypes, of course, but these tend to be entertained only if safely anchored in the past and comfortably entrenched in the compromises and ambitions of the social status quo.

Shri Mataji's role in Sahaja Yoga has certainly been that of a mother. She has undoubtedly played a powerful and prominent part in the unfolding of events but, from the perspective of each individual, she has remained dependably in the background, giving love and support while teaching us what we needed to know. Her most imperative message has always been that we have to do the growing up ourselves.

It has also been noticeable that she has made a point of operating within the parameters of the Sahaja practices and techniques that she taught. Although there have been many miraculous cures, unlikely coincidences and improbable events associated with Sahaja Yoga, these have manifested wherever Sahaja Yogis were operating; they are not exclusively related to Shri Mataji herself. For the most part, other than the subtle manifestations of vibratory awareness, she has not demonstrated mysterious or sensational powers and has rather urged us to have faith in our own potential. In other words, while her role has been that of mother to her spiritual children, she has at the same time been a living example of an ideal realised soul, and has shown us that everything she has manifested in this life, we can become.

It seems pretty clear that a fundamental change is taking place in the dynamic of Sahaja Yoga, with the focus shifting away from a reliance on Shri Mataji's physical intervention to the emergence of something new and substantial within us. It is as if we were being compelled to experience her personality on a higher level; but the established momentum of the familiar takes time to rein in, and it can be hard to separate what is going on inside from an unconscious reaction to Shri Mataji's physical proximity and the collective stimulus of the other Sahaja Yogis. Collective experience with other realised souls is always important, of course, but Shri Mataji does not have to be physically present, and as profound inner experience grows it can be sustained in smaller gatherings.

In my own case, confirmation of these changes could hardly have been more profound. It occurred during an intense episode of high-energy experience that took place over two or three weeks and was preceded by a potent and dramatic dream. In the dream I was a child and encountered a powerful being I recognised as the 'grim reaper' or the 'angel of death'. This was a massive and formidable male figure, a warrior angel whose armour and weapons were covered with the blood and gore of the battlefield. He took hold of my hand:

'You have to say goodbye to everyone,' he said, towering over me.

'Goodbye everyone,' said I, apprehensive but surprisingly resolute.

'Well done,' said he, the ghost of a smile cracking his severe countenance.

I spent a couple of days wondering if this had been a premonition of my death, and quite looking forward to it in some ways; then realised, when I was thrown unexpectedly into high-energy experience, that it was some deep attachment of my ego I had been freed from. My kundalini rose with tremendous force without warning one morning as I stepped out of my car to visit a client:

I become suddenly aware of the ego and superego in my head. They appear to encompass a delicate matrix of golden filaments whose symmetry is blemished at random locations by thickened knots or obstructions of some kind. Simultaneously, some of these 'knots' are struck by bursts of subtle energy with lightning speed and precision, almost like a sequence of laser strikes, and they instantly dissolve. I feel as if I had been stuck or held back somehow by these 'knots', a bit like a parachutist caught in a tree, and enough of these 'snags' have been released for me to slide free.

I have no idea exactly what has happened; it is just another baffling glimpse of divine 'technology' in action; but I have no time to wonder at it for a huge column of energy is rising through my being, so broad it seems wider than my body. By the time I reach the client's front door, I am in another world, my consciousness merged with a greater Self that permeates everything around me. [Why did I carry on with my work? It just seemed normal somehow - naturally occurring high states are very different from the incapacitating disorientation that can occur on drug highs.]

My 'Self' fills every space I enter, and I float serenely around offices and houses, trying smilingly to focus on my job, while people around me glance furtively above and about themselves, sensing something strange is going on but unable to figure out what it is. The consciousness of my greater being recedes and becomes more peripheral as I concentrate on my work, and floods back again when I stop. I spend a lot of time parked up and enjoying the countryside.

I am washing my hands under a tap and I see the water is full of light. I sit down to eat a meal and suddenly I am a small boy again, about to eat a meal my mother has prepared for me. I am fascinated by the intensity of emotion that saturates the food, how conscious I am that my mother had made it, and how much its sustenance expresses her love for me. It is extraordinary how deep I once delved in search of this kind of experience, and I marvel that simple innocence and surrender have revealed more than all of the primal screaming and 'encounter' sessions I struggled through.

It is strange how young my mother is, just a girl she seems, and how much she loves me. Her love is like rich wine or heady nectar, fragrant, intense and devoted to my well-being. Gradually I discern a pure essence of spirit within that love, a sparkling awareness that permeates beyond its boundaries. It is clear, shining consciousness, without colour or form, yet potent with the quintessence of beauty and splendour, like a sea of liquid diamond. Pristine purity intermingles with immaculate love, and the great spirit of the Father and the almighty sacred Mother are one.

A series of vast, ancient beings looks out at the world through my eyes, the embodiment of awesome knowledge and power. They are deities I know. Sitting at my desk in an open-plan office, I drift deeper and deeper into peace and stillness. Letting go is effortless and supremely satisfying; it is as if a single thread is gently pulling apart the patterns of my personality like the knitted rows of a woollen jumper. Finally, gently, my human identity dissolves completely.

Only a pure, hollow being remains, a clear crystal vessel through which the Holy Spirit flows in utter silence, rising steadily through its exact centre. I look down at my hand and it has become completely transparent, as if made of glass, and is full of light. Something uncoils in my head, a last blessed release, and suddenly, shockingly, Shri Mataji jumps into me. This is how I experience it. It is astounding, as if she has 'downloaded' herself from somewhere above me.

There is a flash of incredulity as I feel her entering my being, and a long, astonishing moment in which I become Shri Mataji; utterly pure, suffused with bliss and full of light and power. Suddenly I know everything and all of my chakras go into action like some kind of divine weaponry, releasing vibrations with tremendous force. A last vestige of ego reacts; I feel alarmed at the power and magnitude of it all, at what effect such intense energies might have on those around me, and I 'jump' back out of the experience, sitting stunned at my desk, trying to comprehend what has happened.

Slowly the experience deepens again, but in a gentler way. I see that all of the chakras become one in the Sahasrara as my ego dissolves, and I experience this as Shri Mataji entering my being. For a moment, I realise, the process of self-realisation is complete and has manifested fully.

I had experienced Shri Mataji reflected within me before, of course, but it had been in a far less complete and dynamic way; a glimpse of the future, perhaps, when she had lifted me out of the maya for a moment. Many of the high levels of consciousness I had experienced in Sahaja Yoga were initiated by first 'becoming' Shri Mataji, in fact, and she had appeared in the form of many different archetypes to open doorways into new dimensions of existence.

To those who may feel daunted at the thought of an overwhelming experience of this nature, either because they cannot imagine it happening to them or because they are frightened that it will, I would say that few people seem to have to jump through the kind of cosmic hoops that I have done. It is a legacy, I think, of the damage I did to myself on deep and subtle levels in the bad old days; perhaps the kundalini could only resolve these things on the same kind of high-energy levels where they were created.

Now, when I experience my greater Self manifesting, it is a gentle, subtle process that only slowly gathers pace; awe and wonder remain, but it is like meeting an old friend, a familiar and comforting presence; and the scenario is more that of a grateful child being showered with gifts than of a mountaineer ascending in the teeth of a gale.

The all-pervading power manifests through every realised soul to a greater or lesser degree, and, in higher states of consciousness, joy and beauty are experienced in a state of oneness that renders all distinctions of ego equally redundant. In Sahaja Yoga, collective consciousness grows according to the calibre of the sum total of realised souls, not through any hierarchal elite. Every realised soul is equal in this respect, and there is something to be learned from everyone, however new or inexperienced they may be. I have a great deal of respect for them all because I know how hard they have worked to establish their self-realisation, and against what odds they have kept their dream of a higher life. The chemically charged wild child may laugh at the sedate pace of the Sahaja Yogi as he or she races by at a hundred miles an hour, but Sahaja Yogis are learning how to control and maintain the vehicle and will pass the smoking ruins of their reckless cousins soon enough, speeding up all the time.

Well, I suppose that brings me to the end of my tale, and a rambling, incomplete and untutored one it is, too. Its purpose is to paint a broad picture, and it has already taken me too long to get this far; the details can be filled out according to individual interest and desire.

To be honest, I wish that someone else could have written this book. I have been quite damaged in this life and have gone on to damage myself even more, and I have not particularly enjoyed opening myself up in this way. Still, I could think of no other way to communicate what I wanted to, and I have tried to do it as simply and genuinely as I can.

At a certain level, spiritual experience becomes impossible to describe, and it appears pointless to try to do so. I suppose one advantage of having been shattered in so many ways, and of passing through so many processes as the kundalini put the pieces back together, is that I have at least been able to describe the journey.

I know there are many souls struggling to find truth in this world, and I would like to dedicate what I have written to each of you. I wish that your journey may take you to the immaculate joy and beauty of the divine, to that ecstatic dissolution of selfhood in the fabulous song of creation.

*Shri Mataji passed from this life on 23rd February 2011, so we have our answer, it is up to us. A new era dawns in Sahaja Yoga, much turmoil continues but profound experience multiplies. The world stands poised for huge change and upheaval and something great is rising through the chaos. For me the times are reflected in a powerful dream I had, and in an e-mail from a Sahaja Yogini describing her feelings at one of the first collective puja's held without Shri Mataji's physical presence:

In the dream Shri Mataji asked everyone to build a huge temple for a festival of Krishna (the archetype controlling the Vishuddhi chakra at the throat, which represents, among other things, the collective consciousness of the Virata). This was a vast building whose main structure was already in place, and was both Shri Mataji's home and a public building. Shri Mataji herself was there, directing events, and as luminous, dynamic and encouraging as ever. Much of the inner architecture of the building had already been pre-constructed, and large sections of it were suddenly being delivered in great volume in a succession of big trucks, enabling us to reassemble them easily in situ at tremendous speed. Despite the industrial efficiency of this process, all of the construction components were of very high quality and beautifully finished, and included magnificent arrays of exquisite statues, decorative reliefs and richly carved furniture. Many hundreds of the statues were of Krishna, beautifully hand-carved from marble and gleaming with gold and brilliant colours. Considerable provision had been made for our welfare, with comfortable facilities and support for our needs; and people came to show us how to dance while we worked, so that the whole construction process proceeded like a kind of giant musical stage play, or a huge traditional folk dance in which everyone took part.

In the e-mail about the puja: 'The culminating part was the aarti at the end of the puja.' (Aarti means 'light' and refers to a ceremony in which decorative metal trays containing burning camphor are offered to the divine.) 'A few people at the front held the aarti trays, but lots of other people started to come forward, ladies and men, to touch each other's shoulder and be part of the aarti. I did not plan to go, but something pushed me to go forward as well. All close to each other with the right hand on the shoulder of the person in front. Many, many people joined together, nearly everybody. We all sang the aarti. (a traditional song of the same name) and the vibrations were incredible, I literally felt how we all have become like a wall, one big body and Shri Mataji was completely manifesting in us, through us in oneness. I really felt how she was in all of us, and we had become her body. She really existed within us. It was an overwhelming feeling, of love, divine love, tears of emotion and love were pouring down on many people's faces. Shri Mataji was there so deep, so palpable, so divine.'

Chapter 27
Flowers in the rain

The final words, I think, should belong to Shri Mataji, and to something she wrote long ago:

To My Flower Children

You are angry with life
Like small children
Whose mother is lost in darkness
You sulk expressing despair
At the fruitless end to your journey
You wear ugliness to discover beauty
You name everything false in the name of truth
You drain emotions to fill the cup of love
My sweet children, my darlings
How can you get peace by waging war
With yourself, with your being, with joy itself
Enough are your efforts of renunciation
The artificial mask of consolation
Now rest in the petals of the lotus flower
In the lap of your gracious mother
I will adorn your life with beautiful blossoms
And fill your moments with joyful fragrance
I will anoint your head with divine love
For I cannot bear your torture anymore
Let me engulf you in the ocean of joy
So you lose your being in the greater one
Who is smiling in your calyx of Self
Secretly hidden to tease you all the while
Be aware and you will find him
Vibrating your every fibre with blissful joy
Covering the whole Universe with light.

Shri Mataji Nirmala Devi, early 1970s

Lightning Source UK Ltd.
Milton Keynes UK
178041UK00002B/2/P

9 781456 770310